The Scene of the Mass Crime

The Scene of the Mass Crime takes up the unwritten history of the peculiar yet highly visible form of war crimes trials. These trials are the first and continuing site of the interface of law, history and film. From Nuremberg to the contemporary trials in Cambodia, film, in particular, has been crucial both as evidence of atrocity and as the means of publicizing the proceedings. But what does film bring to justice? Can law successfully address war crimes, atrocities, genocide? What do the trials actually show? What form of justice is done, and how does it relate to ordinary courts and proceedings? What lessons can be drawn from this history for the very topical political issue of filming civil and criminal trials? This book takes up the diversity and complexity of these idiosyncratic and, in strict terms, generally extra-legal medial situations. Drawing on a fascinating diversity of public trials and filmic responses, from the Trial of the Gang of Four to the *gacaca* local courts of Rwanda to the filmic symbolism of 9/11, and from Soviet era show trials to Nazi People's Courts, leading international scholars address the theatrical, political, filmic and symbolic importance of show trials in making history, legitimating regimes and, most surprising of all, in attempting to heal trauma through law and through film. These essays will be of considerable interest to those working on international criminal law, transitional justice, genocide studies, and the relationship between law and film.

Christian Delage is a historian and a film director. He is Professor at the Université Paris 8, and teaches at Sciences Po Paris. Christian is a regular Visiting Professor at the Benjamin N. Cardozo School of Law, New York.

Peter Goodrich is Professor of Law and Director of the Program in Law and Humanities, Benjamin N. Cardozo School of Law, New York. He has authored ten books on legal theory, psychoanalysis, legal history, law and the visual.

Discourses of Law

Series editors: Peter Goodrich, Arthur Jacobson and Michel Rosenfeld
Benjamin N. Cardozo School of Law

This successful and exciting series seeks to publish the most innovative scholarship at the intersection of law, philosophy and social theory. The books published in the series are distinctive by virtue of exploring the boundaries of legal thought. The work that this series seeks to promote is marked most strongly by the drive to open up new perspectives on the relation between law and other disciplines. The series has also been unique in its commitment to international and comparative perspectives upon an increasingly global legal order. Of particular interest in a contemporary context, the series has concentrated upon the introduction and translation of continental traditions of theory and law.

The original impetus for the series came from the paradoxical merger and confrontation of East and West. Globalization and the internationalization of the rule of law has had many dramatic and often unforeseen and ironic consequences. An understanding of differing legal cultures, particularly different patterns of legal thought, can contribute, often strongly and starkly, to an appreciation if not always a resolution of international legal disputes. The rule of law is tied to social and philosophical underpinnings that the series has sought to excoriate and illuminate.

Titles in the series:

Visualizing Law in the Age of the Digital Baroque: Arabesques and Entanglements
Richard K. Sherwin

Novel Judgments: Legal Theory as Fiction
William P. MacNeil

Shakespearean Genealogies of Power: A Whispering of Nothing in Hamlet, Richard II, Julius Caesar, Macbeth, The Merchant of Venice, and The Winter's Tale
Anselm Haverkamp

Nietzsche and Legal Theory: Half-Written Laws
Edited by Peter Goodrich and Mariana Valverde

Law, Orientalism, and Postcolonialism: The Jurisdiction of the Lotus Eaters
Piyel Haldar

Endowed: Regulating the Male Sexed Body
Michael Thomson

The Identity of the Constitutional Subject: Selfhood, Citizenship, Culture, and Community
Michel Rosenfeld

The Land is the Source of the Law: A Dialogic Encounter with Indigenous Jurisprudence
C.F. Black

Sex, Culpability and the Defence of Provocation
Danielle Tyson

Forthcoming:

Shakespeare's Curse
Bjoern Quiring

Crime Scenes: Forensics and Aesthetics
Rebecca Scott Bray

The Rule of Reason in European Constitutionalism and Citizenship
Yuri Borgmann-Prebil

The publisher gratefully acknowledges the support of the Jacob Burns Institute for Advanced Legal Studies of the Benjamin N. Cardozo School of Law to the series *Discourses of Law*.

The Scene of the Mass Crime

History, Film, and International Tribunals

Edited by
Christian Delage and Peter Goodrich

Routledge
Taylor & Francis Group
LONDON AND NEW YORK

First published 2013
by Routledge
2 Park Square, Milton Park, Abingdon, Oxon OX14 4RN

Simultaneously published in the USA and Canada
by Routledge
711 Third Avenue, New York, NY 10017

Routledge is an imprint of the Taylor & Francis Group, an informa business

British Library Cataloguing in Publication Data
A catalogue record for this book is available from the British Library

Library of Congress Cataloging-in-Publication Data
The scene of the mass crime : history, film, and international tribunals / [edited by Christian Delage and Peter Goodrich].
p. cm.
1. War crime trials. 2. Trials (Political crimes and offenses) 3. Trials in motion pictures. I. Delage, Christian. II. Goodrich, Peter, 1954–
KZ1168.5.S34 2012
341.6′9′0268—dc23

2011041913

ISBN: 978-0-415-68894-9 (hbk)
ISBN: 978-0-415-68895-6 (pbk)
ISBN: 978-0-203-12198-6 (ebk)

Typeset in Minion
by RefineCatch Limited, Bungay, Suffolk

Contents

Illustrations

Figures

Portfolio

Table

Notes on contributors

Johann Chapoutot is Associate Professor at the University of Grenoble 2 and a specialist in the contemporary history of Germany, and is currently a member of the Institut universitaire de France. His doctoral dissertation was published in 2008 under the title "Le National-socialisme et l'antiquité".

Vincent Dozol is registered in the Master of History program at the École des hautes études, supervised by Christian Delage. He graduated from Sciences Po and completed an internship of one year at The University of Virginia, College of Arts and Sciences. Vincent's dissertation focuses on the filmic representations of "asymmetric, surgical, and technological" wars in the Gulf and in Iraq.

Hélène Dumas is completing a doctoral dissertation in history at the École des hautes études en sciences sociales on "Judicial processes and national reconciliation: The *Gacaca* juridictions in Rwanda".

Anne Kerlan is a researcher at the Institut d'histoire du temps present, which is part of the Centre national de la recherche scientifique (CNRS). Her research interests include the cultural history of modern and contemporary China, the role of visual culture in Chinese society, film and literature, the culture of images and literate culture. Anne is a specialist in Chinese film.

Pieter Lagrou is a professor at the Université Libre de Bruxelles and at Sciences Po Paris, and a specialist in the comparative history of Western Europe, and post-war restoration.

Stuart Liebman is Professor Emeritus at the Department of Media Studies at Queens College, CUNY. He has published widely about early French cinema and theory, post-war German cinema, and Soviet and Eastern European films, in scholarly and critical journals both in the United States and abroad.

Constance Ortuzar is registered in the Master of History program at the École des hautes études, supervised by Christian Delage. Her dissertation focuses on the practices and uses of moving images in history museums. Constance is presently working on a case study on the recently opened Museum of Memory and Human Rights in Santiago, Chile.

Brice Poirier is currently Coordinator of the "Bureau de défense des parties civiles" for the NGO Avocats Sans Frontières France.

Henry Rousso is senior research fellow at the Institut d'histoire du temps présent (CNRS). His first books dealt with the history and memory of World War II, and he is currently working in a multidisciplinary and comparative perspective on the relationship between history, memory and justice, and more generally on the epistemology of contemporary history.

François Roux is currently Chef du Bureau de la Défense, Special Tribunal for Lebanon in The Hague. He was the defence lawyer of Duch, the first Khmer Rouge tried in Phnom Penh.

William A. Schabas is Professor and Director of the Irish Centre for Human Rights at the National University of Ireland, Galway. He is Chair of the International Institute for Criminal Investigation and chairman of the Board of Trustees of the United Nations Voluntary Fund for Technical Cooperation in Human Rights.

Françoise Sironi is Associate Professor at the University Paris 8. A founder of the Association Primo Levi Association, she is an expert in traumas related to the crimes of genocide, crimes against humanity and war crimes. She was an expert witness for the ECCC in the Duch trial.

Nicolas Werth is a senior researcher at the Institut d'histoire du temps présent (CNRS). He is a specialist in the social history of the USSR (particularly the 1920s and 1930s), the relationship between power and society, forms of state violence and resistance to social policy.

Introduction

Christian Delage and Peter Goodrich

A change in the material relays of knowledge, new modes of transmission, inevitably impact the social order and the legal form. The classical trinity, *ordo, lex, medium*, refers precisely to the co-implication of technology and the institutions of power. The previous seismic change in the material form of knowledge was inaugurated by the printing presses and, borrowing from Debray's *Course on Mediology*, introduced the reign of the graphosphere.[1] Print not only exponentially expanded the social presence of law but also led to the systematization of the discipline. Law became a linear enterprise, in part mirroring the rectilinear form of the typeset book and its various authorized and collated compilations.

Photography, film and now the plethora of digital forms of virtual relay are having a comparably drastic if not yet fully explored impact upon the preconceptions and forms of relay of legality. The videosphere has crept up on lawyers and despite a tradition-based conservatism and a tendency toward hostility to novelty – *novum omne cave*, is the relevant legal maxim – the new media have promulgated images into all dimensions of the practice of law. Graphic presentations of statistics, magnetic resonance body images, animatrix reconstructions of events, private videos that captured crimes in the course of commission, photographs and films have come to play an increasing role both inside and outside of court. Visual literacy is fast becoming the watchword of progressive lawyers and *au fait* legal scholars. This book aims to contribute to the trend and to provide the elements of a history of the growing amity of what is frequently if incorrectly termed "law and film". The encounter between law and the moving image, between the juridical and the virtual, has a highly specific and distinctively peculiar history in the varied quasi-legal forums that have at different times and in diverse ways been instituted by international bodies to record, to judge, to reconcile and to move beyond mass crimes. The story starts in Nuremberg in the aftermath of the Holocaust and World War II.

When the young American architect Dan Kiley was commissioned, in Spring 1945, to design the court room that would house the trial of a number of major Nazi war criminals, he was asked to consider two completely new factors. First, and at the time uniquely, the proceedings were to be filmed. Second, the courtroom was to be organized in such a way as to accommodate the screening of newsreels on a big screen, during the course of the trial.[2] This remit led Kiley to make some major innovations in the plans for the courtroom so as to allow for this double staging of the trial. He first moved the judges from the center to the side of the court so as allow for the installation of the screen. The focal point, the visual center of the forum, became a blank screen which at certain points in the trial would play the novel role of screening documentary footage of atrocities committed by the German authorities though without any necessary or direct connection to the accused. The film screen held center stage and in front of it, with a direct view of this vivid and disturbing evidence, Kiley placed the benches for the Nazi accused. For the first time in courtroom architecture, the accused would not face the judges but rather they would stand in full view of the public sitting on the mezzanine.[3] Previously, it had been thought that both victim and accused were to be protected from people's eyes, so as to preclude any excess of emotion, either of compassion or of hate, disturbing the purported tranquility of reason in the forum.

The new configuration of the courtroom reoriented forensic space so as to allow for the emergence and contestation of the novel charges of crimes against humanity and later genocide.[4] The "atrocities" committed by the Nazis were of such magnitude that they required a new legal architecture, novel spacing and untested displays of evidence. The immensity and the uniqueness of the crimes charged required a drastic adaptation of both the architecture and the procedure of the trial. The space had to be adequate to the horror of the atrocities and the novel forms of proving them. First, the fact of the crimes had to be established, and this required collecting testimony from political leaders, perpetrators, survivors and witnesses. The defendants had to be brought face to face with their crimes, they had to be shown – challenged with and confronted by – the evidence of their atrocities; with the testimony of survivors, for sure, but also with the documentary and filmic record, visual and audible, of their deeds. More than this, the filming of the trial was intending to create both a record and a relay of the fact of the atrocities to prevent subsequent ignorance or denial of such crimes. Film would also allow history to be inscribed in a form that future generations could view, learn from and in turn transmit. In sum, this novel use of filming and of screening footage played a dual role. It brought film to law as a means of making and recording history while at the same time evidencing crime through film. Images here enter the heart of law both as a forensic process and as a mode of historical record, of judging history and so determining the truth of what had happened.

Since 1945, historians and media professionals have played a crucial role in the elaboration, consolidation and relay of the legacy of the Nuremberg trials. These exemplary forensic proceedings became the model for the future development of international justice, and today the literature on this field is impressive and growing.[5] In the first part of this book, Pieter Lagrou, William Schabas and Hélène Dumas discuss the appropriateness and the effects of the impeachment of war criminals and their trial in forums that derive in large measure from Nuremberg. They also address the role that these trials play in the constitution of a shared collective memory and so in the writing of history. Henry Rousso, using the example of the Papon trial in France, addresses the issue of the role of images of the victims in the trial of those responsible for their deaths. Such images were shown, controversially, in the courtroom during the trial of Maurice Papon and Rousso elaborates upon the effects of this decision and its impact both upon the history recorded in the trial and upon the public sphere to which the trial was relayed.

In Part 2, Nicolas Werth, Johann Chapoutot, Anne Kerlan and Stuart Liebman evoke the "show trials" that took place in the Soviet Union under Stalin, in Nazi Germany, in post-Maoist China and in post-World War II Poland. The concept of a show trial is complicated and disputed. All trials are in a sense show trials, theatrical events that are intended to show justice being done, but that is not the meaning generally attached to the specific notion of the show trial. Organized by dictatorships, show trials are political trials whose primary purpose is to advertise and publicize what the dictatorship views as political crimes. They thus display – show – the culprits and have the function of both humiliating and sentencing the accused while at the same time educating the public by way of making an example of "subversive" or "traitorous" elements in society. The political control of the trial process and the regime's goals of publicizing and inculcating its ideology are defining features of show trials and distinguish them as extreme and distinct variations from the norm.

The show trial is a double-edged sword and, as the studies in this volume show, they were more often unsuccessful in their political goals even if they did result in the death or imprisonment of a few political enemies. The Soviet *raion* trials, for example, were widely reported in the local press but the people, knowing their political and staged character, reacted strongly against them. Far from establishing and augmenting centralized power, the *raion* trials paradoxically ended up reviving local power centers. Even though these were show trials, Moscow did not have them filmed, as their purpose was local rather than national, let alone international. The Nazis, on the other hand, chose to film the trial of opponents of the regime who had attempted to assassinate Hitler towards the end of the war, in June 1944. The prosecutor, Roland Freisler, however, so overplayed his role that the film of the proceedings would have outraged even a sympathetic audience and so the film was never shown. Freisler was so arrogant and contemptuous of the defendants that viewers of these images would inevitably have ended up sympathizing with the unfortunate defendants and not with the histrionics of the prosecutor. These images were not shown in 1944, but they were among the first pieces of film found by the Allied forces in 1945 and were subsequently presented as evidence at Nuremberg.

When the Chinese organized the public trial of the so-called "Gang of Four", they could not prevent one of the principal defendants, Mao Zedong's widow, from taking the stand and defending herself and the politics of the Cultural Revolution which she shared with her husband, the semi-sacred figure of Mao himself. Filmed in close-up, her scorn of the proceedings and her screams were particularly spectacular and led to the film of the trial all but disappearing from history. Finally, Stuart Liebman evokes a quite unknown event, the earliest history of Holocaust trials and Holocaust cinema in Poland and USSR. Not only were these the first trials of German concentration camp personnel, but they created an imagery that instituted a virtually complete iconography for the representation of extermination camps that has been employed ever since.

The new research field of "law and film"[6] has extended the range of analysis and reflection upon the manner in which mass crimes, as well as terrorist attacks, may include consideration of their spectacular and specifically "filmic" appeal and intelligibility. Despite the earlier misadventures of filmed trails, film has increasingly become central to the very purpose of war crimes tribunals. In Part 3, the contributors focus on Cambodia, and the Khmer Rouge trials taking place there. The first thing done by the Vietnamese when they invaded Cambodia and removed the Khmer Rouge from power was to film the traces of the crimes committed, especially in a jail located in the heart of the capital city, Phnom Penh, the infamous S-21.

Brice Poirier relates how this film footage was eventually found and considered, or not, as legal evidence of war crimes. The Khmer Rouge trials indeed started with the trial of one individual, the former director of S-21. His lawyer and the expert appointed to perform a psychological examination of the defendant here explain how they worked, before and during a trial that was filmed and aired live on the website of the Tribunal.

In the war in the former Yugoslavia, as in the United States under the threat of al-Qaeda, criminal actions took place before the cameras. Far from hiding their acts, the perpetrators were proud of what they were doing, and sometimes wanted to take advantage of the immediate international resonance of their crimes to assert their political views.

In the West, in more recent years, film has come to play another role in the commission and response to mass crimes. In the former Yugoslavia, proud of their deeds, those perpetrating the genocide filmed their executions of their enemies, in cold blood, with handheld cameras. They wanted a record of their acts and they wanted to publicize and spread the visibility and terror of what was being done. By the same token, al-Qaeda planned the attacks of September 11th in main part as media events. Their symbolic targets, the decision to attack in camera-friendly morning light and the choice of a media capital as the object of the principal attacks all suggest a finely attuned sense of the immediate and international impact that this very visible event would have.

In Part 4, Constance Ortuzar, Vincent Dozol and Christian Delage return in diverse and surprising ways to these attacks on the United States. Images of the attacks against the World Trade Center towers flashed around the world within the hour and came rapidly to form a searingly vivid, pretty much real-time collective memory of the events. At the time, there were some discussions as to the propriety of confronting the public with pictures of horror so as to inform it in real time of the material and human toll of a terrorist act. The first professional witnesses, directors Jules and Gedeon Naudet, refused to film corpses strewn on the ground around the twin towers. Not only that. The images resonated with earlier representations of the destruction of New York in a number of Hollywood movies, and soon generated a post-September 11th filmic aesthetic. The impact of these images on the day of the event was very powerful and the symbolism of destruction created certain visual tropes of terror that ironically came also to be used to commemorate other atrocities and, as Ortuzar shows, had a marked influence upon how Chile now remembers and memorializes its own September 11th, in 1973, when the Chilean President Salvador Allende was killed in a coup. Once unleashed, the images of terror take on a life of their own, as *impresa* – symbolic marks – of the event, as visual tropes of terror, as figures not only of destruction but of structures falling apart.

The essays gathered together in *The Scene of the Mass Crime* allow historians, media experts and lawyers to address for the first time the actual history of the various international tribunals and other more explicit and politically driven "show trials" which first threw law and film together. This intersection of media and law, film and trial has a longer history in theater and in the innumerable film and television courtroom dramas, well-established staples of the entertainment industry, but here, for the first time, an international group of experts look to the history of the real in the form of filmed trials and film's use in trial.

Notes

1 Régis Debray, *Cours de médiologie*, Paris: Gallimard, 1996.

2 On the US jurisprudence of film as evidence, see Pierre R. Paradis, "The Celluloid Witness", *University of Colorado Law Review*, 37, 1965, pp. 235–69. See also Neal Feigenson and Christina Spiesel, *Law On Display: The Digital Transformation of Legal Persuasion and Judgment*, New York: NYU Press, 2009.

3 Christian Delage, "Image as Evidence and Mediation: The Experience of the Nuremberg Trials", *Law and Popular Culture*, edited by Michael Freeman, Current Legal Issues 2004, vol. 7, Oxford: Oxford University Press, 2005, pp. 504–19.

4 Michael M. Marrus, *The Nuremberg War Crimes Trial, 1945–1946. A Documentary History*, Boston and New York: Bedford Books, 1997; Peter Maguire, *Law and War. An American Story*, New York: Columbia University Press, 2000; Donald Bloxham, *Genocide on Trial: War Crimes Trials and the Formation of Holocaust History and Memory*, Oxford: Oxford University Press, 2001.

5 Mark Osiel, *Mass Atrocity, Collective Memory, and the Law*, New Brunswick, NJ: Transaction Publishers, 1997; Gary Jonathan Bass, *Stay the Hand of Vengeance. The Politics of War Crimes Tribunals*, Princeton and Oxford: Princeton University Press, 2000; Lawrence Douglas, *The Memory of Judgement: Making Law and History in the Trials of the Holocaust*, New Haven: Yale University Press, 2001; Antoine Garapon, *Des crimes qu'on ne peut ni punir ni pardoner: Pour une justice internationale*, Paris: Odile Jacob, 2002.

6 Among recent publications, see Neal Feigenson and Christina Spiesel, *Law on Display: the Digital Transformation of Legal Persuasion and Judgment*, New York: NYU Press, 2009; "*In Flagrante Depicto*: Film in/on Trial", *Cardozo Law Review*, March 2010, 31–4 ; Richard Sherwin, *Visualizing Law in the Age of the Digital Baroque: Arabesques and Entanglements*, London: Routledge, 2011.

PART 1

History, trauma, war crimes

CHAPTER 1

'Historical trials': getting the past right – or the future?

Pieter Lagrou

The organisation of 'historical trials', especially in the realm of international justice, is often justified by at least four debatable claims. First, these trials are supposed to help victims overcome their trauma, alleviate their suffering; quench their legitimate thirst for justice. Second, they are expected to reconcile war-torn societies, promote the transition to democracy, restore law, order and human rights. Third, they would prevent repetition, create legal precedent, build a better future. Fourth and last, they purportedly establish historical truth, constitute a record for posterity and thus combat oblivion. Who could oppose an intervention that can promise such an array of eminently desirable results, with, after all, a limited mobilisation of resources – compared at least to almost any alternative mode of intervention in post-conflict societies? But, by raising expectations of this kind, can trials ever deliver anything but crude disappointment?

In this chapter, we will limit ourselves to the last claim. To start, it might be important from the outset to distinguish between 'making history in the courtroom' and 'writing history in the courtroom'. The Iraqi court was most certainly making history by sentencing Saddam Hussein to death, but was it also writing history, creating a useful record of decades of Ba'ath party rule?[1] Historians are addicted to judicial records. They are dependent upon them, not just as raw material, but also as an interpretation and a narrative. Yet, all historians agree that historical truth is superior to judicial truth and that judicial sources are ridden with traps and biases, loopholes and blind spots. In this contribution I will argue that a court case is most often not very good at establishing the truth and, more often still, not really interested in establishing what historians hold to be the truth.[2] As an introduction, I will briefly present two probably rather unexpected examples.

The first example is Emmanuel Le Roy Ladurie's *Montaillou*, a monument of the French *nouvelle histoire* and absolute historical bestseller of the 1970s, with over two million copies sold (including translations – for comparison, Braudel's *La Méditerranée sous le règne de Philippe II* sold eight thousand).[3] Le Roy Ladurie's book is based on one sole source: the registry of the Inquisition of Jacques Fournier, compiled during his judicial campaign in the course of the year 1317.[4] In his introduction, Le Roy Ladurie makes the unlikely claim that Fournier, in his registry, revealed himself to be both a professional policeman and an ethnographer. He would moreover have been a man of great moderation (since he abstained from torturing his suspects) and remarkable intelligence, with a sharp sense of observation and intuition. For Le Roy Ladurie, Fournier's registry offers a fascinating window into the depths of the minds and souls of fourteenth-century peasants and shepherds, thus allowing the historian to probe into the immutable times of rural societies unspoiled by modernity, industrialisation and democracy. Since all pre-modern mountain villages share essentially the same way of life, Le Roy Ladurie suggests, through his matching of primary and secondary sources, that his judicial source gives him equal access to his object of study as that which Pierre Bourdieu obtained through participating observation in *Le Village Kabyle* and that their conclusions can be compared.

Le Roy Ladurie is what the French call a *monstre sacré* and he used to be an academic baron. His work was thus not criticised in France until fairly recently by the iconoclastic medievalist Patrick Boucheron in a sanguine, and for French academic traditions unusually refreshing exchange.[5] Fournier was an exceptionally ambitious young cleric, who built his career on his short stint as an Inquisitioner when Bishop of Pamiers. In the course of just one year, he triumphantly scored several unprecedented, crucial points. First, the regular clergy is perfectly apt to conduct the Inquisition, much better actually than the Dominican and Franciscan orders, which claimed its monopoly. Second, the Inquisition is a superb tool to assert the power of the Church over society. Even though Catharism had long been subdued, Fournier extended the reach of the Inquisition into unexplored realms of heresy, such as superstition, political and fiscal disobedience and sexual mores. All of which was to the delight of Le Roy Ladurie and Fournier's superiors since, third, he went on to be promoted, having proven to be an exceptionally gifted administrator of the Church, ending his career as Pope Benedict XII. All through his steeply ascending career, he carried a leather-bound luxury copy of his Inquisition registry with him, to the papal seat in Avignon, from which it was later transferred to the library of the Vatican. His registry stood witness to his glorious feats of arms in battling heresy, but as such it also became a judicial source and a doctrinal treaty of sorts.

Le Roy Ladurie was very much oblivious of this context. What his source registered was the brutal irruption and unprecedented intrusion of the Inquisition into a village society. What it revealed was trauma and survival strategies when facing persecution, not the *longue durée* of the peasant mentality.[6] Like so many social scientists working on transcripts of the International Criminal Tribunal for Yugoslavia or Rwanda, he also totally evacuated the issue of translation, from *patois* into church Latin and onwards into contemporary French. From the point of view of the historian, Fournier, for his part, proved to be a fourteenth-century Carla Del Ponte, Baltazar Garzón, Antonio di Pietro or Eva Joly: a relentless militant of the extension of the jurisdiction of his court; a great innovator of its mandate and of the legal categories at its disposal; an explorer of new realms for the application of criminal law; a public prosecutor with professional ambitions beyond what the judicial career had to offer. In short, *Montaillou* is methodologically a very poor production. Historians, beware of the Le Roy Ladurie syndrome.

A second example is chosen from a very different context, starting from a rather straightforward question of historical truth: are the *Anne Frank Diaries* a fraud, or do they constitute an authentic document?[7] A series of judicial proceedings tried to tackle this question, but all remained inconclusive. A first court case, started in 1956, opposed Meyer Levin to Otto Frank, Anne's father and only heir.[8] This was a civil law case, involving intellectual and property rights. With Otto Frank's agreement, Meyer Levin had authored a first theatre adaptation of the diaries, but he failed to find a theatre willing to produce his scenario on stage. Frank then entrusted the same task to Frances Goodrich and Albert Hackett, who went on to produce an absolute blockbuster on Broadway and later achieved worldwide success. Levin felt betrayed, claimed financial compensation for his fruitless work and also, in a McCarthyist mindset, very much resented the 'ideological orientation' of the successful and 'leftist' version. The case went on to the Supreme Court, but was finally settled out of court in 1959, with Frank agreeing to pay Levin the sum of $25,000. That same year, a second court case pitched Otto Frank and the editor of the German translation of the diaries against Lothar Stielau, a Lübeck high school teacher.[9] Stielau had written in an article in the student periodical of his school that the diaries were a fake and Frank and his editor sued him for libel and defamation in another civil tort law case. The case was again closed by an out of court settlement in October 1961, the plaintiff accepting the *pretium doloris* proposed by the defendant. Stielau did face a further disciplinary procedure brought against him by his ministry of education. Further libel cases brought against Heinz Roth, Ernst Römer and Edgar Geiss, authors and distributors of rather more straightforward pamphlets on the 'Anne Frank Lie' in 1976, were ultimately inconclusive, dragging on through appeal procedures, statutes of limitation and the trespassing of the defendants.[10] There were also two stalled criminal proceedings: first the investigation into the betrayal of the Frank family's shelter, dropped for dearth of evidence in 1946; and second, in 1963, the case against Karl Silberbauer, the SS agent responsible for their arrest, identified by Simon Wiesenthal while still on active service in the Vienna police corps, but dropped on the request of Otto Frank.[11]

The long series of diverse civil and criminal proceedings before American, German and Dutch legal authorities not only failed to reach a final verdict or state the truth. They also substantially nourished the controversy by new suspicions, undecided issues and rumours. It was obviously and quite legitimately the role and duty of defence attorneys to produce arguments that made the doubts expressed by their clients appear less outlandish or inspired by anti-Semitism and neo-Nazi sympathies only; arguments that did find their way into the public discourse. And court cases did offer a stage for the paranoid interpretations of Robert Faurisson (in the Roth case) and David Irving (in the Geiss case). After all, so ran the rumour, why would Otto Frank agree to pay Meyer Levin $25,000 if really it was his daughter who had written the diaries? Facing this growing controversy, in 1980 the Dutch government commissioned a critical edition of the diaries from a committee of historians. Published in 1986, the critical edition effectively halted the controversy, by establishing through the methods of historical source analysis the firm and simple truth that the diaries are an authentic, and, besides, quite exceptional document.[12]

As far as the capacity of the court to state the truth is concerned, we can draw a few conclusions from this introduction. First of all, only a minority of cases lead to a trial (only in a handful of the 100,000 cases of Dutch Jews deported and killed was a trial investigating the circumstances of their arrest ever organised). Second, most civil law cases never reach a verdict, because a settlement is reached out of court. In these cases, the court helps individuals to reach an agreement, but it does not pronounce any judicial truth. Third, the court as an institution and the judge as an individual pursue a whole set of goals which have overwhelming priority over 'saying the truth'. They want to set legal precedent, affirm or extend the jurisdiction of the court, promote a personal career. These goals do not just interfere with historical truth; they will inform the judicial narrative, select the events under the attention of the court, their legal definition, the witnesses summoned to the court and the stories they will be allowed to tell.

Historians of the Second World War all suffer to some extent from the Le Roy Ladurie syndrome. They are heavily dependent upon judicial sources, which inform their historical narrative in crucial ways, and they are most often not aware of it. In the final analysis, it is the task the judiciary sets itself that dictates the judicial narrative, and the underestimation or ignorance of this agenda by historians has far-reaching consequences. I will try to illustrate this observation through the example of Belgium, but the Belgian case is only a case in kind, which could easily be extended to most occupied territories. Post-war justice in Belgium followed two very different and separate tracks, one concerning Belgian nationals and one concerning Germans.

Belgian nationals were brought to trial on charges of collaboration and treason. The task the judiciary set itself – or at least, the task the political authorities conferred on it – was to purge the national electorate of fascist elements, and to do it quickly and on a large scale. Some 400,000 cases were opened, in a population of eight million inhabitants, which means one out of every 20 citizens of all ages and sexes. As a result 60,000 trials were organised and 40,000 individuals convicted, which is 0.5 per cent of the total population. Compared even to Soviet statistics of the Stalinist purge of occupied territories, this is quite impressive.[13] How did the Belgian judiciary treat this massive volume of cases? The judgement of wartime collaboration, including civilians, was deferred to military tribunals, which were created almost *ex nihilo*, involving the recruitment of 400 judges, freshly graduated from the country's law schools.[14] The tribunals deployed a peculiar legal arsenal, defining crimes such as 'intelligence with the enemy' and 'undermining of national institutions'. Elements of proof included simple membership of criminal organisations, including most collaborationist organisations and parties, defining the crime as essentially a political offence. This made it relatively easy to establish guilt, since collaboration movements had been careful to keep membership lists, which the judiciary only had to compile. It was especially incomparably easier to check membership of criminal organisations than to establish individual responsibility for criminal acts. This in turn had a long-lasting impact on historiography and public memory, where collaboration came to figure as a political, ideological adventure and not primarily as a criminal undertaking or a sum of individual criminal acts of which tens of thousands of fellow citizens were the – often fatal – victims.

German nationals were brought to trial on charges of war crimes and 4,400 cases were opened and transmitted to the United Nations War Crimes Commission.[15] Belgium obtained 530 extraditions from its allies, 314 of whom were called as suspects and 219 as witnesses. Subsequently 37 trials were organised, involving 103 individuals; two individuals were sentenced to death and executed and of the remaining convicts all walked free by 1956. Compared to the record of trying Belgian collaborators, this is of course a record of dismal failure. Singularly, counting the difficulty of obtaining an extradition, the fact that for 530 extradited, only 103 suspects were brought to trial should have been an embarrassment to Belgian authorities facing their allies. This, however, is not at all how Belgian legal tradition recalls this episode. What case, then, did they want to make?

Quite obviously, above all, the Belgian courts wanted to make their case, cancelling out, among others, the Leipzig humiliation, the Nuremberg backlash and the American Malmédy trial.

Belgium was not the only European nation with an experience of German war crimes before 1939, but German atrocities in 'poor little Belgium' had attracted incommensurable attention, in allied wartime propaganda, in post-war controversies and, not the least, in the way Belgians themselves understood their war experience.[16] From the summer of 1914 all through the late 1920s, an enormous effort was made to document the crimes and prepare for legal charges to be brought against the invader and occupier, from the local level of municipalities and parishes, to the national and diplomatic level. The Belgian authorities initially charged over one thousand German offenders for a trial before Belgian courts.[17] The Versailles Treaty had announced in its Article 227 the organisation of a special tribunal to judge Emperor William II of Hohenzollern, with five judges appointed by the USA, Britain, France, Italy and Japan respectively, and Articles 228 through 230 stipulated that Germany recognised the right of allied and associated powers to bring German nationals before their own military tribunals, 'notwithstanding any proceedings or prosecution before a tribunal in Germany', and that it would cooperate through extradition of suspects and provide full record to the investigating judges.[18] The Dutch government never extradited the Emperor and the special tribunal never made it to the starting blocks. As for the extradition of German nationals, the German authorities never submitted to the extraterritoriality imposed by the Treaty and offered to organise their own tribunal instead, in Leipzig. The latter simply dismissed all the charges brought by Belgium (and France), to the utter indignation and frustration of the Belgian public. Belgium then organised a few dozen trials *in absentia*, which, in the absence of any prospect of extradition, was mainly a strategy of diplomatic harassment of an unpunished and unrepentant former enemy and cumbersome neighbour.

The International Military Tribunal in Nuremberg was supposed to demonstrate that the allies had learned from the mistakes in Versailles and Leipzig. This time round, however, Belgium's place in the judicial arena and the attention awarded to the crimes committed on its soil were very modest, compared to 1919. France represented Belgium and, overall, Belgium hardly entered the broad picture of Nazi criminality drawn out in Nuremberg. Emperor William's former protective host, the Netherlands, got a much more prominent showing, thanks to the presence of Arthur Seyss-Inquart, *Reichskommissar* of the occupied country, among the two dozen defendants. By the time the Belgian legislator found the time to draft the framework for the judgment of German war criminals, that is, not before the spring of 1947, the dominant legal opinion shared some of the German misgivings about the Nuremberg precedent. By adopting elements of retroactive justice, the International Tribunal had violated the sacrosanct principle of *nullum crimen sine praevia lege* and thereby allowed German public opinion and the German legal profession to dismiss the trial as an expeditious exercise of victors' justice. The opinion of German lawyers had a very different weight in Brussels than in Washington, especially because the judiciary had been the spearhead of administrative resistance to German *Gleichschaltung* in Belgium. The post-war trials were in this sense merely continuing an ongoing argument on legality and, intrinsically, on the superiority of legal principle in the tradition of the German authoritarian and Belgian liberal state respectively.[19]

Last but not least, the judgement of crimes committed on Belgian soil during the Second World War entailed a third element of judicial competition, this time with the liberating armies, who installed a new military occupation, and, with it, their own jurisdiction. The Battle of the Bulge – otherwise known as the Von Rundstedt offensive, the last desperate counter-attack of the German troops in December 1944 through the snow-covered Belgian Ardennes – was the bloodiest battle of the American army in the Second World War (in terms of the number of American losses). It was also the scene of much publicised American heroism (General McAuliffe refusing surrender in Bastogne with his legendary reply: 'Nuts') and no less publicised German cruelty. In July 1946, an American military tribunal in Dachau sentenced 43 German soldiers to death by hanging for the killing of a hundred American prisoners of war in Malmédy, plus 22 life sentences and eight lengthy prison sentences. The severity of the verdict stirred a huge controversy in the United States. The American defence attorney Everett, soon echoed by Senator McCarthy, accused the prosecutor's office of the use of torture to extract unfounded avowals and insinuated that Jewish judges on the trial had harboured an anti-German bias.[20] The Malmédy controversy went on to discredit the entire American war crime trials programme (the so-called 'Nuremberg successor trials') and contributed in no small amount to their progressive dismantling starting in early 1948. None of the death sentences was carried out and, after appeal and revision, all convicts walked free by 1956.[21] At the very same time of the killing of the American prisoners of war, a greater number of Belgian civilians (120) had been killed in a neighbouring locality. The Stavelot massacre trial opened before a Belgian military tribunal in Liège in June 1948, the very first war crime trial organised in Belgium under the new war crime law and very much intended as a demonstration of Belgian legal craftsmanship.

We will highlight just two aspects of this ambitious project. First, the new law, adopted in June 1947, was hailed as a major legal innovation, amply surpassing preceding experiments with extraterritorial justice. The Belgian law squared the circle of national jurisdiction over international crimes through the principle of the 'double indictment', meaning that in order to be brought before the court any charge had to qualify as both a 'manifest violation of international law' and as a crime defined under the regular, national, penal code.[22] The law was thus simply establishing the jurisdiction of military tribunals over war crimes and organising the procedure, while referring to two distinct sets of pre-existing laws and jurisprudence, both well established and consensual: the regular penal code, with its universal entries of crimes such as manslaughter, murder, arson, theft, illegal arrest, etc. and international law as it was recognised by the belligerents at the time of the perpetration of the crime. As such, the Belgian jurisdiction would be unassailable, even in the legal tradition of the accused.

The consequences of this exemplary frame of reference were not entirely anticipated. The regular penal code proved to provide a very restrictive arsenal of legal qualifications for criminal behaviour, and to be quite unsuited for the exceptional circumstances of Nazi occupation. Individual criminal responsibility was thus limited to the person who pulled the trigger or otherwise physically committed the manslaughter or murder. As a result, the *Schreibtischmörder* or commanding officers were in the main part sent back to Germany without facing trial, while their subordinates could plead obedience to a superior's order – a plea the Belgian judges would then have the greatest difficulty in disqualifying, since only 'manifest violations of international law and humanity' excised the small fry from their routine discipline. It took miracles of inventiveness and perseverance on behalf of the investigating judges to corner some of the most notorious

German officials. Otto Siegburg, a SIPO-SD agent responsible for the manhunt of hundreds of Jews in the Brussels area, was finally sentenced for one single murderous incident during a routine nightly roundup that qualified as manslaughter. Max Boden, head of the internment camp of Mechelen, from where over 25,000 Jews were shipped off to extermination, mostly at Auschwitz, was found guilty of indecent assault on some of his female inmates. The Belgian jurisprudence prefigured in this sense the one the German Federal Republic was to establish, based on the German penal code of 1870. As Rebecca Wittmann convincingly showed for the case of the West German Auschwitz trial of the early 1960s (1963–1965), in the end SS personnel were found guilty of charges that would equally have figured as crimes before an SS tribunal, that is, individual criminal conduct, and not for their participation in a common criminal undertaking; that is, in the end, for their very obedience.[23] Any crime less than manslaughter or the causing of permanent disability was dismissed by the prosecutor's office, because they carried insufficient penalties. The years spent in custody (*détention préventive*) were multiplied by two and deducted from the final sentence in the Belgian judicial tradition. Since the trial took place between 1948 and 1951, only prison sentences of ten years or longer prevented convicts from suing the Belgian State for abusive internment.

This of course narrowed the possible paths the judicial narrative could have chosen into a very cramped alley, one moreover with a lasting impact on the historical narratives. The narrow construction of German guilt, commonly admitted until the 1980s, of a criminal clique around Hitler, of a few rotten apples in the basket of a *Saubere Wehrmacht* and, beyond that, of a relatively clean war in the West, compared to the all-out war in the East, was bound to inform the mainstream historiography of German occupation in Western Europe for the decades that followed the closing down of the military tribunals, if only because of the very limited coverage in terms of individuals the judicial sources allowed historians to have.

A second unintended consequence of the exemplary case the Belgian judiciary wanted to make was caused by its desire to grant German suspects integral access to legal counsel, defence and appeal procedures. Defendants could appeal the judgment, which they overwhelmingly did, and after a failed appeal they could bring their case to the Supreme Court (*Cour de Cassation*). The very restrictive jurisprudence of the Supreme Court, as of 1948, curtailed even further the margins of the judicial strategy of the prosecution. Suspects were entitled to both a Belgian and a German defence counsel. American occupation authorities in Germany, with considerable experience in the matter, strongly advised against this idea and consequently refused exit permits to German lawyers from their zone. The British authorities proved more cooperative and, especially, the *Landesministerium für Justiz* of *Rheinland-Westfalen* agreed to foot the bill for all German *Kriegsverurteilte* in Belgian custody. What Belgian officials initially accepted as an unexpected boon for the financial management of the operation soon turned into the magistrates' nightmare. The German counsel were mostly high-profile lawyers with experience in international law, some of them university professors, while the prosecutor's team was made up of mostly young and inexperienced graduates who had never encountered international law in their university curriculum. The German team was, moreover, backed up by the *Zentrale Rechtsschutzstelle für Kriegsverurteilte* in Bonn, a federal clearinghouse centralising the jurisprudence of German suspects standing trial all over Europe, before American, British, French, Danish, Italian and other tribunals. It took an all-out effort by the prosecutor's office, and the help of Belgian delegations in European capitals, to fight this unequal battle and reverse the intellectual power balance.

The most notorious consequence of the presence of German defence counsel in the courtroom was the rampant internationalisation of the jurisprudential framework. Through their intervention, court decisions in Copenhagen and Dachau, in Rome and The Hague entered the perimeter of the space in which Belgian judges made law. The central contentious issues in the Belgian trials had been addressed in very comparable terms elsewhere: the legitimate means of counterinsurgency by an occupying army, the recourse to torture with terrorism suspects, the shooting of hostages. The post-war jurisprudence was all but avant-garde in this regard. The American Nuremberg successor trials, and the Balkan hostages case in particular, went to some length to reaffirm the rights of a standing army facing insurgency. If German conduct in occupied Yugoslavia, which the American military tribunal had been very careful to qualify, was the yardstick, then German conduct in Belgium could only appear moderate indeed.[24]

The trial of the head of the German occupation in Belgium, General von Falkenhausen, and three of this immediate subordinate generals, and the files it produced, have been a central source for the history of the German occupation in Belgium until this day.[25] Von Falkenhausen got off rather lightly, for the reasons explained above. In March 1951, three weeks after the end of his trial, he was released and returned to Germany.[26] His trial was poor history written in the courtroom – a tale of a righteous general upholding the honourable traditions of the *Wehrmacht* facing a conspiracy fomented by Himmler and his SS stooges in Brussels. As a line of defence in court this was sensible enough, but as a narrative baseline of much of the historiography of Nazi occupation in Belgium, it was very limited. It was also, harking back to the first claim of the usefulness of historical trials laid out in my introduction, decidedly a very poor performance in terms of the satisfaction it offered to the thirst for justice for the victims, whose fate was only cursorily and in oddly dispersed patches evoked in the trial. Still, the von Falkenhausen trial – and with it the experiment in war crime trials before Belgian courts in the years 1948 to 1951 (when reconciliation with the Federal Republic put an end to it) – was hailed as a major accomplishment, a source for pride and a triumph for the Belgian militants of the minor utopia of international law.[27] This short episode is inscribed in a long tradition of commitment to international law, from the founding of the Institute of International Law in Ghent in 1873, the Nobel Prize for the militant of international law Henri La Fontaine in 1913 to the ephemeral law of universal jurisdiction for war crimes and crimes against humanity of 1993. The International Criminal Tribunal for Yugoslavia cites the Belgian jurisprudence of the late 1940s on these precise issues (such as the invalidation of recourse to superior order as a defence argument).[28]

The case the Belgian judiciary first and foremost wanted to make in 1948 was that it was possible, in spite of the unfortunate precedents of Leipzig, Nuremberg and Malmédy, to exercise extraterritorial justice, that is, to bring soldiers, officers and civil servants of a foreign state to court, while adopting the highest standards of procedure, legal reference and rights of defence; that it is possible to judge a defeated enemy without resorting to expeditious victors' justice and – the biggest victory of it all – to do so without leaving the accused the slightest pretext to reject the sentence on formal grounds and thus to reach a verdict the former enemy is forced to accept. That, for once, impunity was defeated. That this implied a subtle negotiation by which all convicts walked free by 1956 then appeared as only a minor compromise. The exercise of post-war justice in Belgium concerning Belgian nationals and Germans thus reached exactly opposite results: impressive quantities but debatable quality of the verdicts for the former, almost negligible numbers of convicts, but unassailable verdicts for the latter. The trials were thus not an exercise in backward-looking justice, they were very much forward-looking; they were, in the eyes of their promoters, a monument for the future.

To conclude: it seems that much historical research that is exclusively or predominantly based on judicial sources falls prey to an epistemological fallacy. At the very least, there is a deep misunderstanding between judges and historians. Historians think that trials are all about the past and that courtrooms serve essentially to churn out historical records for future historians to compile. They are a matter of retrospective analysis, a 'work of memory' or a *gerichtliche Aufarbeitung der Vergangenheit*. Judges, on the contrary, are essentially interested in the future; they want to set legal precedent, they want to make a case, which is what will make their trial a 'historical trial'. They are not so much making history in the courtroom as trying to contribute to the history of the courtroom, affirming their jurisdiction, making legal history. The post-war years were a period of intense legal innovation, of controversy, contestation and severe backlashes. Genocide, crimes against humanity, crimes against peace were first created and then stored in the closet of judicial history for half a century after the end of the International Military Tribunal in Nuremberg, at the least as far as international tribunals are concerned. Since the mid 1990s judges are again experimenting on a wide scale with international justice and legal innovation, but these remain intensely contested. The International Criminal Tribunal for former Yugoslavia, the International Criminal Tribunal for Rwanda, the permanent International Criminal Court, 'hybrid' courts, third country jurisdiction, universal jurisdiction and truth and reconciliation commissions compete in a crowded arena. Each court, each judge, has to make its case. They all have to make sure there is a future for their particular staging of justice, for their contribution to the edifice of international law – be it the 'common criminal undertaking' or the inclusion of rape as a constitutive act of genocide, for instance. All of this is very legitimate, but it is, altogether, very different from what historians hold to be the process of writing of history. Historians should no more expect judges to write history than victims should expect consolation from them or war-torn societies should expect reconciliation. International justice, in its hard-fought battle for existence has had to offer inflated promises and raised expectations it cannot fulfil. Telling judges and the wider public that we are perfectly happy if tribunals just create legal precedent and write legal history, and that any of the indirect rewards of the judicial process lie beyond their direct responsibility, is probably the best contribution historians can offer to the edifice of international justice, which, by all accounts, should never become more than a minor utopia.

Notes

1 See Jennifer Trahan, 'Book review of *Enemy of the State: The Trial and Execution of Saddam Hussein* by Michael A. Newton and Michael P. Scharf' in *Cornell Journal of Law and Public Policy* Summer 2009, Vol. 18, no.3, pp. 831–48 and *idem*, 'A critical guide to the Iraqi High Tribunal's Anfal Judgement: Genocide against the Kurds' in *Michigan Journal of International Law* Winter 2009, Vol. 30, no. 2, pp. 305–412.

2 See also Carlo Ginzburg, *Il giudice e lo storico: considerazioni in margine al processo Sofri*, Torino: Einaudi, 1991.

3 Emmanuel Le Roy Ladurie, *Montaillou, village occitan de 1294 à 1324*, Paris: Gallimard, 1975, 640pp. The entire development on Montaillou in this article is owed to Patrick

Boucheron, 'Le dossier Montaillou' in *Le dossier noir de l'Inquisition* in *L'Histoire*, no. 259, Novembre 2001, pp. 46–7, and a conference given at the Université Libre de Bruxelles on 16 December 2005, 'Relire Montaillou: le témoignage, l'historien et l'anthropologue'.

4 The source had been conveniently edited and translated a decade earlier: *Le Registre d'inquistion de Jacques Fournier (Évèque de Pamiers) 1318–1325* traduit et annoté par Jean Duvernoy, préface de Emmanuel Le Roy Ladurie, Paris/La Haye/NY: Mouton Éditeur, 1978, 3 vols [original edition: Privat, 1965].

5 Boucheron, 'Le dossier Montaillou' in *Le dossier noir de l'Inquisition* in *L'Histoire*, no. 259, Novembre 2001, pp. 46–7. See also Le Roy Ladurie's pathetic response in the next issue.

6 Which did not escape some of Le Roy Ladurie's contemporaries; see, among others, Robert Mandrou, *Magistrats et sorciers en France au XVII siècle. Une analyse de psychologie historique*, Paris: Plon, 1968; Carlo Ginzburg, *Il formaggio e i vermi: il cosmo di un mugnaio nel '500*, Torino: Einaudi, 1976; Giovanni Levi, *L'eredità immateriale: carriera di un esorcista nel Piemont del Seicento*, Torino: Einaudi, 1985.

7 See Harry Paape, Gerrold Van der Stroom and David Barnouw, *De Dagboeken van Anne Frank*, Amsterdam: Bert Bakker, 1986 [for the English edition: New York: Doubleday, 1989].

8 See David Barnouw, 'Het Toneelstuk', *ibid.*, pp. 91–7.

9 David Barnouw, 'Aanvallen op de echtheid van het dagboek', *ibid*, pp. 99–119.

10 *Ibid.*

11 Harry Paape, 'Het Verraad', *ibid.*, pp. 33–56.

12 Paape, Van der Stroom and Barnouw, *De Dagboeken van Anne Frank*, *op. cit.*

13 See Amir Weiner, *Making Sense of War: the Second World War and the fate of the Bolshevik Revolution*, Princeton: Princeton University Press, 2001; Tanja Penter, 'Collaboration on Trial: New Source Material on Soviet Postwar Trials against Collaborators' *Slavic Review* 64, no.4 (Winter 2005) pp. 782–90; Nathalie Moine, 'La Commission d'enquête soviétique sur les crimes de guerre nazis: entre reconquête du territoire, écriture du récit de la guerre et usages justiciers', *Mouvement social*, 222, 2008, pp. 81–109.

14 See Luc Huyse, *Onverwerkt verleden: collaboratie en repressie in België, 1942–1953*, Leuven: Kritak, 1991; and Chantal Kesteloot (ed.), 'Repressie en gerechtelijke archieven: problemen en perspectieven' , in *Dossier bij het SOMA-Berichtenblad*, nr. 38, 2003, 66 p.

15 See Pieter Lagrou, 'Eine Frage der moralischen Überlegenheit? Die Ahndung deutscher Kriegsverbrechen in Belgiën' in: Norbert Frei (dir.) *Transnationale Vergangenheitspolitik. Der Umgang mit deutschen Kriegsverbrechern in Europa nach dem Zweiten Weltkrieg*, Göttingen: Wallstein Verlag, 2006, pp. 326–50.

16 See John Horne and Allan Kramer, *German Atrocities 1914. A History of Denial*, New Haven: Yale University Press, 2001.

17 *Ibid.*, pp. 326–55 and Jules Wolf, 'La question des "Crimes de Guerre" en Belgique', *Journal des Tribunaux*, 3 novembre 1946, no. 3700.

18 See http://avalon.law.yale.edu/imt/partvii.asp (accessed on 8 August 2011).

19 See C.L. Louveaux, 'La magistrature dans la tourmente des années 1940–1944' in *Revue de Droit Pénal et de Criminologie*, July 1981, pp. 619–64 and Cassian Lohest and Gaston Kreit, *La Défense des Belges devant le Conseil de Guerre allemand*, Liège: Pax, 1945.

20 James J. Weingartner, *Crossroads of Death: The Story of the Malmédy Massacre and Trial*, Berkeley: University of California Press, 1979, p. 169 and *idem*, *A Peculiar Crusade: Willis M. Everett and the Malmedy Massacre*, New York: New York University Press, 2000.

21 The company commander, Jochen Peiper, became a sales manager for the Porsche Motor company, in charge of the American market. After a new investigation over his role in a massacre of civilians in Northern Italy in 1964, he withdrew to a tiny village in French

Burgundy. Uncovered by the communist newspaper *L'Humanité*, he was killed in 1976 in a fire-bomb attack on his house. Weingartner, *Crossroads*, p. 263.

22 Loi du 20 juin 1947 relative à la compétence des jurisdictions militaires en matière de crimes de guerre, published in the *Moniteur Belge*, No. 177–8, 26–27 June 1947, p. 6304.

23 Rebecca Wittmann, *Beyond Justice: the Auschwitz trial*, Cambridge MA: Harvard University Press, 2005.

24 See Pieter Lagrou, '1945–1955. The Age of Total War' in: Frank Biess and Robert Moeller (eds) *Histories of the Aftermath*, New York and Oxford: Berghahn Books, 2010, pp. 287–96 and *idem*, 'Guerre honorable sur le front de l'Ouest: crime, punition et reconciliation' in Gaël Eismann et Stefan Martens, *Occupation et répression militaire allemandes*, Paris: Autrement, 2007, pp. 201–20.

25 See particularly Albert de Jonghe, 'De strijd Himmler – Reeder om de benoeming van een HSSPF te Brussel', *Bijdragen tot de Geschiedenis van de Tweede Wereldoorlog*, Brussels, 1974, pp. 9–82; 1976, pp. 5–52; 1978, pp. 5–178; 1982, pp. 97–186; 1984, pp. 5–234 (also available in French translation in the parallel editions of the *Cahiers d'Histoire de la Seconde Guerre mondiale*).

26 In September 1960 he would marry Cécile Vent, a Belgian resistance heroine who had regularly visited him in prison, a couple incarnating European reconcilation. See Pieter Lagrou, 'Guerre honorable sur le front de l'Ouest', *op. cit.*

27 See Jay Winter, *Dreams of Peace and Freedom: utopian moments in the twentieth century*, New Haven: Yale University Press, 2006.

28 See for instance http://www.un.org/icty/erdemovic/appeal/judgement/erd-adojcas971007e.htm (accessed on 4 June 2012).

CHAPTER 2

Building the narrative

The UN Tribunals for the former Yugoslavia, Rwanda and Sierra Leone

William A. Schabas

In 2004, the United Nations Secretary-General published 'The rule of law and transitional justice in conflict and post-conflict societies'. The document considered the range of initiatives undertaken at the international level over the previous decade or so, including the special criminal tribunals. The Secretary-General noted that these tribunals sought to advance a number of objectives, 'among which are bringing to justice those responsible for serious violations of human rights and humanitarian law, putting an end to such violations and preventing their recurrence, securing justice and dignity for victims, *establishing a record of past events*, promoting national reconciliation, re-establishing the rule of law and contributing to the restoration of peace'.[1] He added that criminal trials 'can also help societies to emerge from periods of conflict by establishing detailed and well-substantiated records of particular incidents and events'.[2]

The role of international criminal tribunals as arbiters of historical truth has been contested since the first manifestations of this modern phenomenon, at Nuremberg and Tokyo. Referring to a national trial, but one subject to provisions of international law and widely regarded as part of the corpus of international criminal law, Hannah Arendt, in *Eichmann in Jerusalem*, wrote:

> The purpose of the trial is to render justice and nothing else; even the noblest of ulterior purposes – 'the making of a record of the

> Hitler regime which would withstand the test of history', as Robert G. Storey, executive trial counsel at Nuremberg formulated the supposed higher aims of the Nuremberg Trials – can only detract from the law's main business: to weigh the charges brought against the accused, to render judgment, and to mete out due punishment.[3]

Storey's remarks, cited by Arendt, cannot be found in the published proceedings of the trial and the source of her quotation is not evident. Ironically, the closest resemblance in the transcripts of the International Military Tribunal is a comment by Otto Freiherr von Londinghausen, who was counsel to Konstantin Freiherr von Neurath:

> In this age it may be said that one cannot imagine any avowed dictator or omnipotent despot who can rule without or against the will, or at least the tacit approval of the nation, at least its majority. And so – it is necessary to make this known to the world – invisible behind the defendants, there sits also in the prisoners' dock our poor beaten and tortured German people, because it placed upon a pedestal and selected as leader a man who led it to its doom. From this follows of necessity the inescapable demand that, contrary to the concept of a conspiracy applied in regard to ordinary criminals, application of the concept of conspiracy applied in international law must first proceed to investigate and examine how it happened – how it could happen that an intellectual, high-ranking people, a people who gave so much to the world in terms of cultural and spiritual gifts as the German people did – that it could hail a man such as Hitler, follow him into the bloodiest of all wars, giving him the best it had. Not until you, Your Honours, have taken this into consideration and examined this question, will you be able to establish a just verdict in regard to the individual defendants themselves, with due consideration for their dissimilarity – a judgment which will stand the test of history.[4]

Von Neurath was judged to be a relatively less egregious figure by comparison with his co-accused, and he was one of the few Nuremberg defendants to be condemned to a fixed term of imprisonment. His counsel never received an answer from the Tribunal. The question was left to genuine historians.

The era of the modern-day international criminal tribunals begins in 1993, when the United Nations Security Council decided to establish the International Criminal Tribunal for the former Yugoslavia.[5] Largely modelled on the precedent of Nuremberg, the Tribunal was deemed to be superior in some respects, notably in the fact that it seemed impervious to the charges that it had been established by the victors to judge those they had vanquished, and that it applied law that had not been previously accessible and foreseeable. The following year, in 1994, the Security Council established a similar institution to address the genocide in Rwanda.[6] The huge costs of the two international criminal tribunals prompted the United Nations to explore less costly options. In 2002, it reached agreement with the Government of Sierra Leone to establish a Special Court composed of national and international personnel, including judges, with modest aspirations in terms of the number of trials it might undertake and a funding model based upon voluntary contributions from interested states rather than a draw on the general budget of the organization.[7]

There is now a fourth United Nations international criminal tribunal, the Special Tribunal for Lebanon, but its work is still at a preliminary stage and although the first indictments were issued early in 2011, nobody has yet been taken into custody.[8] The Lebanon Tribunal has an extremely narrow mandate. It is charged with prosecuting those responsible for a single assassination of a leading politician that took place in February 2005. The broad sweep of recent history of Lebanon seems to be far from its concerns. Indeed, it might be said that the reason for the narrowly drafted remit of the Special Tribunal is precisely to avoid some of the major historic events in that country in recent times, such as the 2006 war between Israel and Hezbollah.

The three fully operational United Nations international criminal tribunals, for the former Yugoslavia, Rwanda and Sierra Leone, were established to address major conflicts in different parts of the world. Each has now generated an enormous volume of case law. The tribunals have held many dozens of major trials. In most of these, there have been important debates about the history of the situations being considered. These have gone well beyond the specifics of the charges against the individual accused. In a general sense, the pattern of prosecutions has confirmed perceptions of the conflict that are widely shared by contemporary historians. In some respects, however, they disappoint. Observers of the conflicts in the Balkans have noted the prevalence of rape, and its use as a weapon of war. There have been only a few prosecutions for sexual violence, and they do not reveal the sort of plan or pattern described in the literature.

Expert testimony, from historians, has often been adduced, generally in order to provide some background for the charges or, from the defence standpoint, to provide perspective and sometimes offer evidence in mitigation. But in the Milošević trial, when the Prosecutor put someone identified as a historian on the witness list, presiding Judge Richard May said that

> according to your list, you're going to call somebody who is simply identified as a historian who will apparently deal with the historical context of relations between Serbs and Albanians in Kosovo. Now, again, let me put you on notice that we shall look very carefully at this sort of evidence. While it's right that historians have been called before this Tribunal, there must be a limit to the amount of evidence which we can obtain or have put before us, particularly in the light of history. The amount of historical evidence we will want to hear is very limited.[9]

Many others had already been tried before the Milošević case, however, and Judge May was probably satisfied that most of the historic context had already been elucidated in earlier judgments.

In a presentation to the United Nations General Assembly, the first president of the International Criminal Tribunal for the former Yugoslavia, Antonio Cassese, said the institution was creating 'an historical record of what occurred during the conflict thereby preventing historical "revisionism"'.[10] The 1998 Annual Report of the Tribunal stated:

> Ensuring that history listens is a most important function of the Tribunal. Through our proceedings we strive to establish as judicial fact the full details of the madness that transpired in the former Yugoslavia. In the years and decades to come, no one will be able to deny the depths to which their brother and sister human beings sank. And by recording the capacity for the evil in all of us, it is hoped to recognise warning signs in the future and to act with sufficient speed and determination to prevent such bloodshed.[11]

Similar pronouncements appear, but only relatively occasionally, in judgments of the tribunals: 'It is one of the purposes of the International Tribunal to establish a historical record of the event [*sic*] in the former Yugoslavia. It is also a purpose of the International Tribunal, and a duty owed by the prosecution to the International Tribunal, to look for the "truth" of those events.'[12] In one case, a Trial Chamber said that the ethnic cleansing of the village of Ahmići which was at issue in the proceedings, had

> gone down in history as comprising one of the most vicious illustrations of man's inhumanity to man. Today, the name of that small village must be added to the long list of previously unknown hamlets and towns that recall abhorrent misdeeds and make us all shudder with horror and shame: Dachau, Oradour sur Glâne,

> Katijn, Marzabotto, Soweto, My Lai, Sabra and Shatila, and so many others.[13]

The Trial Chamber cautioned, however, that its 'primary task . . . was not to construct a historical record of modern human horrors in Bosnia and Herzegovina. The principal duty of the Trial Chamber was simply to decide whether the six defendants standing trial were guilty of partaking in this persecutory violence or whether they were instead extraneous to it and hence, not guilty.'[14] Slightly later, another Trial Chamber said it preferred to avoid 'expressing rhetorical indignation that these events should ever have occurred at all'. It said it would leave it 'to historians and social psychologists to plumb the depths of this episode of the Balkan conflict and to probe for deep-seated causes. The task at hand is a more modest one: to find, from the evidence presented during the trial, what happened' during the brief period relevant to the indictment.[15]

Sometimes, historical truth has been presented as a by-product of the international criminal proceedings rather than as an objective, even a secondary one. In *Milutinović* et al., a Trial Chamber said that it had 'one core task: to determine whether the Prosecution had proved the guilt of any of the Accused on any of the charges'.[16] Nevertheless, '[c]oincidentally, the narrative of this Judgment includes information which may help to provide a fuller understanding of events in 1998 and 1999 in Kosovo. This Judgment is, however, simply one element in an array of material from which historians will derive a complete historical account.'[17] In a judgment of the International Criminal Tribunal for Rwanda, judges noted that defence and prosecution evidence was not necessarily contradictory and that 'when viewed in combination as a whole' it provided 'a broader historical record of the killings at Kabuye hill'.[18]

Sometimes, judges have refused to address issues that are of undoubted historical importance but essentially irrelevant for the purposes of a determination of criminal liability. For example, the International Criminal Tribunal for Rwanda has ignored the issue of responsibility for the shooting down of the presidential aeroplane, an event that sparked the killings in April 1994. Even if it could be proven that the Rwandese Patriotic Front forces were responsible for the assassination, this could in no way provide a defence to persons charged with subsequent acts of genocide.[19]

Some commentators have assessed the function of tribunals as writers of history with favour. For example, Professor Richard Wilson has written that '[j]udgments handed down by the International Criminal Tribunal for the Former Yugoslavia (ICTY or Tribunal) challenge the long-held assumption in socio-legal scholarship that courts are inappropriate venues to construct wide-ranging historical explanations of past conflicts.'[20] But a former judge of the Yugoslavia Tribunal, Patricia Wald of the United States, has written that

> ... dozens of pages in ICTY judgments focus on the causes and precursors of the 1991 outbreak of hostilities. However, commentators, citizens, and officers of the implicated countries increasingly suggest that the adversarial trial process and the findings of judges may not produce the best approximations of history. Moreover, the 'adjudication' by ICTY of who started, prolonged, or ended the war and why in the context of criminal proceedings without the states themselves having input is basically unfair, or at least does not contribute to future reconciliation.[21]

Indeed, the role of the tribunals as authors of history is controversial. At various times, prosecutors, defence counsel and judges have all insisted that this is not a burden that should be placed upon the shoulders of judicial institutions. It has the potential to distort both prosecution and defence, they have argued. On other occasions, however, these actors in the process have acknowledged that their role as historians is inescapable.

For example, one of the earliest trials at the International Criminal Tribunal for the former Yugoslavia involved brutality in a concentration camp in central Bosnia, located not far from the road between Sarajevo and Mostar. It was quite typical of the first cases in that it focused on low-level perpetrators. This did not lend itself to discussions about the broad features of the conflict and its background. According to the judgment,

> The Indictment at issue in the present case is solely concerned with events in the municipality (*opstina*) of Konjic, in central Bosnia and Herzegovina, during a period of months in 1992. The Trial Chamber does not consider it necessary to enter into a lengthy discussion of the political and historical background to these events, nor a general analysis of the conflict which blighted the whole of the former Yugoslavia around that time. The function of the Trial Chamber is to do justice in the case at hand and while this naturally involves presenting its findings in context, we will limit this background section to those facts which are necessary to situate the evaluation of the present case.[22]

Often, judges have insisted that the portions of their decisions concerning history be viewed as background information rather than as proven facts.

What they have labelled 'historical context' should be considered as 'essentially a brief explanation of events in deliberately neutral language aimed at allowing the Trial Chamber to form some idea of the historical backdrop'.[23]

Debates about the history-recording function of the international prosecutions have arisen in the context of determining the scope of a given trial. In order to shorten the length of proceedings, judges have often requested that the scope of indictments be reduced. In reply, prosecutors have maintained that broad indictments are necessary for the purpose of establishing the historical record. For example,

> As a final argument, the Prosecution submits that reducing the scope of the Indictment would risk the creation of an inaccurate historical record. It argues that '[t]he loss of the Slobodan Milošević Judgment left an inevitable void in terms of the historical record of the scope of the atrocities committed by Milošević and his co-perpetrators' and that 'the Tribunal is now faced with the opportunity [. . .] to create a permanent historical record of these atrocities and to bring justice to the victims of these heinous crimes'. In this regard, it also submits that a further reduction of the Indictment 'would result in a historically and factually inaccurate record, and a loss of possibly the last opportunity the Tribunal has to achieve one of its core goals [. . .] – to bring effective redress to the victims of international humanitarian law violations'. However,

Figure 2.1 Slobodan Milošević, ICTY, The Hague, 2002. © Paul Vreeker/POOL/AP.

> the Tribunal was established to administer justice, and not to create a historical record. The Trial Chamber will therefore not consider this argument as relevant . . .[24]

The reference to the *Milošević* trial is apt but perhaps mistaken. The former Serbian President died of natural causes after proceedings had been under way for four years. Arguably, had the charges against him been more focused, and the different aspects of the conflicts in the former Yugoslavia addressed through distinct trials, at least one set of proceedings might have been completed. So the search for the more exhaustive historical portrait may ultimately have backfired. Even the determination of the mode of participation in the offence has been presented as being useful for purposes of the 'historical record'.[25] In one case on appeal, judges rejected the defendant's argument that a detailed reasoned opinion was required in order to establish the 'historical record'.[26]

In *Milošević*, judges decided to join the indictments so as to hold one long trial, covering the distinct conflicts in Croatia, Bosnia and Herzegovina and Kosovo, rather than two shorter ones. Arguing for the joinder of the different indictments, the Prosecutor unsuccessfully invoked an argument related to the role of the Tribunal as historian. According to one commentator, the thrust of Carla Del Ponte's approach was that 'the separation of the charges against Milošević into two distinct trials would work to establish two distinct historical narratives, constituting the conflicts in Croatia and Bosnia and Herzegovina as one event, and the conflict in Kosovo as an entirely distinct historical event'.[27] Del Ponte insisted that the two conflicts were linked, and that 'the constitution of two separate narratives actually causes prejudice to victims . . . provid[ing] an alternative to the discriminatory historical narratives which form the legitimating basis for the violence perpetrated upon them'.[28] James Cockayne has noted that

> . . . the decision crucially affected the construction of the historical narrative through the Milošević trial. The Appeals Chamber's decision required the Trial Chamber to hear the Kosovo Indictment first. In effect, this makes the players in the drama act out Act III before Acts I and II. Inevitably, the Prosecution has had to engage in a number of re-writes of the script along the way, to help the trial's audience contextualize the drama it sees played out in the Churchillplein courtrooms.[29]

As he explained, the making of decisions by prosecutors and judges about 'the process of determining individual legal liability is, in the context of trying the architects of mass violence, inevitably bound up with a larger project of constructing an alternative public historical narrative'.[30] Milošević contested the proposal to join the indictments in a single trial as a gambit by the Prosecutor to push back the Kosovo charges. He said: 'It is a consequence of the 11th of September. They wish to place in the background the charges for Kosovo because those charges of Kosovo inevitably open up the issue of the cooperation of Clinton's administration with the terrorists in Kosovo, including the bin Laden organisation.'[31] Milošević said that a single trial would aim at 'creating an historical fallacy that will be [used] to accuse those who defended Yugoslavia of breaking it up'.[32]

These issues have also been considered in the context of guilty plea proceedings, of which there have been several, especially at the Yugoslavia Tribunal. In effect, a defendant acknowledges guilt and proposes not to contest the charges of the Prosecutor, in exchange for a reduction in the list of crimes for which a conviction will be registered. An agreed statement of facts is filed with the Court. This is said to be beneficial to victims, because they are saved the trauma of testimony, while critics argue that such proceedings deprive victims of their voices. Guilty pleas save precious resources, expedite proceedings, and avoid the risk of full acquittals. Guilty pleas are taken as mitigating circumstances because they 'may contribute to the process of national reconciliation'.[33]

Concerns have been expressed that guilty plea proceedings may distort the historical record that some contend the tribunals are expected to construct.[34] Judges have noted that a plea agreement may impede the fulfilment of their mandate, 'which is to bring the truth to light and justice to the people of the former Yugoslavia. Neither the public, nor the judges themselves come closer to knowing the truth beyond what is accepted in the plea agreement.'[35] As a result, they have warned, there might be 'an unfortunate gap in the public and historical record of the concrete case'.[36] Accordingly, '[a] public trial, with the presentation of testimonial and documentary evidence by both parties, creates a more complete and detailed historical record than a guilty plea, which may only establish the bare factual allegations in an indictment or may be supplemented by a statement of facts and acceptance of responsibility by the accused.'[37] Nevertheless,

> when coupled with an accused's substantial co-operation with the prosecution, an agreement grants more insights into previously undiscovered areas. However, while treating plea agreements with appropriate caution, it should be recalled that this Tribunal is not the final arbiter of historical facts. That is for historians. For the judiciary focusing on core issues of a criminal case before this

> International Tribunal, it is important that justice be done and be seen to be done.[38]

It has been said that, before accepting a plea agreement, the court 'may seek to ensure that the totality of the accused's criminal conduct is reflected and that an accurate historical record exists'.[39]

Sometimes, trial chambers have underscored the limited extent of their assessments, pointing out that for the purposes of 'history' their account is inadequate. Momčilo Krajišnik was a Bosnian Serb leader who was closely associated with Radovan Karadžić. Convicting him of crimes against humanity and war crimes, a Trial Chamber concluded that there had been 3,000 Muslim and Croat victims during the indictment period, a figure that would be generally perceived as a grotesque understatement. The judgment explained '[t]o avoid any misunderstanding' that its conclusion was 'not a historical finding, but a legal one'.[40] It said it could only base its conclusions on the evidence received, and that it could not 'exclude the possibility that more Muslims and Croats were killed in these municipalities during the relevant time period'.[41]

One of the major decisions of the International Criminal Tribunal for Rwanda, concerning military leaders, resulted in the dismissal of charges of conspiracy to commit genocide, although the accused were convicted of other crimes. The judges explained that they were not asked to determine 'whether there was a plan or conspiracy to commit genocide in Rwanda' but rather 'whether the Prosecution has proven beyond reasonable doubt based on the evidence in this case that the four Accused committed the crime of conspiracy'.[42] The acquittal on the conspiracy charges provoked a chorus from genocide deniers, who said the judgment proved they were right all along. Bagosora's defence counsel, Peter Erlinder, wrote that 'after seven years of receiving the best evidence the [Rwandese Patriotic Front] could muster, three judges of the UN tribunal for Rwanda unanimously concluded that the story of the Rwanda genocide told by the victors . . . of a "long-planned conspiracy to commit a genocide of Tutsi civilians" by top military officers was *not supported by the evidence.*'[43] Professor Charles Jalloh has properly described this as mischaracterization, noting that the Trial Chamber was well aware of 'the weightiness of its finding in the specific case before it but also for Rwanda's contested history'. He has pointed to portions of the judgment where the judges said they '*cannot exclude that there were in fact plans prior to 6 April [1994] to commit genocide in Rwanda*', and that 'there are certain indications in the evidence of a prior plan or conspiracy to perpetrate a genocide as well as other politically motivated killings in Rwanda, which could have been triggered upon the resumption of hostilities between the government and the RPF or following some other significant event'.[44]

Indeed, earlier rulings of the International Criminal Tribunal for Rwanda described the 1994 genocide as a proven fact that was no longer subject to dispute. Relying on a precedent applicable at the Nuremberg Tribunal,[45] the modern international criminal tribunals may take judicial notice of 'facts that are not subject to reasonable dispute, including common or universally known facts, such as general facts of history'. According to one Trial Chamber, these must be facts 'so notorious, or clearly established or susceptible to determination by reference to readily obtainable and authoritative sources that evidence of their existence is unnecessary'.[46] Judicial notice can only be taken of 'facts not subject to reasonable dispute'.[47] The mission of the tribunals as historians has been invoked as one of the justifications for judicial notice. To attain this objective, it is said to be desirable that they arrive at relatively similar conclusions.[48] In *Karemera* et al., the Appeals Chamber of the International Criminal Tribunal for Rwanda stated:

> The Appeals Chamber agrees with the Prosecution: the fact that genocide occurred in Rwanda in 1994 should have been recognized by the Trial Chamber as a fact of common knowledge. Genocide consists of certain acts, including killing, undertaken with the intent to destroy, in whole or in part, a national, ethnical, racial or religious group, as such. There is no reasonable basis for anyone to dispute that, during 1994, there was a campaign of mass killing intended to destroy, in whole or at least in very large part, Rwanda's Tutsi population, which (as judicially noticed by the Trial Chamber) was a protected group. That campaign was, to a terrible degree, successful; although exact numbers may never be known, the great majority of Tutsis were murdered, and many others were raped or otherwise harmed. These basic facts were broadly known even at the time of the Tribunal's establishment; indeed, reports indicating that genocide occurred in Rwanda were a key impetus for its establishment, as reflected in the Security Council resolution establishing it and even the name of the Tribunal. During its early history, it was valuable for the purpose of the historical record for trial chambers to gather evidence documenting the overall course of the genocide and to enter findings of fact on the basis of that evidence. Trial and Appeal Judgements thereby produced (while varying as to the responsibility of particular accused) have unanimously and decisively confirmed the occurrence of genocide in Rwanda, which has also been documented by countless books,

> scholarly articles, media reports, U.N. reports and resolutions, national court decisions, and government and NGO reports. At this stage, the Tribunal need not demand further documentation. The fact of the Rwandan genocide is a part of world history, a fact as certain as any other, a classic instance of a 'fact of common knowledge'.[49]

Although the International Criminal Tribunal for the former Yugoslavia and the Special Court for Sierra Leone have also determined the existence of 'historical facts of common knowledge',[50] there are no comparable defining events like the Rwandan genocide that have been adjudicated in this manner.

Unlike the International Criminal Court, where the Prosecutor has enormous leeway in the choice of 'situations' for prosecution, the exercise of discretion at the ad hoc tribunals for the former Yugoslavia, Rwanda and Sierra Leone is limited to the selection of specific offenders within relatively narrow temporal and territorial jurisdictional parameters. But even these determinations can have an enormous impact on the narrative that emerges from the work of the institutions. For example, although the International Criminal Tribunal for the former Yugoslavia had jurisdiction over the NATO bombing campaign in early 1999, the Prosecutor chose not to pursue charges of war crimes directed against military leaders of the United States and some countries in Western Europe.[51] Accusations of one-sided prosecution have also been levelled against the International Criminal Tribunal for Rwanda. Human Rights Watch has said the failure to prosecute atrocities perpetrated by the Rwandese Patriotic Front 'would be a failure of justice – not merely victor's justice' that 'will taint perceptions of the Tribunal's impartiality and undermine its legitimacy for years to come'.[52] The Special Court for Sierra Leone provides a remarkable contrast. Its first Prosecutor chose to pursue the various combatant groups in the conflict, including leaders of the popular pro-government Civilian Defence Forces. In making such discretionary choices, the international prosecutors frame the narratives of the conflicts themselves, although they generally defend their choices as being based upon allegedly objective assessments of the gravity of specific crimes rather than a more policy-oriented approach rooted in the didactic function of the judicial record or the need for historical accuracy.

The paradigm of one-sided trials is the International Military Tribunal at Nuremberg. Holocaust deniers charge that the silence of Nuremberg about Allied war crimes manifests an underlying hypocrisy.[53] An obnoxious slogan of some German neo-Nazis reads 'Auschwitz + Dresden = 0'. But such a dismissive view of Nuremberg is not limited to extremists, and finds much currency in the academic literature of international criminal justice. Recently, in proceedings before the European Court of Human Rights, Latvia argued that a recent prosecution of an anti-Nazi partisan 'helped to make up for the inadequacies of the Nuremberg trial, a trial that had to a large extent been an example of justice for the victors, punishing crimes perpetrated by the Nazis, while allowing notorious criminal acts by the Allies to go unpunished'.[54] Similar critiques were made of the International Military Tribunal for the Far East (the 'Tokyo Trial'). They were dramatically highlighted in the famous dissent by Judge Pal. He was concerned both about the retroactivity issue and the one-sided nature of the proceedings. For Judge Pal, the European allies in the Pacific conflict were just as egregious as the Japanese, and he consequently voted to acquit all of the defendants.[55]

The historical narrative that results from the post-World War II trials is one of a conflict between good and evil, where atrocities perpetrated by one side cannot be compared with the breaches of the other. It is a view of the War that would be shared, in a broad sense, by historians. To that extent, the narrative generated by the courts corresponds to that of the academy. Is not the same process at work at the modern tribunals? The Rwanda Tribunal depicts a conflict marked by a crime so heinous and appalling that prosecution for offences committed by the 'other side' might actually distort history rather than enhance it, just as prosecutions of Allies and Nazis alike might have done the same sixty years earlier. Similarly, the prosecutorial choices with respect to the conflicts in the former Yugoslavia may also find their legitimacy from a broader historical perspective. Of course, these matters remain subject to debate, but then so too do many aspects of the Second World War.

The anomaly of the Special Court for Sierra Leone, with its apparent attempt at even-handedness, may be explained by the circumstances of the conflict, where the just war scenario does not fit with the same degree of comfort. To be sure, there were many in Sierra Leone who viewed the civil conflict of the 1990s as a 'rebel war' for which responsibility could be imputed to one side and not the other. The more nuanced view adopted by the Prosecutor in the selection of suspects was in fact largely corroborated by the work of the Truth and Reconciliation Commission, which operated from 2002 to 2004 when the Court was beginning its first trials but before any had been completed. The Commission issued its final report in October 2004. There were some initial suggestions that the Truth Commission might provide the historical background for the prosecutions before the Special Court.[56] Indeed, the two institutions were considered to be broadly complementary, each having its own field of action and specific mandate. Perhaps unexpectedly, the historic narratives that have emerged from them are not identical. The Court has tended to emphasize external causes for the conflict, such as political manipulation by foreign political leaders and the international diamond trade, while the Commission's conclusions focused on internal factors, such as governance for several decades by a corrupt oligarchy. It is not apparent, however, that the different perspectives of the Truth and Reconciliation Commission and the Special Court can be explained by its mandate or its structure. Rather, this is probably attributable to the assessments of the individuals who were involved.

In his 2004 report on the rule of law, the United Nations Secretary-General acknowledged that 'other transitional justice mechanisms', such as truth and reconciliation commissions, may address 'the inherent limitations of criminal justice processes — to do the things that courts do not do or do not do well — in particular . . . to meet the need for a full, comprehensive historical record of what happened during the period of conflict and why'.[57] But it is probably better to recognize that international courts and truth commissions contribute in distinct ways, each providing an element of the historical narrative, in much the same way as we speak about the product of historians who work with different types of sources, such as archival materials and live interviews with participants. International criminal tribunals contribute to the historical narrative, but they provide a version that is flat and lacking in nuance. Truth Commissions provide different perspectives, and help to generate a portrait in three dimensions, not two.

Notes

1 'The rule of law and transitional justice in conflict and post-conflict societies', UN Doc. S/2004/616, para. 38 (my emphasis).
2 *Ibid.*, para. 39.
3 Hannah Arendt, *Eichmann in Jerusalem: A Report on the Banality of Evil*, New York: Viking, 1964, p. 253.
4 (1948) 19 IMT 221,
5 UN Doc. S/RES/827 (1993).
6 UN Doc. S/RES/955 (1994), annex.
7 Statute of the Special Court for Sierra Leone, (2002) 2178 UNTS 138, annex.
8 Statute of the Special Tribunal for Lebanon, UN Doc. S/2006/893, Attachment.
9 *Milošević* (IT-02-54-T), Transcript, 9 January 2002, pp. 242–3.
10 UN Doc. A/52/PV.44, p. 2.
11 'Fifth Annual Report of the International Tribunal for the Prosecution of Persons Responsible for Serious Violations of International Humanitarian Law Committed in the Territory of the former Yugoslavia since 1991', UN Doc. A/53/219-S/1998/737, para. 296.
12 *Halilović* (IT-01-48-T), Motion for Judicial Notice, 1 March 2005, para. 9 (references omitted).

13 *Kupreškić* et al. (IT-95-16-T), Judgment, 14 January 2000, para. 755.
14 *Ibid.*, para. 756.
15 *Krstić* (IT-98-33-T), Judgment, 2 August 2001, para. 2.
16 *Milutinović* et al. (IT-05-87-T), Judgment, 26 February 2009, para. 4.
17 *Ibid.*
18 *Kalimanzira* (ICTR-05-88-T), Judgment, 22 June 2009, para. 386.
19 *Bagosora* et al. (ICTR-98-41-T), Decision on Request for Subpoenas of United Nations Officials, 6 October 2006, paras 12–18.
20 Richard Ashby Wilson, 'Judging History: The Historical Record of the International Criminal Tribunal for the Former Yugoslavia', (2005) 27 *Human Rights Quarterly* 908, at p. 908.
21 Patricia Wald, 'The International Criminal Tribunal for the Former Yugoslavia Comes of Age: Some Observations on Day-to-Day Dilemmas of an International Court', (2001) 5 *Washington University Journal of Law & Policy* 87, pp. 116–17.
22 *Delalić* et al. (IT-96-21-T), Judgment, 16 November 1998, para. 88.
23 *Kayishema* et al. (ICTR-95-1-T), Judgment and Sentence, 21 May 1999, paras 32–3; *Bizimungu* et al. (ICTR-99-50-T), Decision on Prosecutor's Motion for Judicial Notice, paras 14–15.
24 *Stanisić* et al. (IT-03-69-PT) Decision Pursuant to Rule 73*bis* (D), 4 February 2008, para. 21.
25 *Brđanin* (IT-99-36-A), Separate Opinion of Judge Meron, 3 April 2007, para. 7.
26 *Babić* (IT-03-72-A), Judgment on Sentencing Appeal, 18 July 2005, para. 17.
27 James Cockayne, 'Commentary', in André Klip and Göran Sluiter, eds., *Annotated Leading Cases of International Criminal Tribunals, The International Criminal Tribunal for the former Yugoslavia 2001–2002,* Vol. 8, Antwerp/Oxford: Intersentia, 2005, pp. 175–83, at p. 179.
28 *Ibid.*
29 *Ibid.*, at p. 181.
30 *Ibid.*
31 *Milošević* (IT-02-54-T), Transcript, 11 December 2001, p. 134.
32 *Milošević* (IT-02-54-T), Transcript, 30 January 2002, p. 337.
33 *Seregundo* (ICTR-2005-84-I), Judgment and Sentence, 12 June 2006, para. 57.
34 Nancy Amoury Combs, *Guilty Pleas in International Criminal Law, Constructing a Restorative Justice Approach*, Stanford: Stanford University Press, 2007, at pp. 67, 207.
35 *Dragan Nikolić* (IT-94-2-S), Sentencing Judgment, 18 December 2003, para. 122 (references omitted). Also: *Deronjić* (IT-02-61-S), Sentencing Judgment, 4 March 2004, para. 135.
36 *Ibid.*
37 *Momir Nikolić* (IT-02-60/1-S), Sentencing Judgment, 2 December 2003, para. 61.
38 *Dragan Nikolić* (IT-94-2-S), Sentencing Judgment, 18 December 2003, para. 122 (references omitted). Also: *Deronjić* (IT-02-61-S), Sentencing Judgment, 4 March 2004, para. 135.
39 *Momir Nikolić* (IT-02-60/1-S), Sentencing Judgment, 2 December 2003, para. 52.
40 *Krajisnik* (IT-00-39-T), Judgment, September 2006, para. 71.
41 *Ibid.*
42 *Bagosora* et al. (ICTR-98-41-T), Judgment and Sentence, 18 December 2008., para. 2092.
43 Peter Erlinder, *Rwanda: Flawed Elections and the Politics of 'Genocide Denial'*, JURIST – Forum, 28 August 2010, http://jurist.org/forum/2010/08/rwanda-flawed-elections-and-the-politics-of-genocide-denial.php. (accessed 5 June 2012; emphasis in the original).

44 Charles Jalloh, *(Re)Writing History After Rwanda's Genocide: A Response to Peter Erlinder*, JURIST – Forum, 31 August 2010, http://jurist.org/forum/2010/08/rewriting-history-after-rwandas-genocide-a-response-to-peter-erlinder.php (accessed 5 June 2012).

45 Agreement for the Prosecution and Punishment of Major War Criminals of the European Axis, and Establishing the Charter of the International Military Tribunal (IMT), (1951) 82 UNTS 279, annex, art. 21.

46 *Semanza* (ICTR-97-20), Decision on the Prosecutor's Motion for Judicial Notice and Presumptions of Fact Pursuant to Rules 94 and 54, 3 November 2000, para. 25. Also: *Norman* et al. (SCSL-04-14-PT), Decision on Prosecution's Motion for Judicial Notice and Admission of Evidence, 24 June 2004; *Sesay* et al. (SCSL-04-15-PT), Decision on Prosecution's Motion for Judicial Notice and Admission of Evidence, 24 June 2004.

47 *Simić* et al. (IT-95-9-PT), Decision on Pre-trial Motion by the Prosecution Requesting the Trial Chamber to take Judicial Notice of the International Character of the Conflict in Bosnia Herzegovina, 25 March 1999; *Nsabimana* et al. (ICTR-98-42-T), Decision on the Prosecutor's Motion for Judicial Notice and Admission of Evidence, 15 May 2002; *Kajelijeli* (ICTR-98-44A-T), Decision on the Prosecutor's Motion for Judicial Notice Pursuant to Rule 94 of the Rules, 16 April 2002, para. 17.

48 *Semanza* (ICTR-97-20-I), Decision on the Prosecutor's Motion for Judicial Notice and Presumptions of Facts Pursuant to Rules 94 and 54, 3 November 2000, para. 20; *Bizimungu* et al. (ICTR-99-50-T), Decision on Prosper Mugiraneza's First Motion for Judicial Notice Pursuant to Rule 94(B), 10 December 2004, para. 6; *Norman* et al. (SCSL-04-14-AR73), Fofana – Decision on Appeal Against 'Decision on Prosecution's Motion for Judicial Notice and Admission of Evidence', 16 May 2005, para. 21.

49 *Karemera* et al. (ICTR-98-44-AR73(C)), Decision on Prosecutor's Interlocutory Appeal of Decision on Judicial Notice, 16 June 2006.

50 *Strugar* (IT-01-42-T), Judgment, 31 January 2005, para. 13.

51 'Committee Established to Review the NATO Bombing Campaign Against the Federal Republic of Yugoslavia, Final Report to the Prosecutor', The Hague, 13 June 2000, PR/P.I.S./510-e. See: Paolo Benvenuti, 'The ICTY Prosecutor and the Review of the NATO Bombing Campaign against the Federal Republic of Yugoslavia', (2001) 12 *European Journal of International Law* 503; Michael Bothe, 'The Protection of the Civilian Population and the NATO Bombing in Yugoslavia: Comments on a Report to the Prosecutor of the ICTY', (2001) 12 *European Journal of International Law* 531; William J. Fenrick, 'Targeting and Proportionality during the NATO Bombing Campaign against Yugoslavia', (2001) 12 *European Journal of International Law* 489; Michael Mandel, 'Our Case Against NATO and the Lessons to be Learned from it', (2001) 25 *Fordham International Law Journal* 95; N. Ronzitti, 'Is the non liquet of the Final report by the Committee Established to Review the NATO Bombing Campaign Against the Federal Republic of Yugoslavia Acceptable?', (2000) 82 *International Review of the Red Cross* 1017; Robert Cryer, *Prosecuting International Crimes, Selectivity and the International Criminal Law Regime*, Cambridge: Cambridge University Press, 2005, at pp. 213–20.

52 'Kenneth Roth to Hassan Jallow', 14 August 2009. See also: Human Rights Watch, 'Rwanda: Tribunal Risks Supporting "Victor's Justice": Tribunal Should Vigorously Pursue Crimes of Rwandan Patriotic Front', 1 June 2009.

53 David Irving, *Nuremberg, The Last Battle*, London: Focal Point, 1996.

54 *Kononov* v. *Latvia*, no 36376/04, Judgment, 24 July 2008, para. 92.

55 Neil Boister and Robert Cryer, *Documents on the Tokyo International Military Tribunal*, Oxford: Oxford University Press, 2008, at pp. 811–930.

56 *Prosecutor* v. *Norman* (Case No. SCSL-2003-08-PT), Decision on Appeal by the Truth and Reconciliation Commission for Sierra Leone ('TRC' or 'The Commission') and Chief Samuel Hinga Norman JP Against the Decision of His Lordship Mr Justice Bankole Thompson Delivered on 30 October 2003 to Deny the TRC's Request to Hold a Hearing with Chief Samuel Hinga Norman JP, 28 November 2003.

57 'The rule of law and transitional justice in conflict and post-conflict societies', UN Doc. S/2004/616, para. 47.

CHAPTER 3

Competitive narratives: an incident at the Papon trial

Henry Rousso

This chapter, which is part of a larger work, deals with an incident that lasted around six minutes, in a major trial that lasted about six months. It involves two major players: the president of the *cour d'assises* de Bordeaux, the first level of the criminal court in the French system that gives him a kind of absolute power to run a trial, and Arno Klarsfeld, Beate and Serge Klarsfeld's son, a provocative activist like his mother and a lawyer like his father, defending the victims. Since he was a teenager, Arno Klarsfeld had been active in Nazi hunting and the fight for the recognition of Holocaust survivors in the French national memory. The Klarsfeld family contributed greatly to the holding of all the trials for crimes against humanity in France, in the 1980s and 90s. They adopted in and outside the courtrooms judicial and political strategies that influenced the nature and the meaning of these "show trials," which had no real precedent in the history of French justice. The idea of this chapter came also from Christian Delage's work, which enlightened me on a topic I didn't pay attention to before reading his book: what is at stake when images are shown in a courtroom? Do the images dramatically change the nature of the narratives provided in a tribunal? Are they central pieces for the prosecution or just a way to provoke emotion and curiosity?[1] I will focus here on how a brief and vivid exchange between the president and an attorney about the possibility of showing some photos of the victims could have led to a major incident, in a trial that had been throughout its course a dramatic event.

The incident raises several general questions in the field of memory, and in the field of "restorative justice." What about the violence of the victims, and what about the fact that talking and remembering such crimes as those committed during the Holocaust may arouse mixed feelings among the victims, including revenge, anger, hate, fear? This question is rather a taboo, or at least an uncommon issue when observers of various kinds comment on such trials. Some witnesses or some of their representatives may refuse to follow the symbolic rules, the polite speeches, and the formal respect for the magistrates, for the lawyers, for the accused himself. A courtroom is a place where restraint, self-control, even a bit of hypocrisy is absolutely necessary to oblige the different players to restrict themselves, to control their emotions, to replace a possible desire for revenge with an oral, cold-blooded and patient confrontation under the supervision of a third party. Nevertheless, some of the players, for different reasons related to the nature of the crimes and the impact of their long-term effects, may refuse to play the game.

As a matter of fact, this was the case in the three major French trials for crimes against humanity. In the trial of Klaus Barbie, in July 1987, held at the *cour d'assises* of Lyons, the defendant refused to participate in his own trial, rejecting the legitimacy of the court: "*C'était la guerre, et la guerre c'est fini*" ("It was war, and the war is over"), as he said in French, at the very end of the last session, before the verdict that sent him to jail for life. These words were among the very few that he expressed, and all through the trial (except on two or three occasions) he avoided having to face his victims, who protested in vain about the empty dock. It led to a quasi-absence of any direct confrontation between the perpetrator and the victims, to the contrary of what was expected in this the first "historical trial" of the Holocaust in France. This was a very different situation than the one observed in Jerusalem, in 1961 and 1962, at the Eichmann trial – the "standard" of such trials – where the defendant himself was the main witness, becoming a non-ordinary accused completely involved in his own trial.[2] In the case of Paul Touvier, a former militiaman indicted in 1973, and judged in March and April 1994, at the *cour d'assises* of Versailles, Arno Klarsfeld, who pleaded for the first time and was guided by his father, played the role of the maverick. He didn't follow his colleagues and most of the magistrates, who all accepted the official version of the historical facts examined in the court. On June 29, 1944, at Rillieux, near Lyons, Touvier gave the order to execute seven Jewish hostages, sparing a non-Jewish one. This murder was the main incrimination and the only one that can be identified, fifty years after, as an indelible crime against humanity – war crimes benefit in France from a statute of limitations after twenty years. According to a 1992 jurisprudence, only members of the "Axis forces" could have committed crimes against humanity during World War II. Then, Touvier was indicted as an accomplice who obeyed a German order, which was at the very least a historical mistake, or at worst an official lie. Actually, Touvier followed the orders of the French *Milice* to avenge the murder by the French partisans, the day before the execution of the hostages, of one of its leaders, Philippe Henriot. There was not then any single intervention from the occupiers. It was a "French crime," as Arno Klarsfeld pointed out afterwards.[3] Meanwhile, defending this interpretation could have jeopardized the trial, and run the risk of an acquittal. Because of the legal constraints, very few wanted to deal with a major contradiction: at its very beginning, the Touvier case was supposed to focus more on the French behavior towards the Jews and genuine anti-Semitism, which were not taken into account in the post-war trials, than to emphasize again the process of collaboration, which was at the core of the purges, in 1944 and 1945.[4] Last but not least, at the Papon trial, the same Arno Klarsfeld, representing some "*parties civiles*" (the victims in the French system who participate as such in a criminal trial), refused to accept the rules established by the president and tried literally to take the power within the courtroom "on the behalf of the survivors."

The incident also raised the issue of competitive narratives in a judicial process involving political crimes. In any trial, there is of course a competition between the defense and the prosecution, who adopt by definition contradictory perspectives on the same event. In any trial there is a confrontation between professional magistrates and lawyers, on the one hand, and ordinary people among the victims, the witnesses or the defendant himself, who may be hurt by the specific rules of a tribunal, by the way one talks about violence and suffering, by the absence of emotion or empathy. But in the so-called "show trials" such as Nuremberg, Eichmann, Barbie or Papon there is another kind of competition between two different groups: on one side, those who wish to limit the debates to the judicial case, or want to control emotion, even if it is necessary to maintain a large space for the victims who come to talk not only to the court but to the whole world; on the other side, those who wish to transform the courtroom into a political arena, or into a "*lieu de mémoire*," a realm of memory. We have plenty of historical examples of these oppositions: the cool-blooded President Moshe Landau, at the Eichmann trial, trying to contain the invasive general attorney, Gideon Hausner, or the general prosecutor Pierre Truche, at the Barbie trial, calmly denouncing the strategy of the defense attorney, Jacques Vergès, and his "*défense de rupture*," aiming to politicize the trial and compare the German atrocities during World War II to the French colonial crimes of the 1950s. The incident at the Papon trial belongs to the same kind of confrontation, which seems to be a singularity of "trials for memory."

Georges Gheldman testimony

The main issue in the Papon trial was to prove that Maurice Papon, the former secretary general of the *Préfecture régionale* of Bordeaux during the war, in the occupied zone, and then the local representative of the Vichy government, was personally involved in the deportation of around 1600 Jews, mostly foreigners, between 1942 and 1944, who almost all perished at Auschwitz. More generally, the trial focused on the role of the French administration and the French police in the Holocaust, even if the Papon trial was a kind of a "substitute" for the aborted case of René Bousquet, the head of the Vichy police, who was murdered in June 1993 after his indictment for crimes against humanity but before he could be judged.

When the trial began, the president, Jean-Louis Castagnède, decided to accept the demand of the defense attorney, and let the defendant go free. Even if it is supposed to be the rule in criminal trials, this was a very unusual and surprising decision in the French judicial context, especially if one takes into account the nature of the crimes. Castagnède's idea was to encourage Maurice Papon to participate fully in his trial, in order to avoid what happened during the Barbie trial where the accused was absent, or in the Touvier trial, where the accused didn't really cooperate. This decision provoked a clash among the victims' attorneys, especially Arno Klarsfeld, even if some of them defended it in principle – this was their traditional claim in other trials. Then, from the opening, a kind of a suspicion surrounded the president, with the idea – completely unfounded – that Maurice Papon may be "protected" as a former Gaullist or a former minister.

The incident on which I will focus occurred on December 15, 1997 when the court was examining the rounding up of July 16, 1942 in Dax, near Bordeaux, the same day as the Vél d'Hiv rounding up, in Paris. It followed the trial of a victim, Georges Gheldman, whose mother was arrested, deported and killed. Arno Klarsfeld was then 41 years old, a handsome guy, dressed like a teenager, already well known because of his name or his own action during the Touvier trial. He was also a kind of media figure, who had an affair with the international model Carla Bruni – later France's First Lady – creating a strange link between what were supposed to be two different worlds: those of the survivors and of the jet set. Regarding the trial itself, and as was the case in the Touvier trial, he was under the control of his father, Serge Klarsfeld, who never appeared in the courtroom but was demonstrating practically every day outside with the *Fils et Filles des déportés juifs de France*, the association he founded in the early 1980s and which Arno represented in the trial. Arno Klarsfeld had a very particular style compared to the other lawyers, who were all professionals, with long experience in the courts. On the contrary, he participated mainly, not to say only, in a very few cases involving Holocaust survivors, either in France or in the USA. Actually, Arno was like his father, an activist more than a practicing lawyer. Serge Klarsfeld even declared on many occasions that neither he nor his son liked the law. It was just an instrument for their cause. Nevertheless, the name of Klarsfeld aroused respect in this place because their action opened the path for such trials.

President Castagnède was a serious-looking 53-year-old magistrate who had followed a local career. He was chosen with the idea that the Papon trial should be an "ordinary trial" – a goal that was central as well in the Eichmann and Barbie trials. Full of restrained feelings, mastering his emotions, he actually ruled over one of the longest and hardest trials in France's history. Like other magistrates in the same situation, nothing prepared him to face the challenges of such an event, and he had to take decisions during the sessions on many unusual issues. He agreed, for example, to show on a screen, visible to the entire courtroom including the public, a number of important documents, which was at that time still an uncommon behavior in French courts. Traditionally, only the judges, the prosecutors, and the attorneys could view these pieces of visual evidence, and only the president could decide whether or not to *read* them, in order to let the public follow the debates – in the French criminal procedure, only the president leads the debate, conducts the hearing, and asks the questions. This respects the basic rule that any element of the court trial has to be orally exposed. In this perspective, the Papon trial was the first of the three French trials on the Holocaust to propose a real public and visible cross-examination of many crucial documents, shown to everybody at the same time, as in an academic seminar, an important issue regarding its "historical" and "educational" ambitions.

Georges Gheldman was a ten-year-old child born into a Jewish family from Hungary. The French police arrested them in Dax, on July 16, 1942, and transferred them to the Germans, who released the child. According to the decisions made by the Sipo-SD at a national level, the Nazis didn't want at that moment to arrest children under 16 years old, whereas the Vichy government didn't want to take care of thousands of lonely children, separated from their parents. Georges Gheldman's testimony was a very brief, sober, and moving one:

> On July 16, 1942, when I was ten and a half years, I went home. I probably went to play outside. I returned at teatime and I found a note from my mother asking me to join her at the police station. So I picked up my bike, I went to the police station where I was arrested. My mother was already there, with other people. And

> then we stayed a few hours, after which, under guard, we were taken to the prison of Dax where we were delivered to the Germans. There about a dozen of us spent the night in a large cell. And the next morning, we got out of prison. My mother and the others went, still under German guard, and I was released, I was expelled. I am . . . So I . . . It was the last time I saw my mother. And so I went to a friend of my mother, M. Paul Cougouille, we called him "Father Cougouille," who lived in Dax, who took me, and wrote at that moment a letter to the younger sister of my mother who lived in Paris at that time. And that very evening, in the afternoon, I was so traumatized that I had such a strong bilious attack that I was admitted to the Dax hospital. [. . .] I've been sick for several days. And there I stayed long after I was healed. And when Father Cougouille came to pick me up – I would not say how long later, but at least two weeks later perhaps, even more surely, but now I really have absolutely no concept of time – directly to [take] a bus. There was a smuggler who brought me to the free zone. And when I asked him why I stayed so long, he said it was because the French police were looking for me and that he had left me in the hospital to protect me. That's it.[5]

Then Georges Gheldman went to Brive, in the free zone, and when the Germans invaded the south of France, he went to many other places, protected by civilians or partisans. He never got any news of his mother, but knew she was deported thanks to Serge Klarsfeld's Memorial, listing all the names of the different convoys, published in 1978. After his brief testimony, Maurice Papon asked him to give some "details" about this "drama." He could hardly enter into a sophisticated speech dealing with such a simple tragic situation explained by a first-hand witness. This episode was clear for everybody in the court: the child and his mother were arrested by the French police, given to the Germans, and then the boy was released by the Germans while the Vichy police were looking for him again and while the mother was sent to the death camps. The complicity of Vichy was indubitable. Then Papon played the part of someone who doesn't understand what was going on. He cautiously asked the president: "May I ask the witness when this drama occurred?" as if he didn't know. He talked about the victim in a very formal way as "*Madame votre mère*," trying to deny any responsibility for what happened, and unable to justify the behavior of the Vichy police towards a child that the Germans didn't want to arrest. Later, the president agreed to show a very moving and important handwritten document: the letter sent to the witness's aunt, who lived in Paris, as he referred to it.

Because it was difficult to see it on the screen (the ink was partly erased), Arno Klarsfeld took the initiative and read it loudly to the court, despite this being the exclusive privilege of the president. In this brief letter, the boy explained that his mother "has gone with other Jews to Mérignac [a transit camp] where they will be gathered, then they will go to Germany." Arno Klarsfeld reacted with irony: "This suggests that a ten-year-old boy was better informed than a civil servant from the *préfecture régionale.*" Then, the attorney gave a new and a core element. The Gheldmans were Hungarian Jews. According to the situation in Hungary in 1942, which was an ally of the Third Reich, the Nazis did not target them. But the Vichy administration declared and delivered them to the Germans as "Polish," which led to the death of the mother. Georges Gheldman did not know this and only learned it during the trial from the documents shown. This was clear proof that the French administration falsified the lists in order to abandon a foreign family it wanted to get rid of, and by the same means, to achieve the deportation statistics required by the Nazis.

To summarize the context, this was one of the worst moments for the defendant. He was cornered by the documents, by the victim and his attorney, and by the president. The last two were acting in the same fashion, giving many arguments to the court to prove the complicity of Maurice Papon in this specific case. Nevertheless, and unexpectedly, a few minutes after these exchanges, one of the major incidents of the trial occurred.

Showing the photos of the vanished

When he was describing the faith of the Gheldman family, in the context of vivid emotion in the courtroom – Georges Gheldman couldn't contain himself from crying, as were other participants – Arno Klarsfeld asked the president to show on the wide screen above the court some photos of them, especially of the mother:

> Arno Karsfeld: Perhaps, even so, we can show the photographs, Your Honor? In any event, I would like to show the photographs of Mrs Gheldman . . .
>
> President Castagnède: Yes . . . no . . . I will not show them, I will not show them.
>
> AK: Why?
>
> Pres.: Because I will only show those items that are essential to an understanding of the proceedings.
>
> AK: Your Honor, I believe that these are essential!
>
> Pres.: And that is your opinion. I have made my ruling.

AK: I have asked you several times to show these photographs, to show the photos of [deported] children, and on several occasions you have refused. I have not yet been able to understand why. It is standard procedure in trials to show photographs. You have not read out the names [of the victims], you have only read the names of those persons who are represented here by civil parties to the proceedings. You have not read the others. You too might be interested in some of these Jews, Your Honor, how am I to know?

Pres.: Sir! . . .

AK: So, I would like you to show the photographs . . .

Pres.: Mr Klarsfeld . . .

AK: . . . because that is even so the third time . . .

Pres.: I will not authorize it! . . .

AK: I represent the Sons and Daughters of the Deported, and but for that organization you would not have the honor of presiding over this court, so, seriously, I would like to have these photographs shown and the jurors can then get an idea, imagine, and see who it was that was deported.

Pres.: Mr Klarsfeld, I decided on the goals of this trial at the very outset and as a consequence I am determined, as far as possible, not to waste my time and energy on matters that do not merit attention . . .

AK: (interrupting) This is not a digression, this is worth the effort . . .

Pres.: You have brought to my attention two matters, of a general nature, that would be impermissible and which, without doubt, would normally lead me to rule against you. I want to move to a witness, who can testify as to matters of importance. I am going to prepare for this testimony by studying the documentation that you told me was essential. As for the other matters, I do not wish to hear anything further . . .

AK: . . . so they are flung back into anonymity. This is what you want me to conclude!

Pres.: . . .

AK: I have an obligation, Your Honor, because I represent the voice of those who were killed, and even if it does not give me any pleasure to address you in this manner, I am obliged to do so. I am compelled to take these arguments forward because I have to represent these people. I have to say that I do not understand why we spend a lot of time showing documents which are often of little import and yet the photograph of a woman whose life was shattered cannot be shown on screen? Really, I do not understand.

[*The President talks sotto voce with one of the two other judges.*]

AK: And I believe that many of the civil parties will not be able to understand why the photographs cannot be screened.

Pres.: I appreciate that. At the end of the trial, when the arguments and proofs of what seems to me to be necessary along the way is completed. My concern at the moment – and I do not want us to be led astray – is that, to the extent that the proceedings permit, we present to the jury the evidence that will crystallize the facts and allow them to deliberate and make their decision. And I do not, at this time, want at this stage of the argument, such as it is, to introduce anything other than what witnesses say and the documents show. There are very many important things that will need to be said later [during this trial], and I understand that the witness might hope to see the face of his mother, just as I understand very well that those people who are not civil parties will hope to hear their name read out. All of that, however, is beyond my remit. My role, and I want to fulfill it to the letter, is already onerous without adding anything more to it.

AK: You have a discretionary power, you could exercise it.

Pres.: Again! I don't know if you have understood what I said, but it was extremely clear.

AK [*addressing the witness*]: And so, in any event, Mr Gheldman, I am sorry that the President is opposed to showing the photograph of your mother . . .

Pres.: Once the proceedings are completed I can show as many photographs as I want to!

AK: I remember also [the requests] for the photos of the French internment camps. You said: "Later, Mr Klarsfeld," and it is later and they have still not been shown.

[. . .]

Pres.: Certainly, because we have not finished yet . . .

AK: [*interrupting him*]: . . . and so, I am distressed for good reason because the photo of Mrs Gheldman will never be shown.

Pres.: Enough. Do you have any other questions to ask?

AK: No, I simply have to formulate my apologies to Mr Gheldman for the failure to show the photograph of his mother, like [the photos, the names?] of the 165 other people on the convoy of 18 July [1942] who were sent to hell. I regret that their names will not be read either. That is it, Your Honor.[6]

Who has the power in a show trial?

We clearly have here a competition between two main conceptions of such trials. On the one hand, the president, unsurprisingly, wants to follow his own path. He tries to limit the debates to the specific case examined, to establish the truth and let all the protagonists recount their role. He clearly adopts a historical narrative: Who? When? Where? Why? To the contrary of what has been written here and there, the historical posture was not assumed by the historians, who were heard at the beginning of the trial and delivered very general speeches on Vichy France, without mentioning the Papon case itself.[7] The historical narrative was actually delivered by the president, and some lawyers who had a real knowledge of the case, like Michel Zaoui, Alain Lévy, Gérard Boulanger and Arno Klarsfeld himself. This last one, on the other hand, wanted to transform the courtroom into a place for memory and for mourning. He knew that the trial was being videotaped. Consequently, showing the faces of the victims and providing what he calls "a living trace" of them in the official archives became an obsessional aim for him. He followed what his father did in earlier decades: he gave a name and a face to those who were killed and burned without a burial.

Meanwhile, the real issue was not just a question of memory, nor a noble preoccupation for the victims, but rather the control of the trial. There is, here, a clear will to grasp power in the courtroom and to impose Klarsfeld's very particular views on the case. Serge and Arno Klarsfeld wanted to see Papon condemned, but they pleaded for a lighter sentence than Barbie or Touvier so as to respect the hierarchy of responsibility for the Holocaust in France. In this perspective, they didn't consider Papon to be a "monster," nor did they see him as a fascist but rather as a faithful civil servant. They also assimilated the professional magistrates of the 1990s to the elites who betrayed the country in the 1940s. This is the meaning of the insulting accusation towards the president, suspected of distinguishing between "interesting Jews" and others, an unbearable reference to some practices of the Nazis and of the Vichy Regime. Many activists in the 1990s shared the same caricatured view of the French elites, as engaged primarily in protecting the memory of their predecessors in Vichy France. This was also the case of the former president François Mitterrand, who covered up for his "friend" René Bousquet, but it was a sociological nonsense considering the generation gap between the 1940s and the 1990s.

In his harsh exchange with the president, Arno Klarsfeld showed that some of the victims were trying to take control of what they considered to be *their* trial: "You have the honor to preside over this court thanks to the *Fils et Filles des déportés juifs de France*," the Klarsfelds' association. This statement was legally unacceptable, and historically a mistake, not to say a lie: justice was done on behalf of the French people, and the Papon case was not brought by Klarsfeld but by other activists and lawyers, in the early 1980s.

Epilogues

Two days after the incident, during the December 17 session, after having delivered some clear statements about discipline to the court, the president agreed to show the photos brought by a victim, Elianne Alisvaks-Dommange, whose parents were arrested by the Vichy police and deported by the Germans. End of the story? Not exactly. In 1998, after the end of the trial, Arno Klarsfeld published a book where he gave his own view of the incident: "My 'interesting Jews' were not a gratuitous insolence, but a strategic thrust to force the president to reconsider what I viewed as being 'essential.' Three days later the President will give up and show the pictures. A trial is sometimes a battle; one can't win it with courtesy."[8] A month after the incident, on 28 January 1998, Serge and Arno Klarsfeld revealed that President Castagnède had a further familial link with one of the plaintiffs – which he pretended to ignore; and he was probably in good faith. This was a real *coup de théâtre* threatening his position, but he finally refused to abandon his chair, even if he lost part of his authority. This was a kind of total victory for the Klarsfelds. Maurice Papon was finally declared guilty, and condemned to ten years in prison, the sentence publicly expected by Klarsfeld even if the attorneys have no right to ask for a specific penalty. He was released in January 2001, considered to be too old to remain in jail, a decision that raised a new controversy about the case.

I shall conclude by addressing the reluctance of the president to show images during the trial. From his point of view, the trial was not supposed to produce such a face-to-face confrontation with a lawyer who was also playing an important role in the public debates. The president was respecting the traditional principle of oral proceedings, a pillar of modern law since the eighteenth century. The French Revolution introduced it in France with the 1791 Constitution: "Examination of witnesses is always made orally and without their testimony being written."[9] One wanted to avoid any secret justice, any crooked proof, any supremacy of written documents in establishing the truth. One wanted to open up the judicial debates as well. That is the reason why, in a French criminal trial, only the president, the prosecutor and the attorneys have a copy of the files: the historians, for example, supposed to be the "experts," do not have the right to see any single official document from the case. All the documents mentioned have to be read, usually by the president, as we have already seen.

> The link between oral hearing and the judge's impartiality lies in the guarantee given to the defendant that the judge will base his personal conviction only upon the elements he has acquired during the hearing, which have been submitted to cross-examination by the parties. The aim is to prevent the judge from being influenced by information and evidence gathered during the preliminary stage [for example by the police], which would not have been cross-examined. The truth must appear to everyone at the hearing. The trial stage, oral and totally adversarial, appears to be an opportunity given to the defense to correct the orientation transmitted to the procedure from the investigation phase [before presenting the case to any court, which refers to the French inquisitorial system]. It also protects the accused from the effects that media coverage of a case may have on the impartiality of the *siège* [the judges].[10]

But, in line with the growing use of new technologies, this principle has changed progressively in the last two decades. In a strange coincidence, in March 1998, just before the end of the Papon trial, a French court of appeal, dealing with the case of a president who showed photos in the courtroom, argued that this behavior was contradicted by the principle of oral proceedings. In 1999, the *cour de cassation* (Supreme Court) dismissed this judgment, declaring: "This right does not violate the principle of oral proceedings, since the documents in question do not concern the statements of witnesses and experts established during the hearing and not yet heard."[11] In the USA, the possibility of showing photos has been allowed since 1930, under the condition that the producer of the images shown was willing to come to court to explain how they were taken.[12]

Oral proceedings allow the court to ignore unnecessary information, as well as assumptions abandoned during the investigative stage of the trial. An impartial judgment must rely only on what has been said within the court, even if the written documents are decisive elements – but after their cross-examination during the debates. In a way, that is what the president wanted to express in refusing Klarsfeld's demand. He acted as if such a trial was really an "ordinary" trial, examining "ordinary" crimes, committed by an "ordinary" criminal. "Ordinary justice" has been a leitmotiv of the French magistrates since the Barbie case – as it was in the Eichmann trial. It has been theorized by Pierre Truche, the prosecutor, and it refers both to the legacy of Nuremberg, which was a court of exception *par excellence*, and to the legacy of the purges, in post-war France, when justice was based on special courts and left quite bad memories. But nothing was ordinary in the trial of Maurice Papon, as nothing was ordinary in the Barbie, Eichmann and other comparable cases. Arno and Serge Klarsfeld's behavior, even if it is disturbing because it disregards a judicial system they solicited themselves, had at least the merit of showing the flagrant limits of such a fiction.

Notes

1 Christian Delage, *Truth in Images*, Philadelphia: University of Pennsylvania Press, forthcoming [1st edition: *La Vérité par l'image: De Nuremberg au procès Milosevic*, Paris: Denoël, 2006].

2 For a reassessment of the Eichmann trial, see the recent researches made for an exhibition held in Paris, in 2011: Henry Rousso (ed.), *Juger Eichmann. Jérusalem, 1961*. Paris: Mémorial de la Shoah, 2011; and Henry Rousso and Fabien Théofilakis, "Eichmann: No ordinary defendant", *Dossiers de l'Institut d'histoire du temps présent*. Online. Available at <www.ihtp.cnrs.fr/spip.php%3Farticle1111&lang=en.html> (accessed June 5, 2012).

3 Arno Klarsfeld, *Un crime français*, Paris: Fayard, 1994.

4 On this complex issue, see Éric Conan and Henry Rousso, *Vichy, An Ever-Present Past*, translation by Nathan Bracher, foreword by Robert O. Paxton, Hanover: University Press of New England, 1998 [1st edition: 1994], and Richard J. Golsan (ed.), *Memory, the Holocaust and French Justice. The Bousquet and Touvier Affairs*, Hanover: University Press of New England, 1996.

5 "Le 16 juillet 1942, j'avais alors 10 ans et demi, je suis rentré chez moi. J'étais sûrement allé jouer à l'extérieur. Je suis rentré à l'heure du goûter et j'ai trouvé un mot de ma mère qui me demandait d'aller la rejoindre au commissariat. J'ai donc repris mon vélo, je suis allé au commissariat de police où, là, j'ai été arrêté. Ma mère était déjà là, avec d'autres personnes. Et puis on est restés quelques heures, et ensuite de quoi, sous bonne garde, nous avons été amenés à la prison de Dax où nous avons été livrés aux Allemands. Là, nous avons passé la nuit dans une grande cellule où nous étions environ une dizaine. Et puis, le lendemain matin, nous sommes sortis de la prison. Ma mère et les autres sont partis, toujours sous bonne garde, allemande, et moi on m'a mis libéré, on m'a chassé. Je suis . . . J'ai donc . . . Ça a été la demière fois où j'ai vu ma mère. Et je suis donc parti chez un ami de ma mère, Monsieur Paul Cougouille, que nous appellions le père Cougouille, qui habitait à Dax, qui m'a recueilli, et qui a écrit à ce moment-là une lettre à la jeune sœur de ma mère qui habitait à Paris à l'époque. Et le soir même, dans l'après-midi, j'ai été tellement éprouvé que j'ai eu une crise de foie tellement forte qu'on m'a hospitalisé à l'hôpital de Dax. Ce qui fait que j'étais à l'hôpital de Dax, j'y ai été malade pendant quelques jours. Et là je suis resté bien longtemps après que j'ai été guéri. Et quand le père Cougouille est venu me rechercher – je ne saurais pas dire combien de temps plus tard, mais au minimum quinze jours plus tard, peut-être plus, sûrement plus même, mais là je n'ai vraiment absolument aucune notion du temps – pour m'ammener directement voir . . . un autocar, il y avait un passeur qui m'a amené en zone libre. Et quand je lui ai posé la question pourquoi j'étais resté si longtemps, il m'a dit que c'était pace que la police française me recherchait et qu'on m'avait laissé dans cet hôpital pour me protéger. Voilà." Transcription and translation from the original videotape, from the broadcast of part of the trial on the cable TV channel *histoire* in 2005 (33rd hearing, program #11, December 15, 1997, personal archives of Henry Rousso). The so-called "minutes" of the Papon trial – *Le Procès de Maurice Papon*, vols 1 and 2, Paris: Albin Michel, 1998 – is a useful tool but there are important and numerous changes compared to the original tapes (see here: vol. 1, pp. 722–34).

6 **Arno Klarsfeld**: *Peut*-être on peut montrer quand même les photos, Monsieur le Président? Je voudrais quand même qu'on montre les photos de Mme Gheldman ... **Le président**: Oui ... non ... moi, je ne les montre pas, je ne les montre pas. **AK**: Pourquoi? **P**: Parce que je montre les pièces qui sont essentielles à la compréhension des débats. **AK**: Je crois que cela, c'est essentiel, Monsieur le Président ! **P**: Et c'est votre sentiment. Moi, j'ai tranché. **AK**: Je vous ai demandé plusieurs fois de montrer les photos, de montrer les photos des enfants [déportés], plusieurs fois vous avez refusé. Je n'arrive pas à comprendre pourquoi. Alors que normalement, dans tout procès, on montre les photos, vous n'avez pas lu les noms [des victimes], vous avez lu seulement les noms des personnes pour qui des gens se sont portés partie civile. Vous n'avez pas lu les autres. Il y a peut-être des juifs intéressants pour vous aussi, Monsieur le Président, qu'est-ce que je peux en savoir? **P**: Maître !... **AK**: Alors, je voudrais qu'on montre ces photos ... **P**: Maître Klarsfeld ... **AK**: ... ou alors qu'il soit pris acte que vous ne voulez pas montrer ces photos ... **P**: Maître Klarsfeld ... **AK**: ... parce que cela fait quand même trois fois ... **P**: Je ne vous autorise pas ! ... **AK**: Je représente ici les Fils et Filles des déportés, association sans laquelle vous n'auriez pas l'honneur de présider cette cour, alors je voudrais, sérieusement, que l'on montre ces photos et que les jurés puissent se faire une idée, imaginer, voir ce qu'étaient les gens qui étaient déportés. **P**: Maître Klarsfeld, j'ai décidé que ce procès irait, autant que je pourrai, à son bout et, par conséquent, je ne vais pas m'acharner, ni même dépenser mon énergie, sur des incidents qui ne méritent pas la peine ... **AK, l'interrompant**: Ce n'est pas un incident ! Ça mérite la peine ... **P**: Vous venez d'avoir à mon égard deux propos qui, d'une manière générale, seraient intolérables et qui, sans doute, devraient normalement m'incliner à prendre des dispositions. Je viens d'avoir un témoin, qui vient de déposer sur des choses importantes. Je viens de baliser son témoignage par les documents que vous versez qui me paraissent essentiels. Pour le reste, je ne souhaite pas aller au-delà. **AK**: ... Donc les replonger dans l'anonymat. C'est ce que je dois comprendre ! **P**: ... **AK**: Je suis obligé, Monsieur le Président, j'ai derrière moi les voix de ceux qui sont morts, et même si cela ne me fait pas plaisir de vous parler ainsi, j'y suis obligé. J'ai comme une sorte de chose qui me pousse en avant et c'est vrai que ces gens doivent être représentés. C'est vrai que je ne comprends pas pourquoi on montre des documents qui souvent, parfois, ne sont pas d'une grande importance, on y reste pendant des minutes et des minutes. Et la photo d'une femme qui a vu sa vie brisée, on ne peut pas la projeter à l'écran? Réellement, je ne comprends pas.
[Le président parle à voix basse avec l'un des deux autres juges.]
AK: Et je crois que de nombreuses parties civiles ne doivent pas comprendre aussi pourquoi on ne peut pas présenter ces photos. **P**: J'apprécierai. J'ai jusqu'à la fin de l'audience, jusqu'à la fin des débats pour montrer tout ce qui me paraîtra nécessaire au fur et à mesure. Mon souci pour le moment – et je ne voudrais pas que nous nous égarions –, c'est de faire en sorte que ces débats permettent à la cour et aux jurés d'avoir de façon cristallisée des éléments de fait sur lesquels ensuite ils se prononceront et ils prendront leurs responsabilités. Et je ne veux pas, pour le moment, de ce débat, tel qu'il est là, je ne veux pas ajouter autre chose que ce que ce témoin a dit, et que ces documents montrent. Il y a des choses très importantes qui viennent d'être dites [durant cette audience], et je comprends que, pour le témoin, peut-être souhaite-t-il que l'on voit le visage de sa mère, comme je comprends très bien aussi que les gens qui ne se sont pas constitués parties civiles souhaiteraient que je lise leur nom. Tout ça, c'est au-delà de ma fonction. Ma fonction, je veux la remplir toute entière, c'est déjà beaucoup sans que j'ai à aller au-delà. **AK**: Vous avez un pouvoir discrétionnaire, vous pouvez le faire. **P**: Voilà !

Je ne sais si vous comprenez le sens de mon propos, mais il est très clair. **AK, s'adressant au témoin**: Eh bien, Monsieur Gheldman, en tous les cas, je regrette que le Président s'oppose à ce qu'on montre votre mère . . . **P**: J'ai jusqu'à la fin de ces débats pour montrer toutes les photos que je voudrai ! **AK**: Je me souviens aussi [les demandes] sur les photos des camps d'internement français. Vous avez dit: "Plus tard, Monsieur Klarsfeld", et on est plus tard et elles n'ont toujours pas été montrées.
[. . .]
P: C'est sûr, et on n'est pas encore au bout . . . **AK, l'interrompant**: . . . donc, je peux m'inquiéter à juste titre que la photo de Mme Gheldman ne soit pas montrée non plus. **P**: Bien. Est-ce que vous avez d'autres questions à poser? **AK**: Non, j'ai simplement des regrets à formuler à Monsieur Gheldman que l'on ne montre pas la photo de sa mère, comme [les photos, les noms?] des 165 autres partants du convoi du 18 juillet [1942] qui ont été emmenés vers l'enfer. J'ai des regrets qu'ils n'aient pas été cités non plus. Voilà, Monsieur le Président.
Transcription and translation from the original videotape. The transcription in *Le Procès de Maurice Papon*, *op. cit.*, vol. 1, pp. 728–9 presents many distortions of this dialogue.

7 One historian, Marc Olivier Baruch, was cornered by the defense attorney, Jean-Marc Varaut, because he had explicitly mentioned the case of the secretary general Maurice Papon in his PhD on the Vichy administration. The book was opportunely published just before the trial but the hearing of the author showed obviously the limits of the historian's expertise in such circumstances.

8 "Mes 'juifs intéressants' n'étaient pas une gratuite insolence, mais une poussée stratégique pour contraindre le président à céder sur ce que j'estimais 'essentiel'. Trois jours plus tard, le président cédera et montrera les photos. Un procès est parfois une bataille, on ne peut la gagner avec des amabilités." Arno Klarsfeld, *La Cour, les nains et le bouffon*, Paris: Robert Laffont, 1998, p. 135.

9 "L'examen des témoins sera toujours fait de vive voix et sans que leurs dépositions soient écrites," Assemblée nationale constituante, Titre VII, Article 5, September 16, 1791.

10 "Le lien entre l'oralité des débats et l'impartialité du juge réside dans la garantie [donnée] à la personne poursuivie que le juge ne fondera son intime conviction que sur les éléments dont il a pu acquérir connaissance à l'audience et qui ont été soumis à la libre contradiction des parties. L'objectif est que le juge ne puisse être influencé par des informations et éléments recueillis lors de la phase préparatoire qui n'auraient pas subi l'épreuve de la contradiction. La vérité doit apparaître aux yeux de tous à l'audience. La phase de jugement, orale et totalement contradictoire, apparaît comme une opportunité donnée à la défense de corriger l'orientation imprimée à la procédure depuis la phase d'instruction. Elle garantit encore la personne poursuivie des dérives que la médiatisation d'une affaire peut avoir sur l'impartialité du siège." Franklin Kuty, *L'impartialité du juge dans la procédure pénale. De la confiance décrétée à la confiance justifiée*, Bruxelles: Éditions Marcier, 2005, p. 155.

11 *Rejet du pourvoi contre un arrêt de la cour d'assises du Maine-et-Loire du 3 mars 1998:* "Le moyen soutenait que le président, en donnant lecture de nombreuses pièces de la procédure et en communiquant aux assesseurs et aux jurés une planche photographique figurant au dossier, avait porté atteinte au principe de l'oralité des débats. La Cour de Cassation estime qu'il n'en est rien. En effet, il appartient au président d'apprécier si, en vertu de son pouvoir discrétionnaire, il lui apparaît utile de donner lecture de pièces de la procédure et de communiquer aux assesseurs et aux jurés une planche photographique figurant au dossier. Cette faculté ne contrevient pas au principe de l'oralité des débats,

dès lors que les pièces en cause ne concernent pas des déclarations de témoins ou d'experts acquis aux débats et non encore entendus." *Chambre criminelle, 14 avril 1999 (98-83.692 – non publié)*. Available online at <www.juripole.fr/ANAPCA/A199902.htm> (accessed June 5, 2012).

12 Delage, *op. cit.*, p. 101.

CHAPTER 4

Gacaca courts in Rwanda

A local justice for a local genocide history?

Hélène Dumas

Between April and July 1994, the Tutsi community in Rwanda became the target of a mass killing campaign, which was organized at the higher levels of state and perpetrated by a large fringe of the civil population. The Hutu, who were opposed to the violence, suffered the same tragic fate. The figures are still debated, regarding the number of victims as well as the number of perpetrators. Nevertheless, in general, the estimations of the victims oscillate between 500,000 and one million (Des Forges, 1999: 22–3, Republic of Rwanda [RoR], 2004a). The number of perpetrators also oscillates between large scales: from 200,000 to more than one million people (Straus, 2004, 2006: 117, RoR, 2010). The degree and the nature of implication of the civilians in the genocide remain more difficult to establish. Indeed, the participation in the genocide takes on many varied forms – from denunciation to murder. This large spectrum of acts contained behind the general designation of "participation" is one of the most important aspects to keep in mind when describing and analyzing the *gacaca* process.[1] The other main specificity of the Tutsi genocide relies on the huge scale of violence which destroys all social bonds (family, religion, neighborhood, etc.).

This remark raises the main question we can address to a post-violence society: What kind of "justice" could account for the different specificities of such a crime? Indeed, the most striking aspect of *gacaca* jurisdictions is their originality, which can be analyzed as an attempt to acknowledge the specific characteristics of the Tutsi genocide. When the process was launched at the beginning of the 2000s,[2] many observers (Sarkin, 1999, 2001) described the *gacaca* in reference to the South African Truth and Reconciliation Commission (TRC), emphasizing the social healing which could be brought about by that kind of restorative justice. Some NGOs (Amnesty International, 2002) also expressed their fear about a justice which would not respect human rights standards. In Rwanda, the *gacaca* process was first promoted as a means to resolve the huge judicial contentions related to the genocide and to promote "national reconciliation" (RoR, 2004c). During the process, especially until March 2005, the Rwandese government continued to stress the argument of national reconciliation to reinforce its necessity and legitimacy. Many arguments, in order to promote or criticize the *gacaca* jurisdictions, were used.[3] But none of them emphasizes the possible contribution of the trials to a historical narrative of the genocide. This preoccupation came up at the end of the process in 2009 when the question of the archives became salient.

The International Criminal Tribunal for Rwanda (ICTR) could also be asked the same question.[4] Established by Security Council Resolution 955 in November 1994, and located in Arusha (Tanzania), the ICTR is in charge of the prosecution and the judgment of the main persons responsible for the genocide, essentially the members of the former government, militias and military high command. The ICTR mandate is coming to its end soon and it has already achieved the most important part of its activities. Many criticisms had been addressed to this jurisdiction. Its legitimacy is regularly questioned (Reyntjens, 2009, Peskin, 2011) but the content of the documents produced by the inquiries and the judgments is rarely analyzed from the perspective of the social sciences,[5] especially history.

And yet the ICTR's contribution to the establishment of a historical narrative about the Tutsi genocide is important. First, the huge documentation both gathered and produced by the tribunal could be useful to research on genocide history. The tribunal has means that stay out of reach of the historians such as medico-legal inquiries, undertaken at the request of the ICTR prosecution (Koff, 2004).[6] For some regions in Rwanda, the extensive information produced by these inquiries allows historians to draw quite a precise map of the massacres, with reliable indications about the victims' number and the way they have been killed.

But the contribution of the ICTR to the history of the genocide also relies on some very specific questions addressed by the tribunal to this history. First, if we look at the functions held by the accused during the genocide, we can measure the extent and the radicality of the violence. Indeed, all the categories of people who would normally be considered as social barriers against the eruption of violence took an active part in genocide (Audoin-

Rouzeau, 2009): priests (Elizaphan Ntakirutimana, Anastase Seromba, Emmanuel Rukundo), doctors (Gérard Ntakirutimana), and women (Pauline Nyiramasuhuko).[7] Moreover, many other actors have been brought to court. For each case, inquiries and judgments highlight one particular aspect of the mobilization of the state organs in the violence: the media (Media Trial), the army (Military I and II), the militias (Georges Rutaganda), the local administration (Jean-Paul Akayesu, Clément Kayishema, Laurent Semanza, Vincent Rutaganira), the government (Gouvernement I and II), and business (Obed Ruzindana). Besides, the ICTR trials underline some violent practices which have characterized the Tutsi genocide. Thus, rape and sexual violence have been the object of specific attention by the judges (Magnarella, 2002: 319). Despite these remarks, the historiography of Tutsi genocide should not be exclusively dependent on the judicial process. Notwithstanding the huge amount of data collected by this tribunal, the history of the genocide must not fully rely on juridical conclusions. As some trials showed, with regard to the conspiracy of the genocide or the propaganda, the juridical categories are not always relevant to account for questions which are not part of the legal case.

If the ICTR is concentrated on the high-level responsibilities in the genocide, the *gacaca* courts are focused on the grassroots perpetrators. This dichotomy between the mastermind judged in Arusha and the crowd of local perpetrators fits the official narratives, especially in Rwanda,[9] but does not fit the reality of the slaughters, especially the way it appears in the *gacaca* trials. By conducting a comparison between international and national justice, we would like to underline the importance of the formal framework in the construction of the historical narrative. The procedures, the languages, the spaces differ from one jurisdiction to another and shape the narrative very differently. As a survivor who has experienced both jurisdictions states: "In *gacaca* we understand each other, we speak the same language. When I was in Arusha, I could not understand the proceedings . . . I was more afraid of the court than Kayishema [the accused, former *préfet* of Kibuye] I had in front of me" (interview with a survivor in Bisesero, June 2010).

Gacaca courts were designed to be close to the population and this preoccupation shaped their legal framework. The conditions in which the people have to face their past influences the narrative they build.

History of genocide through the legal framework

Looking at the legal framework of the *gacaca* jurisdictions, one can notice the will to find a kind of justice fitting the way the crime was committed. Two examples can illustrate this statement.

Popular dimension

The literature devoted to the Tutsi genocide stresses its popular dimension (Straus, 2006, Kimonyo, 2008, Fujii, 2009a). When looking for explanations to account for the massive implication in the killings, the most recent studies rarely pay attention to the variety of the forms of participation in the genocide. Beyond the striking figures, another particularity of the genocide should be underlined: the intimacy between victims and perpetrators. The *gacaca* laws take into consideration these two dimensions. Thus, they develop a specific view about the history of the genocide. They first insist on the massive participation, but distinguish different degrees. This distinction is an indication that trials will explore the local dynamics and practices of violence.

The *gacaca* system is based on the participation of the population. As the former prosecutor, Jean-Marie Mbarushimana, explained to prisoners in 2001: "Your prosecutor will be your neighbor, your lawyer will be your neighbor, your judge will be your neighbor" (Aghion, 2009). The link between the way the genocide was committed and the legal organization of justice is one of the patterns of the creation of the *gacaca* courts, as it is clearly expressed in a Supreme Court report in 2003: "The main motivations which support the *gacaca* system rely on . . . the will to choose a form of prosecution and judgment which will best conform to the way the crimes were perpetrated" (RoR, 2003). The entire *gacaca* legal skeleton is based on popular participation: the judges are elected within the local population and the sessions have to be held with the participation of the population.

Linked to the importance of popular participation in the prosecution and judgment, the *gacaca* legal framework insists on the public nature of the proceedings:[10] "Considering that such crimes were publicly committed in the eyes of the population, which thus must recount the facts, disclose the truth and participate in prosecuting and trying the alleged perpetrators" (RoR, 2004b). The law echoes many statements of both victims and perpetrators who insist on the fact that genocide was committed publicly. The direct consequence of this imperative is the importance of oral testimonies, which represent the main material of the proceedings.[11] The entire procedure relies on testimonies, from the inquiry sessions to the judgment. In other words, testimony remains the pillar of the evidential system. The emergence of testimony about what happened during the genocide is strongly supported by the confessions of the accused. By reducing the penalty, the legal system encourages people accused of genocide to confess their crimes and to denounce their accomplices. This disposition is not only pragmatic but also reflects the way the genocide was committed. Indeed, the slaughter was perpetrated by large groups of people, increasing the number of potential accomplices. The encouragement of the guilty plea has had consequences to the extent that it has massively increased the number of the alleged perpetrators (Bugingo, 2004, RoR, 2010). The legal encouragement for denouncing accomplices relies on the fact that the majority of the massacres were perpetrated by groups of killers (Straus, 2006, Mironko, 2004).

The categorization of the suspects also indicates the particular apprehension of history by the lawyer. Indeed, they are gathered in several categories depending on the gravity of the accusations. This system pays attention to the practices of violence perpetrated during the genocide. This point is very salient for two main reasons. First, the early inquiries led by the Rwandese authorities in the months following the end of the genocide were very attentive to the practice of cruelty (interview with Tito Rutaremara, Rwandan Patriotic Front (RPF) spokesman in 1994, June 2010). The violent practices are striking in their diversity.[12] That is the reason why we can assume that this aspect of the genocide will be taken into account in the legal system. Second, the way the killings were committed is very significant for the survivors (Kagabo, 1995: 122). In addition, the categorization system also takes into consideration the lootings, which were very important during the genocide, especially in terms of socialization of the violence. For example, for the former commune of Gitesi (Kibuye), Jean-Paul Kimonyo notes the function of lootings as a motive for entering into the violence, and also notices that they represented a means for the local authorities to maintain their power (Kimonyo, 2008: 461).

Besides attention to the popular nature of the genocide and to some practices, the legal framework of the *gacaca* system gambles on a social specificity: the intimacy that characterized the relationships between all the participants in the trials.

Intimate links

The main criticism addressed to the *gacaca* system is also the condition of its implementation. Indeed, many human rights activists and even the survivors' association, Ibuka, denounced the intimate relation between judges, accused, victims and witnesses (Ibuka, 2007, 2008, PAPG, 2006, 2007). The survivors' association, lawyers and human rights watchdogs all questioned the impartiality of the judges. In fact, from the experience I collected during my fieldwork in Rwanda, the judges explain their strategies as being to make people speak about the genocide by virtue of the knowledge they have themselves about the event. In the countryside, *gacaca* judges often are long-time inhabitants of the hill. The more they know the people

Figure 4.1 Survivors of the genocide, along with one defendant, *gacaca* of Kanyinya, 5 October 2006. © Hélène Dumas.

they have to judge, the more they can manage to lead them to speak. For example, in a place called Shyorongi, almost all the judges were born and had grown up there and knew the people they had to judge. A lot of reports (interviews with SNJG member, 2004 and 2007) on early *gacaca* state that inquiries and trials work better in the countryside than in towns. They often raise the question of individualism linked to the urban way of life in order to explain this difference, but we can assert that the main reason relies on the dissolved social links among the *gacaca* participants. In places where the entire community has been living in the same place for a long time, the information is easier to gather.[13] As people know each other, judges can set up strategies to make people talk:

> During the first session of data collection, I was aware that everybody has at least one relative in jail or on the victims' side. So, I put forward the survivors who were accusing a lot of people. The relatives of the accused persons reacted and people began to talk. That's how I bring people to talk about genocide. (Interview with a *gacaca* judge, May 2010)

The intimacy between the actors in the trials also reflects the intimacy of the murderers. The genocide destroyed the closest social bonds, such as those of the family. Sometimes members of the same family were sitting on opposed benches, as victims and as accused. In a trial that took place in a town located in the Western province, named Kibuye, a man was accused by his sisters – among other witnesses – of being an *interahamwe.*[14] One of his sisters explained the reason for her brother's implication in the genocide: "Look at R., his mother was a Tutsi. She is dead. He was a killer. He was the killer of my family. After his mother died, he said: 'My mother just died, I have to kill Tutsi, I'm not expecting anything anymore'" (*Gacaca* trial, Kibuye, 12 October 2006). Intimacy is not restricted to the family but covers the entire spectrum of the activities of social life: cultivation, sharing of drinks, cows, weddings, football, etc. These aspects of social life are consistently present during the trials. Their evocation enables us to discover the existence of the community before the genocide. This process of path-to-path life rebuilding before and during the genocide is possible by the way the *gacaca* were designed. The organization of the judicial arena is also significant for the intimacy it generates between judges, victims, perpetrators and witnesses. The trial scene does not generate distance from the past by strict separation of the actors. The language reinforces this physical proximity. The way people speak about past events in Kinyarwanda is very lively due to the structure of the language itself. All these elements contribute to making the past very much present during the trials.

The *gacaca* process is like a window that unveils the past. But a window opened from the present. And this dimension of temporal imbrication remains crucial: the past is examined from the perspective of present necessities. The evolution of the *gacaca* process, from the first 2001 law to the last one in 2008 can also be considered as a product of post-genocide Rwandan history. Indeed, the legal evolution indicates the pre-eminence of the reconciliation policy on the punitive aim primarily assigned to *gacaca* jurisdictions. In addition, the *gacaca* process and the history of the memory of the genocide are closely linked. For instance, the more the judicial process approaches its end, the more the genocide commemorations euphemize the violence. On the contrary, the eleventh genocide commemoration in 2005 was hardly emotional for the survivors because of the nationwide launch of the *gacaca* (Kimonyo's communication 2010). *Gacaca* trials represent a good opportunity to explore various historical dimensions: the past – before and during genocide – and the present – essentially the post-genocide Rwanda.

In post-genocide Rwanda, the historian can follow the construction of the history of memory. If the legal form of justice influences the way the past is evoked – in this case stressing the popular, intimate and cruel nature of the event – what kind of narratives will emerge from the proceedings?

History on the grass

The *gacaca* process – from inquiries to judgment – embodies the first moment in which all the actors in the genocide are gathered to talk about the past. Despite the fact that the initiative comes from the state and is closely framed by national and local authorities, the narratives deployed during the sessions largely escape official control. It would be exaggerated and untrue to assert that the state-sponsored judicial process dictates the people's narratives. On the contrary, local narratives regularly refute the official narrative of the past.

Aspects of genocide history in the trials

The historiography of the Tutsi genocide is still budding despite some important publications (Chrétien, 1995, Des Forges, 1999). The first studies published in the years after the genocide were mostly stamped with a judicial perspective and thus concentrated on the organization of the genocide at national and international level. Most of these publications – and their authors – participated in the international judicial process, at the ICTR.[15] The most recent studies – written by political scientists – are devoted to explaining the mobilization of the peasantry in the mass killings (Mironko, 2004, McDoom, 2005, Straus, 2006, Kimonyo, 2008, Fujii, 2009a). In Rwanda, some historians have published monographs with a clear memorial perspective (Rutazibwa and Rutayisire, 2007, Rutembesa and Mutwarasibo, 2009).

Some of the questions raised by the *gacaca* process, and, above all, the archives it has produced, are likely to pursue and deepen this historiography. In a certain way, the *gacaca* process participates in the construction of this historiography. Indeed, the trials can be analyzed as a "historiographical experience," to borrow Carlo Ginzburg's words (Ginzburg, 1991: 32). Only 17 years after the genocide, many facts remain unclear, especially the exact number of the victims, for example. The *gacaca* process contributes – to some extent – to highlighting basic facts (the place, the identity and the number of victims and perpetrators) but also the violent practices (especially cruelty) which occurred during the genocide. This desire to discover the past may be more important than the punishment, as a survivor expresses in a trial:

> I'd like to ask a question to the court. You will decide about that case but I wonder if you can make your decision upon what you've heard. I wonder if *gacaca* is worthy for a person like me if I don't know exactly how and where my family was killed. I don't really care about the penalty, I want to know what happened to my relatives. (*Gacaca* trial, Kibuye, 12 October 2006)

Deeply rooted in the local experiences of the genocide, the narratives that appear in the *gacaca* are very telling about the dynamics of formation and action of the *ibitero* (groups of assailants), the various degrees of participation but also the concrete execution of the killings.

The ibitero *and degrees of participation in the genocide*

The majority of the killings were perpetrated in the hills (RoR, 2004a) by bands of killers, more or less numerous. The decision was made by a little group of the hardest killers. They chose their target and went from house to house to look for other participants. The reasons why the people joined the *ibitero* vary from one person to another, from one day to another day. Constraint, fear, necessity to show zeal in order to protect hidden people, greed, hatred and other contingent motives can account for the popular participation. These explanations have been explored in the scientific literature but without taking into consideration the contingency of the motivation. This aspect is very striking when observing *gacaca* since the killers are gathered to talk about each attack they participated in. During the proceedings, the killers explained their participation according to diverse patterns.

Besides the organization of the *ibitero*, the collective narratives recorded during the *gacaca* trials disclose a kind of phenomenology of violence. Indeed, through the examination of the accusations during the proceedings, all the degrees of participation reveal various forms of involvement in the violence. And violence is not confined only to the act of killing. A large array of actions were evoked during the trials: laughs, denunciations, cries, songs, bringing the victims to the execution sites, thefts of belongings from corpses, torture.[16] The evocation of this large spectrum of acts has two goals. Firstly, by examining acts that surround the murder itself, the judges try to establish respective responsibilities. Thus, in a location called Butamwa near Kigali, the *gacaca* session lasted a long time in order to find the man who shouted when he saw a Tutsi refugee fleeing from his plot of land (*gacaca* trial, Butamwa, 4 October 2006). In Kibuye, the court examined with great attention those who brought the sticks which a group of killers had used to assassinate a man in the Kivu lake (*gacaca* trial, Kibuye, 12 October 2006).

On the other hand, the evocation of these kinds of acts also arose from the survivors. The way their relatives had been killed was very meaningful, especially when it concerned children. Telling us about her experience as survivor and judge, a woman remembers the slaughter of her nephews by her neighbors: "I can't understand how a mother like this woman could put my youngest child on her back in order to give him to the killers" (interview with a judge, Kanyinya, May 2010). Still concerned with the murder of these children, one of the members of the group of killers says: "There were a lot of people around the septic tank by which the children had been killed. Men, women and children had come to see the killing and I could hear some of them laughing at the children because they cried when they had been struck the first time" (interview with a sentenced perpetrator, Kigali prison, 17 June 2010).[17] What the judge says about the women who participated in the death of her nephews is quite paradigmatic of the routine and everyday context and quality of the violence. We can also take the example of the weapons – mostly machetes, clubs and hoes – which used to be employed for the field work. It is interesting to observe the evocations of the routine in the trials in so far as the survivors denounce it as an aggravating circumstance whereas the accused use it as an argument in their defense. This assertion could be sustained by the special cases of women involved in the genocide. They refute the accusations in the name of their gender. They could not have done what they are accused of because they are women and mothers.[18]

In another trial, the judges thoroughly examined the looting of the corpses after a huge massacre for which they had difficulty finding the perpetrators. Exploring the peripheral acts that surround the murder itself is a judicial imperative. But it also represents an access to the entire killing process, which is very rich and useful to account for the history of the genocide.[19]

Besides the disclosure of a phenomenology of violence, the trials help to perceive another very important element of the genocide: the way the physical ground, the topography, was used to kill, and – more rarely – to escape.

Execution of the genocide

Gacaca sessions mostly take place in the locations where the killings have been perpetrated. The actors in the trial are mostly native to the place. The intimacy evoked before is also relevant for the geographical environment.

This remark is very important to the extent that the genocide was not committed in dedicated spaces, but mostly on the hills. In many cases, the natural environment holds a very important place in the explanations of the killings. For example, a lot of people were drowned in the Nyabarongo river.[20] Forests were also used as execution grounds.[21] People who attend the trials have a deep knowledge of the topography of the hills and so they can check the truthfulness of testimony. The topography of the massacres also illustrates the contingency mentioned above. Perpetrators often used the natural environment to kill (*gacaca* trial, 7, 12, 19 and 26 August 2008). This point enlightens one basic *gacaca* characteristic: all the actors in the trials share a common knowledge about the place they are living and its history. This minimal common knowledge constitutes a huge difference with the ICTR, where the crime of genocide had to be proved for each case before the June 2006 judicial notice. In other words, the *gacaca* trials offer a large view of the ways the genocide was executed in the hills but also in some areas where victims were gathered in churches or administrative buildings.

By examining the intimacy of the execution of the genocide, the trials can be regarded as an attempt to build a global narrative of this key event in Rwandan national history. But this attempt is not yet achieved in so far as the *gacaca* remain focused on local narratives which do not follow the national historical narrative imposed by the government since 1994.

National and local narratives

The analysis of the gap between national and local narratives about genocide in Rwanda reveals the contradictions of the reconciliation policy. Firstly, whereas the government tries to portray the grassroots perpetrators of the genocide as a manipulated crowd, forced to enter the slaughters by "a bad policy,"[22] the local trials highlight the perpetrators' autonomy. The national narrative, moreover, does not take into consideration the survivors' perception of the killers. Indeed, survivors pay more attention to killing perpetrated by their neighbors than to the masterminds of the genocide. Borrowing Jose Kagabo's interrogation (Kagabo, 1995: 111), we know the general watchword of killing Tutsi. But the *gacaca* trials reveal how basic citizens executed this watchword. In the trials attended, it is possible to see how local inhabitants completed the decision to kill, sometimes without any local administrative orders. It does not mean that the killings were a spontaneous flash of violence. On the contrary, the local trials are a means of focusing on the execution of the genocide under the general political motto of killing Tutsi.

The killers' autonomy appears in the undaunted cruelty of their practices, as in this narrative of the killing of a man in Shyorongi who was tortured to death:

> When I arrived, I saw that they had caught A. There was a big crowd. A man, called D., brought pins. And he push these pins into his A's flesh in order to make him reveal the whereabouts of the *inkotanyi*.

In the same testimony, S., a 14-year-old perpetrator, talks about the murder of P.'s children:

> When I arrived at P.'s house, I saw the assailants throwing the children into the septic tank. . . . T. struck one of the children with a club. I could hear them crying. They threw bricks on the people in the tank and they died. (*Gacaca* trial, Kanyinya, 5 October 2006)

In the same region, a perpetrator who has confessed his crime talks about the way he was deliberately targeted by the neighborhood to murder his Tutsi neighbor's children (interview, Kanyinya, 6 May 2006).

As mentioned before, violent practices span a very wide spectrum and unveil the perpetrators' criminal autonomy. This element, which is central to the *gacaca* trials, contradicts the current official tendency to conceal the violence of the genocide. Indeed, if we consider the evolution of commemorative ceremonies since 1995, it is clear that the memory of violence is progressively banished. If we look at the first ceremonies (Kabera, 2004, CNLG archives), the survivors were remembering their loved ones, always stressing the way they were killed. With the creation of the National Commission for the Fight against Genocide (CNLG) in 2008, the expression of sorrow was well framed by the official organizers. In each ceremony, even the most local ones, the organizers ask the survivors to banish violent memories from their testimonies (interview with commemoration ceremony organizer, Bisesero, 26 June 2010). The question raised by the public expression of violence remains an issue for the government in so far as the officials in charge of public education are still debating the way to teach the history of the genocide (Rutembesa and Mutwarasibo's communication, 2010). Another example of the contradiction between official and local narratives can be illustrated by the way the *gacaca* were promoted at the beginning of their national implementation. They were portrayed as a path to reconciliation, to heal past wounds.[23] After three years of existence, the officials in charge of the *gacaca* were compelled to recognize that *gacaca* were a factor in the tensions between people (Mukantaganzwa, July 2008). The survivors' umbrella association, Ibuka, expresses its fears in face of the increasing number of assassinations of survivors (Ibuka 2007, Simburudali 2009, Burnéous, 2008). The rise in violence, in the harassment of survivors and other witnesses challenges the common statements praising *gacaca* justice as a means to "reconcile" and "forgive."

Beside the question of the violence, another element can illustrate the gap between local and official narratives. Indeed, since 1994, the new government led by the RPF has banished ethnic reference from public life. The *gacaca*, encouraging people to speak about genocide, raised the ethnic reference. It was impossible to deal with the genocide without referring to Hutu, Tutsi and sometimes to Twa. Ethnic identity still strongly structures Rwandan society and the trials represent a good way to see this reference arising and being debated.[24] Linked to this question, the official reconciliation injunctions were often questioned by people during the trials (*gacaca* trial, 11 November 2007). The formal framework that rules *gacaca* does not prevent concurrent narratives from emerging. Thus, *gacaca* trials highlight how people can deal with their past in a very specific configuration that mixes contradictory aspirations.

Conclusion

Almost 20 years after the genocide, Rwanda still has to face its past. The historical work is beginning. If the *gacaca* courts were designed for punishment and reconciliation, the work they did will feed the historical data on the genocide. The judicial process finished its work this year but it has collected fragmented narratives. The constitution of a global narrative on genocide remains a huge challenge, especially in respect to national education. The history of Rwanda and, furthermore, the history of the genocide is not taught in the Rwandan classroom. This issue is critical if we consider the fact that youth make up 67 percent of the Rwandan population and yet they have never heard about the history of the genocide outside of their family memories.[25] But the *gacaca* process did not disclose the entire "truth" about the genocide. For many events, the trials did not manage to reconstitute the facts. Many contradictions and silences remain, especially for some huge massacres. In addition, the *gacaca* process depended on the national political agenda. For example, at the end of 2007, the National *Gacaca* Service urged the courts to close the trials, without considering their own agenda. This situation led to slapdash trials.[26] Finally, for some regions it would have been significant to gather testimonies about the RPF war in so far as it influenced the execution of the genocide.

Seventeen years after the genocide, the historian faces the difficulties linked to the "history of the present." She depends on national political stakes (Audoin-Rouzeau and Garapon, 2010) but also on the personal memory of the witnesses. For some of them, especially the survivors, the genocide remains alive in their daily life. Asking them to remember the past – even before the genocide – may provoke trauma. In spite of the government's willingness to definitively close this black page of national history,[27] the shadow of the genocide is still present, above all in a country where victims and perpetrators have to live alongside each other.

Acknowledgements

This contribution greatly benefits from the invaluable comments of Etienne Smith and Marion Roche. I would like to thank them.

Notes

1 This point is neither visible in the global statistics about the *gacaca* process nor in some scholars' studies. For example, Straus develops a very restrictive definition of the notion of "perpetrator" (Straus, 2004) and does not examine the varied cruel acts that often surrounded the murder itself (Straus, 2006).

2 *Gacaca* jurisdictions were officially created by the organic law of 26 January 2001.

3 It is impossible to indicate the huge literature devoted to *gacaca* courts. The literature is mostly due to lawyers or human rights activists and explores the *gacaca* achievements in terms of "national reconciliation." See Ingelaere (2008), Rettig (2011) and Clark (2010).

4 Dennis Byron's (ICTR President) statement in the conference "International Criminal tribunal for Rwanda. Model or Counter Model for International Criminal Justice? The Perspectives of the Stakeholders," Geneva, 9 July 2009.

5 Lawyers mainly write scientific literature related to the ICTR. An anthropologist, Nigel Eltringham, is now conducting research about the ICTR. See Eltringham (2009).

6 See Haglund, ICTR transcripts ICTR-95-1T, *Kayishema et al.*, 24, 25, 26 November 1997 and Koff (2004).

7 Pauline Nyiramasuhuko was minister in charge of Family and Women Promotion in the government that implemented the genocide. She has been brought to court with a charge of rape incitation and the sentence is still pending.

9 The hierarchy between high rank and grassroots perpetrators is reflected in the categorization process in the genocide prosecutions law. See for example the first one: Organic Law 30 August 1996, Article 2.

10 Except for rape and sexual violence cases.

11 Even if one has to be careful about the orality in order not perceive it as part of a so-called African folklore. In this regard, we have to mention the fact that all proceedings are written down by the *gacaca* secretary, producing a huge archives database.

12 Tito Rutaremara, who held an RPF inquiry commission in 1994, made a list of 52 lethal forms employed during the genocide (interview, June 2010). The Rwandan national census of the victims of the genocide indicates 14 lethal means (RoR, 2004a).

13 In other places like Bisesero, the *gacaca* process went through many difficulties (police commander's personal communication) partly because the killers came from many other hills (interview with genocide survivors in Bisesero, June 2010).

14 *Interahamwe* ("those who work together") is the name of the most important militia implicated in the genocide. By extension, survivors often depict the perpetrators as *interahamwe* even if they were not part of the militia.

15 Alison Des Forges and Jean-Pierre Chrétien were "expert witnesses" in ICTR trials.

16 It is interesting to note that the panel of the crimes increases in the different *gacaca* laws. For instance, the crime of profanation against corpses is taken into account in the second *gacaca* law (RoR, 2004).

17 The large participation in the genocide is also present in the testimonies collected by Jean-Paul Kimonyo: ". . . everybody was participating, even girls, women, children and old persons. Nobody stays home. . . . Even the one who didn't kill, at least cried. . . . They were like hunters running after game" (Kimonyo, 2008: 329).

18 About women's participation in the genocide see African Rights (1995), Hogg (2001) and Baraduc (2010).

19 Access to that phenomenology of violence is not always easy to explore by the way of interviews; see Fujii (2009b: 158).

20 The number of the victims drowned in the river remains uncertain in so far as the bodies were not found (Mugesera, 2010).

21 As in Mukana, a place near Kigali. A mass killing occurred on 12 April 1994 and occupied the *gacaca* jurisdiction for several sessions.

22 This vision is still present nowadays. See for example President Kagame's speech during the 2010 genocide commemoration: "Why must we always remember? We must do so because that which caused us the pain is bad politics, bad politicians and bad leaders. Bad politics that killed people – we don't even need to waste our time on numbers, whether it is 500,000 or one million, those who play with numbers should know that the pain of 500,000 people is not negligible and there is no difference between the politics that caused 500,000 deaths and that which caused one million deaths – both are bad politics."

23 Thus, in 2004, a year before the national *gacaca* implementation, advertisings declared "*Ukuri kurakiza*" (truth heals).

24 In an informal discussion I had after an interview with the president of a *gacaca* jurisdiction, he seemed very preoccupied by his "Hutu likeness" although he is a Tutsi. He tried to demonstrate that ethnicity has nothing to do with physical stereotype but also how he used these stereotypes to conceal his "ethnic" identity – and his potential impartiality – during the trials (Shyorongi, May 2010). Another interview with a woman who is a survivor shows the plasticity of the "ethnic" representation as she considered one of her close Hutu friends as a "Tutsi" because she had lost her Tutsi husband during the genocide (interview in Kanyinya, March 2010).

25 This issue was raised by the Executive Secretary of the National Commission for Fight Against Genocide, Jean de Dieu Mucyo, *New Times*, 18 April 2009.

26 The example of the Shyorongi trials at the end of 2007 can illustrate this statement. In one trial the survivors expressed their anger after the release of a man after only thirty minutes of proceedings.

27 This official willingness is quite ambiguous in so far as the memory of the genocide contrasts with the encouragement of socio-economic development. Indeed, as I stated before, the actual official trend relies on the resilience of the nation more than on a suffering identity. Among the social actors, some young and rich Tutsi take advantage of the commemoration period to flee Rwanda in order to have some fun in the neighbor

countries (personal statement of 24-year-old man who returned to Rwanda after the genocide and who belongs to the "golden youth" of Kigali. April 2009).

References

African Rights (1995) *Not So Innocent: When Women Become Killers*, London.

Aghion, A. (2009) *My Neighbor, My Killer*, Gacaca film.

Amnesty International (2002) *Rwanda. Gacaca: a question of justice*, London.

Audoin-Rouzeau, S. (2009), "Les violences extrêmes du XXe siècle à l'aune de l'histoire et de l'anthroplogie. Le génocide des Tutsi au Rwanda", *Revue d'histoire de la Shoah*, 190, 137–51.

Audoin-Rouzeau, S. and Garapon A. (2010) "La France et le Rwanda quinze ans après le genocide. Responsabilité, brouille et reconstruction", *Esprit*, 364, 80–82.

Baraduc, V. (2010) 'Paroles de Bourreaux. Enquête ethnographique à la Prison centrale de Kigali. Itinéraires et violences de femmes pendant le génocide des Tutsi rwandais', Master thesis, Paris, Ehess.

Bugingo, S. (2004) "Genocide suspects list to hit 500,000", *New Times*.

Burnéous, K. (2008) "Truth-Telling as a Talking Cure? Insecurity and Retraumatization in the Rwandan Gacaca Courts", *Security Dialogue*, 39: 1, 55–76.

Chrétien, J.P. (ed.) (1995), *Les médias du génocide*, Paris: Karthala.

Clark, P. (2010) *The Gacaca Courts, Post-Genocide Justice and Reconciliation in Rwanda. Justice without Lawyers*, Cambridge: Cambridge University Press.

Des Forges, A. (1999), *Aucun témoin ne doit survivre. Le génocide au Rwanda*, Paris: Karthala.

Eltringham, N. (2009) "We are not a Truth Commission. Fragmented narratives and historical record in the International Criminal Tribunal for Rwanda", *Journal of Genocide Research*, 11: 1, 55–79.

Fujii, L.A. (2009a) *Killing Neighbors: Webs of Violence in Rwanda*, Ithaca and London: Cornell University Press.

—— (2009b) "Interpreting truth and lies in stories of conflict and violence", in Sriram, C.L., King, J., Mertus, J., Martin-Ortega, O. and Herman, J. (eds) *Surviving Field Research: Working in violent and difficult situations*, London and New York: Routledge, pp. 147–62.

Ginzburg, C. (1991) *Le juge et l'historien: Considérations en marge du procès Sofri*, Lagrasse: Editions Verdier.

Hogg, N. (2001) "'I never poured blood': Women accused of genocide in Rwanda", graduate thesis, McGill University, Montréal.

Ibuka (2007) *Rapport d'activité de l'année 2006*, Kigali.

Ibuka (2008) *Rapport d'activité de l'année 2007*, Kigali.

Ibuka (2009) *Rapport d'activité de l'année 2008*, Kigali.

Ingelaere, B. (2007) "'Does the Truth Pass Across the Fire without Burning?' Transitional Justice and its Discontents in Rwanda's *Gacaca* Courts", Discussion paper, University of Antwerp/IOB.

—— (2008) "Les juridictions *gacaca* au Rwanda", in Salter M. (ed.) *Transitional Justice and Reconciliation after a Violent Conflict: Learning from African Experiences*, IDEA. Available online at: http://www.idea.int/ (accessed 5 June 2012).

Kabera, E. (2004), *Les gardiens de la mémoire/Keepers of Memory*, Kigali: Link Media Production.

Kagabo, J. (1995) "Rwanda. Notes de voyage", *Les Temps Modernes*, 50: 583, 102–25.

Kimonyo, J.P. (2008) *Rwanda. Un genocide populaire*, Paris: Karthala.

Koff, C. (2004) *La mémoire des os*, Paris: Héloïse d'Ormesson.

Magnarella, P.J. (2002) "Recent Developments in the International Law of Genocide. An Anthropological Perspective on the International Criminal Tribunal for Rwanda", in Hinton A.L. (ed.), *Annihilating Difference. The Anthropology of Genocide*, Berkeley: University of California Press, pp. 310–22.

McDoom, O. (2005) "Rwandan's Ordinary Killers: Interpreting Popular Participation in the Rwandan Genocide", Working paper no.77, London: Crisis States Research Centre, LSE.

Mironko, C.K. (2004) "*Ibitero*: Means and Motive in Rwanda Genocide", in Cook, S. (ed.) *Genocide in Cambodia and Rwanda: New Perspective*, New Haven: Yale University Press.

Mugesera, A. (2010) "Les noyés du genocide: aveux et témoignages", *Dialogue*, Kigali.

PAPG (Projet d'appui au processus gacaca) (2006) *Rapport: juillet, août, septembre 2006*, Kigali.

—— (2007), *Rapport: janvier, fevrier, mars 2007*, Kigali.

Peskin, V. (2011), "Victor's Justice Revisited: Rwandan Patriotic Front Crimes and the Prosecutorial Endgame at the ICTR", in Straus, S. and Waldorf, L., *Remaking Rwanda: State Building and Human Rights after Mass Violence*, Madison: Wisconsin University Press.

Reyntjens, F. (2009) *Les risques du métier: Trois décennies comme "chercheur-acteur" au Rwanda et au Burundi*, Paris: L'Harmattan.

Republic of Rwanda (RoR) (2003) Cour Suprême, Département des Juridictions *Gacaca*, "Les juridictions *gacaca* comme solution alternative au règlement du contentieux du génocide", Kigali.

—— (2004a), *Dénombrement des victimes du génocide. Rapport final*, Kigali.

—— (2004b), *Official Gazette*, 19 June 2004.

—— (2004c), Commission nationale pour l'Unité et la Réconciliation (CNUR), *Rapport sur le troisième sommet national pour l'unité et la reconciliation*, Kigali.

—— (2008), Service national des Juridictions *gacaca* (SNJG), Domitille Mukantaganzwa, "Le processus des Juridictions Gacaca au Rwanda", Colloque international "Genocide au Rwanda et reconstruction des champs du savoir", Kigali, 24 July 2008.

—— (2010) Service national des Juridictions *gacaca*, Denis Bikesha, "The Genocide perpetrated against Tutsi: Handling the Aftermath of *Gacaca*", International symposium on the genocide perpetrated against Tutsi, Kigali, 6 April 2010.

Rettig, M. (2011) "The Sovu Trials: The Impact of Genocide Justice on One Community", in Straus, S. and Waldorf, L., *Remaking Rwanda: State Building and Human Rights after Mass Violence*, Madison: Wisconsin University Press, pp. 194–209.

Rutazibwa, P. and Rutayisire, P. (2007), *Génocide à Nyarubuye*, Kigali: Editions rwandaises.

Rutembesa, F. and Mutwarasibo, E. (2009), *Amateka ya Jenoside yakorewe Abatutsi muri Mugina*, Kigali: CNLG, 2009.

Sarkin, J. (1999) "The Necessity and Challenges of Establishing a Truth and Reconciliation Commission in Rwanda", *Human Rights Quarterly*, 21: 3, 767–823.

—— (2001) "The Tension between Justice and Reconciliation in Rwanda: Politics, Human Rights, Due Process and the Role of the *Gacaca* courts in dealing with the Genocide", *Journal of African Law*, 45: 2, 143–72.

Simburudali, T. (2009) "Survivre au genocide des Tutsi au Rwanda", *Revue d'histoire de la Shoah*, 190, 267–80.

Straus, S. (2004). "How many perpetrators were there in the Rwandan Genocide? An Estimate", *Journal of Genocide Research*, 6:1, 85–98.

—— (2006) *The Order of Genocide. Race, Power and War in Rwanda*, Ithaca and London: Cornell University Press.

PART 2

Show trials

CHAPTER 5

The *raion* trials in the USSR (1937–1938)

Nicolas Werth

The three Moscow show trials of the "Old Bolsheviks" staged in August 1936, January 1937 and March 1938 figure among the most famous examples of a denial of justice performed by a totalitarian state. The same cannot be said of the hundreds of other political show trials which were held in 1937 and 1938 in a number of district (*raion*) centers. These trials remained outside the scope of historical research until the beginning of the 1990s when Sheila Fitzpatrick, one of the leading American historians of the "revisionist" school, wrote the first article on these "forgotten" trials, based on the reports published in the local Soviet press at the time.[1] During the last decade, newly declassified archival sources have thrown new light on the making of these trials, on their political and social functions, on their place and role in the "Great Terror" of 1937 and 1938, this paroxystic moment of the Stalinist State violence. As we now know, far from being a unitary process centered on the purges of the communist political, military and economic elites, this frenzied stage of Stalinist repression was the convergence of several repressive lines. The "Great Terror" clearly had two sides: a public side and a hidden one. The public side was that of the show trials – the famous Moscow trials and the provincial trials of local officials. All these trials were more or less successfully staged political theater and, in Annie Kriegel's words, "a formidable mechanism of social prophylaxis."[2] Show trials unmasked conspiracies, singled out scapegoats, denounced "new lords whose inhuman attitudes end up encouraging the formation of an army of embittered people and Trotskyites."[3]

The public side of the "Great Terror" was also the promotion of a new elite, younger, better educated and more obedient, brought up in the strict "Stalinist spirit of the 1930s." The hidden side of the "Great Terror," recently uncovered, was that of the "NKVD operational orders," taken in compliance with top-secret Politburo resolutions. These were completely hidden transcripts not designed for circulation or discussion in the Communist Party (CP), state or society. The "mass secret operations" launched in the summer of 1937 were a prophylactic measure in the case of a future war, a form of murderous social engineering aimed at ridding the country "once and for all" of its "socially harmful" and "ethnically suspect elements." This mass crime (1.5 million arrests, 800,000 executions) was planned as an operation of social cleansing, with its targets, its victimized groups, its execution quotas allotted to every region and republic by Stalin and Iejov, the People's Commissar of the Interior.[4]

In this knot of "cumulative radicalization," what were the functions of the *raion* show trials, which Stalin despisingly called "agricultural trials," the majority of the accused being kolkhoz or MTS (Machine Tractor Stations) chairmen, low- and middle-ranking Party officials in rural administration accused of sabotaging the harvesting of grain and animal husbandry? These trials, which were intended to single out scapegoats responsible for disastrous agricultural results, show at one and the same time that Stalin's concern for the "little people" downtrodden by local "new lords" masks "secret mass operations" unfolding simultaneously and mobilizes the "masses" for the hunt for "enemies."

The starting point of the *raion* show trials was given by Stalin himself in a secret instruction sent on August 3, 1937 to all Regional and Republican First Party Secretaries. "Enemies of the people," wrote Stalin, "have wormed their way into kolkhozes, MTS and cattle breeding farms in order to sabotage harvests and cattle farming and to cause dissatisfaction with the Soviet system among kolkhoz workers subjected to systematic and intentional harassment from their bosses." In the name of the Central Committee, Stalin instructed every Regional and Republican Party Committee to stage, in carefully chosen *raion* centers, "two or three show trials" per region. The defendants, Stalin specified, should be picked up among "the directors of the *raion* MTS, cattle farming administration officials, kolkhoz chairmen, *raion* Party Committee officials." All these show trials were to be widely publicized in the local press.[5]

During the following weeks, Stalin and Molotov, the Head of the Soviet Government, sent two other top-secret instructions ordering every Regional

Party Committee to organize another round of "three to six show trials" along the following two "lines": "sabotage in the storage of grain" and "sabotage in cattle farming" (the second instruction on the latter topic gave, on several pages, vivid details about the various "acts of bacteriological terrorism" allegedly performed by "false vets," who "systematically inoculate kolkhoz cows, pigs and horses with the germs of anthrax, brucellosis and anemia [*sic*]." In their instructions, Stalin and Molotov specified that "these show trials are to be held with the active participation of peasant masses, a full-length coverage in the local press and end up with the execution of the accused."[6]

Stalin's personal involvement in the show trials can be further traced in a number of telegrams sent in the course of this "political campaign," which lasted several months, from August 1937 until January 1938.[7] In fact, Stalin's addiction to the exemplary "show trial" dates back to the 1920s. Let me just quote one sample of Stalin's correspondence with Menjinski, the Head of the OGPU, dated June 26, 1927, at a time of strong international tensions (marked by the breaking of the diplomatic relations between Great Britain and USSR): "It would be excellent to organize a few show trials on the topic of British espionage. The collected material and confessions could be usefully exploited by our propaganda all over Europe!"[8] The recently published Stalin–Molotov letters (for the period from 1925 to 1936) also reveal the direct implication of Stalin in the scenario of the main "show trials" of the late 1920s and early 1930s (the Shakhty trial, the Prompartia trial, the so-called "Peasant Labour Party" trial, and so on). In these matters, Stalin was indeed Lenin's "best disciple." I will quote here Lenin's letter, dated February 20, 1922 (the NEP "relaxation policy" had been under way for nearly a year) to Kourskii, the People's Commissar for Justice, severely criticizing the laxity of the whole judicial apparatus: "You don't seem to understand the militant role of our revolutionary justice. May I remind you that its three main tasks are: 1 – to intensify the repression against the enemies of Soviet power and the agents of the bourgeoisie; 2 – to implement this repression in the swiftest way through our revolutionary tribunals; 3 – to stage a number of public show trials, exemplary by their swiftness and harshness, exemplary by their educational and political scope, exemplary by their coverage in the press."[9]

Trotsky also praised the practice of show trials highly. On May 4, 1922, at a time when the regime was staging a number of public trials of priests who had tried to resist the campaign of confiscating objects of worship, Trotsky (at the time the second most important Bolshevik leader after Lenin) sent the following letter to the editorial boards of the main Soviet newspapers (*Izvestia*, *Pravda*, *Rabotchaia Moskva* and a number of others):

> What is going on? There has not been a single line in today's papers about the priests' trial! We had to interrupt the trial so that the press could atone for its sins, for not having enlightened the toiling masses about the crimes of clericalism . . . The result of all this? A downright boycott, a downright sabotage by the press of this exemplary trial, the importance of which, in matters of political education, is huge. I urge all the editorial boards to devote the next editions of the newspapers to the trial of the clergy along the following lines: a vast, centralized, counter-revolutionary organization, hiding itself behind the mask of religion, has been uncovered. This organization is controlled from abroad by a clerical-tsarist center, which has plenty of money, transferred abroad by the hierarchy of the Russian Orthodox church headed by Tikhon. This center is preparing for the re-establishment of the tsarist regime in Russia, etc. The participants to this counter-revolutionary clerical-tsarist plot are to be sentenced to death, etc.[10]

Let's now go back to the 1937 and 1938 *raion* show trials. A top-secret report sent on December 19, 1937 by Andrei Vychinski, the General Prosecutor of the USSR, to Stalin, indicates that "between September 10 and December 10, 1937, 626 show trials have been held: 181 in the field of sabotage in cattle farming and 445 in the field of sabotage in the storage of grain. First line: 3,559 sentenced, of whom 1,193 were sentenced to the death penalty by shooting. Second line: 2,053 sentenced, of whom 762 were sentenced to the death penalty by shooting. Grand total: 5,612 sentenced, of whom 1,955 were sentenced to the death penalty by shooting. Before this day, 1,044 have already been shot."[11]

Considering that the "*raion* show trial campaign" ended at the beginning of 1938, the total number of trials must have been around 700, with over 2,000 people sentenced to death and another 4,000 or so people sentenced to long-term forced labour (usually for ten years). True enough, these figures represent only approximately 0.25 percent of the people shot or sentenced during the "Great Terror." Nevertheless, they are very much higher than the rough estimates given by Sheila Fitzpatrick in her study based on a sample of local Soviet press.

I shall now try, by means of the example of one particular public show trial which took place in Severnyi, a small Siberian *raion* center, to analyze the making of this specific denial of justice, performed like an assembly line, with largely – but not totally – standardized "topics," "plots," "scenarios" and defendants.[12]

On the day following the receipt of Stalin's telegram of 3 August, Robert Eikhe, the First Secretary of the Western Siberia Party Committee in

Novosibirsk, summoned a meeting of the Party Bureau, which assigned to the Regional Prosecutor and to the Regional Head of the NKVD the task of picking up, within ten days, among the preliminary investigations on hand against local officials, a number of cases which might comply with Stalin's request. On 15 August the Party Bureau ratified a first list of "wreckers" presented jointly by the Regional Prosecutor and the Regional Head of the NKVD – a group of fifteen Party officials from the remote Severnyi *raion*. Only two of them were already under arrest for some minor embezzlement. On the following day, a dozen low- and middle-ranking officials (three kolkhoz chairmen, three MTS chairmen, three vets and a few other agricultural technicians working in the rural administration) were arrested and subjected to interrogation. Two weeks later, on 4 September, the local "Party boss," Matrossov, the Severnyi District Party Secretary, who was to be in the limelight during the show trial, was in his turn arrested.

For years, the Severnyi district had been considered as behind, never completing the production nor the collection plans. Far away from Novosibirsk, Matrossov, a communist with a "good" social background (he had been a worker from the bench, promoted, as many other *vydvizhentsy*, to a high Party position in the early 1930s), had woven his "family circle" made up of the local Party *nomenklatura* members. Like many other local Party bosses, Matrossov ran his district with an iron hand, abusing people under his jurisdiction, and especially peasants. For people like Matrossov, promoted during the harsh years of collectivization, dekulakization and famine, "fulfilling State and Party duties" meant making free with things, people and laws. "Lords in their fiefdom," in the words of Stalin, Party bosses like Matrossov were at the same time very vulnerable – not only did they permanently infringe "Soviet legality" but they never succeeded in fulfilling the totally unrealistic production or collection plans imposed on them. The preliminary investigation easily gathered incriminating documents against the "Matrossov clique," using in particular the innumerable letters of complaint sent, over the years, by peasants and other citizens abused by local officials. Until then, these letters had remained unanswered, abuses being part of the extremely brutal and arbitrary *modus operandi* of the regime, but they had nevertheless been kept as a *kompromat* (compromising material) which might be used some day. The abuses committed by the Severnyi *raion* administration were indeed innumerable and astonishing: peasants were, as in the time of serfdom, flogged on every pretext, submitted to illegal "special taxes" (a "smoke tax" on stoves, a "dog tax" etc.) and fines (for "anti-sanitary keeping of houses" or "wandering of domestic animals") invented by Matrossov and his team. The proceeds of these "taxes" and "fines" were distributed among the members of the "clique." All these abuses were qualified, by the prosecution, as a deliberate action aimed at "producing a cohort of embittered people ready to stand up against the Soviet power." As for sabotage, the prosecution had a wide choice of incriminating facts among the numerous failures and problems affecting the miserable Severnyi *raion* agriculture and cattle farming: low yields, huge losses of grain during storage and transportation, poor tractor maintenance, epizootics, etc.

According to the Soviet Penal Code, for crimes of counter-revolutionary sabotage (Article 58, clauses 7 and 9), the defendants were granted access to their case only 24 hours before the trial, which opened, in Severnyi, on 18 September. The trial was preceded by numerous meetings held in all the kolkhozes and MTS of the *raion*. On the eve of the trial, Robert Eikhe sent accurate instructions to the local press ordering the editors "to give a full coverage on the crimes of the Boukharin-Trotskyite saboteurs in the Severnyi *raion*." For three days on end, over thirty witnesses (mostly kolkhoz peasants) related the numerous misdeeds of the accused. Matrossov avowed himself to have been in the wrong, but denied the qualification of his acts as "counter-revolutionary" and "boukharino-trotskyite." Some of the other defendants, however, confessed to everything: Novgorodtsev, for example, the head of the zootechnical district department, described in detail how, acting on the orders of an unspecified "foreign country," he had inoculated the livestock of 18 kolkhozes with anthrax, thus causing the death, in 1937, of 1,740 horses, 1,925 cows and 3,304 pigs! The different defence strategies of the accused, combined with the unpreparedness of the proceedings, hastily wrapped up in less than two weeks, resulted in incoherent, contradictory hearings attended by a large audience of hundreds of peasants especially chosen to represent "the abused common people." Contrary to what happened in several other *raion* trials, the witnesses did not indulge in a general criticism of the "abuses" which were a major part of the *modus operandi* of the regime. At the end of the third day, on September 20, 1937, all the defendants were sentenced to the death penalty. Dozens of telegrams were, in the following days, sent to Stalin and to the CP Central committee, on behalf of "workers and kolkhoz peasants" approving of the sentence and thanking Stalin and his "staunch bolshevik team" for "having defended the little people and restored justice." In return, "kolkhoz collectives" promised "to fulfill the collection plans and to subscribe to the 20th Anniversary of the Great October Revolution State loan."

As political theater, these "*raion* trials" were indeed very different from the great Moscow show trials. The accused were not famous Bolshevik leaders, accused of horrible, incredible, inconceivable crimes to which they had admitted their guilt. In the *raion* show trials, the accused were local eminent people, who were suddenly brought to trial for ordinary misdeeds which had been going on for years and which were now qualified as "counter-revolutionary crimes." Held with all solemnity in the district "Palace of Soviets," in the presence of a large audience, these show trials had a different political and educational function from the one assigned to the Moscow trials. They were supposed to illustrate Stalin's and his team's concern for "little people" downtrodden by "new lords" who had betrayed the cause of socialism and had become "enemies of the people." The populist scenario of this political theater ran like this: the "enemies of the people" organized in "local cliques" had wormed their way into key positions commanding the whole of agricultural and cattle farming production in order to perform "sabotage." By abusing "little people," they tried to set them against the Soviet regime. Fortunately, active and politically minded kolkhoz peasants had written letters of complaint, which had been for a time blocked by the "enemies" – this explained the late staging of the trials. Finally, thanks to the fatherly vigilance of Stalin and of his closest associates, the "enemies of the people" had been unmasked. These show trials marked the triumph of the "little people," of Soviet democracy as asserted in the 1936 Constitution, the triumph of Stalinism. This scenario, widely "popularized" in the local press, featured a central dimension of Stalin's populism, based on a somewhat archaic conception of politics – the myth of the "good tsar." But, as Sheila Fitzpatrick underlined in her groundbreaking article, "the peasants did *not* believe in it, the witnesses did *not* credit Stalin with bringing corrupt lower officials to justice."[13] Had it ever existed, the "good tsar" myth had already been curtailed by the time of Stalin's famous article of March 2, 1930, "Dizzy with success," when the dictator tried to shift the blame for collectivization to those local officials who had committed "excesses."[14] With the relentless pursuit of the collectivization drive, the imposing of the kolkhoz system – considered by many peasants as a "second serfdom" – the deportation of millions of "kulaks," dearth and famine, the huge majority of the Soviet peasants, a fact underlined in regular police reports on the mood of the population, did not trust Stalin, whom they rightly held responsible for their misfortunes.

The speedy setting up, in a matter of weeks, of hundreds of show trials did not go without hitches. The scenario sometimes did not work. In Kady, for example, a *raion* center in the Ivanovo region, not only did the accused reject the charges brought against them, but the witnesses "went too far," openly criticizing not only the "abuses" of the local *nomenklatura*, but, more generally, the "new serfdom" introduced by forced collectivization and the imposition of the kolkhoz system. At the end of the first day, the Party authorities decided to clear the court and hear the case behind closed doors.[15] The Kady case was indeed quite exceptional, but it often happened that the testimonies of the witnesses contained several "politically incorrect" remarks. In a trial held in a *raion* center near Novgorod, a peasant witness concluded her testimony by saying: "All the same, our side won, not yours!" – a statement which clearly showed the deep antagonism between "us" (the "little people," the "oppressed," the "new serfs") and "them" (the communists, the bureaucrats, the "new lords").[16] More embarrassing than these awkward statements was the refusal of a certain number of judges to deliver the required death sentence. If we go back to Vychinski's report on the "*raion* show trial campaign" we notice that, contrary to Stalin's and Molotov's instructions to sentence "all the saboteurs to the death penalty by shooting," only a third of the accused were in fact sentenced to the "highest measure of punishment," all the others being sentenced to a ten-year term in a forced labour camp. Local judges and prosecutors often belonged to the same *nomenklatura* circle as the accused and resorted to different stratagems in order to spare their colleagues' lives, the most common being the requalification of the charges of "sabotage" into "complicity in sabotage." In this case, those sentenced to the death penalty were usually "old specialists" (trained in tsarist times) – agronomists or vets were ideal targets – who did not belong to the local Party *nomenklatura*, the latter being often spared (that is sentenced to a long term in the Gulag camps). These manœuvres, however, were quite risky: in Uglitch, for example, after the completion, at the end of August 1937, of the *raion* show trial, which ended up with four death sentences and five sentences to work camps, the judges were summoned by the First Regional Party Secretary in Iaroslavl, who charged them with not having conformed to the "projected verdict" (the death penalty for *all* the accused) that he had sent them before the opening of the show trial. The verdict they had returned was "Trotskyite in essence" and could only lead to the arrest of the whole district Party *nomenklatura*. The judges were dismissed on the spot. However, they somehow escaped arrest (several hundred judges were arrested in the second half of 1937 only in the Russian Federation (RSFSR)).[17] The regional prosecutor appealed against the verdict, but for unknown reasons, the Uglitch case dragged on for over a year first in the RSFSR Supreme Court, and then in the USSR Supreme Court. When it was finally examined, at the end of 1938, the Great Terror was over, the verdict was quashed and the five survivors were freed.[18]

The Uglitch case was certainly not unique. In Alechki (Voronej region), the verdict of the local show trial (two death sentences, seven to forced labour) also went to appeal in front of the regional prosecutor. The RSFSR Supreme Court did not intervene in this case. The trial was re-staged two months later, under the fallacious argument that "new evidence of even more vicious counter-revolutionary crimes had been unearthed." This time, the judges delivered six death sentences, instead of two.[19]

In this mass fabrication of hundreds of trials all over the country, the "master plot" could hardly be entirely standardized. In fact, it could vary considerably. Thus, in Sychevka, a *raion* center in Smolensk region, five of the ten accused were arrested neither for sabotage in agricultural or cattle farming matters, nor for having "intentionally produced, by their abuses, a cohort of embittered people ready to stand up against the Soviet power" but for "having failed in mobilizing the Party organization for the eradication of the enemies." In NKVD and Party quarters, the expression "eradication of the enemies" referred at that time (summer 1937) to the "secret mass operation" launched by the NKVD "Order no. 00447" dated July 30, 1937, targeting "socially harmful elements." Among the accused of the Sychevka *raion* trial figured Krasilnikov, the district Party secretary, accused of having raised, in public, his doubts as to the necessity of another campaign against "saboteurs," "kulaks" and other "enemies"; Bogdanov, the president of the executive committee of the district soviet, was accused of having destroyed a number of lists, dating from the beginning of the 1920s, of peasants catalogued as "kulaks"; and Koudriavtsev, the district prosecutor, who had refused to qualify as "counter-revolutionary" a number of minor offenses. Clearly, in this case, the show trials featured not local officials who had conducted themselves as "lords in their fiefdom" but officials who had been reluctant to engage in the new, unprecedented in its scope, extermination campaign. The Sychevka trial was to show that no foot-dragging would be tolerated in the implementation of the "mass secret operations." It might also have had another aim: to help the local NKVD to fulfil its "quota of enemies" for the 00447 operation. In the days preceding the trial, meetings took place in nearly every kolkhoz, every "family head" being urged to speak out against the "Krasilnikov gang" and – better – to denounce unmasked, hidden "enemies of the people."[20] Notwithstanding the fact that small boxes had been put in the meeting halls so that people could slide in letters of denunciation, the NKVD seems to have gathered very little information that way. For the "mass operations," recent studies have shown that the NKVD had to rely mainly on information gathered over the years by police informants and compiled in a decentralized and rather primitive, often badly kept, system of card-cataloguing.[21] Clearly, further research is necessary to understand the interaction between the two sides of the Great Terror: the public side, that of the show trials, and the hidden side, that of the "secret mass operations."

The "*raion* show trials campaign" ended abruptly at the beginning of February 1938, nine months before the end of the "secret mass operations."

The reason for this is still unclear. Maybe Stalin considered that the staging of these trials was too amateurish. While emphasizing the "positive reactions of the masses to the holding of the show trials," the NKVD and Party secret reports sent to Stalin also revealed the numerous failures of these parodies of justice. The successful fabrication and staging of hundreds of show trials required, for each single case, a solid experience, a long training of the witnesses and a full confession of the main accused – all prerequisites which required time, energy and know-how.

On November 17, 1938 the Politburo, under the signature of Stalin, issued a top-secret instruction stopping all mass operations, and sharply criticizing "major deficiencies and distortions" in the work of the NKVD and the Procuracy (the Soviet legal administration). According to the Politburo resolution (sent only to a few selected Party, police and judiciary officials), "these intolerable defects had occurred because enemies of the people who had wormed their way into the NKVD and into the Procuracy attempted with every means at their disposal to cut off the NKVD and the Procuracy from Party organs, to evade the Party's control and leadership, thereby to make it easier for themselves and their confederates to continue their anti-Soviet subversive activities."[22]

A new wave of purges followed this "new turn."[23] But only a handful of people sentenced in the *raion* show trials to long terms of forced labour in the Gulag camps were set free. Krasilnikov and Bogdanov, two of the accused in the Sychevka trial, were among the lucky few. Thanks to the interference of influential Party colleagues who had somehow managed to come into contact with Vychinski, the death sentence passed upon them had been suspended and they were still alive when the "Great Terror" came to an end. Not a single one of the 6,000 or so people sentenced to death or to a long term in the Gulag camps in the course of the 1937 and 1938 *raion* show trials was, however, rehabilitated until the mid-1950s. As for the great majority of the victims of this mass injustice, most of them were rehabilitated (as were the other victims of the Great Terror) many years after their death, in the 1990s, after the fall of the Soviet regime.

Notes

1 Sheila Fitzpatrick, "How the Mice buried the Cat: Scenes from the Great Purges of 1937 in the Russian provinces", *The Russian Review*, vol. 52 (3), 1993, 299–320. Several points of Sheila Fitzpatrick's article have since been discussed and disputed by Michael Ellman. See his "The Soviet 1937 Provincial Show Trials: Carnival or Terror?", *Europe-Asia Studies*, vol. 53, no. 6, 1221–34.

2 Annie Kriegel, *Les grands procès dans les systèmes communistes*, Paris: Gallimard, 1972, p. 160.

3 From Stalin's speech, dated March 3, 1937.

4 On this aspect of the Great Terror, see Nicolas Werth, *L'ivrogne et la marchande de fleurs. Autopsie d'un meurtre de masse, 1937–1938*, Paris: Tallandier, 2009.

5 RGASPI, 558/11/57/26.

6 Top-secret telegrams from Stalin and Molotov to the Regional and Republican First Party Secretaries, dated September 10, 1937 and October 2, 1937, RGASPI, 558/11/57/71 and 558/11/57/124.

7 See, for example, the two telegrams sent by Stalin on the same day, August 27, 1937, to Krasnoiarsk and Smolensk. "To com. Sobolev, Krasnoiarsk. The fire in the grain elevator you mentioned to me is undoubtedly the result of sabotage. Find the culprits at once! They must be immediately brought to trial. Public trial. Verdict: death sentence, to be reported in all local papers." "To com. Korotchenkov, Smolensk. I advise you to sentence to the death penalty by shooting all the saboteurs of the Andreievskii raion. Public show trial. Publish the proceedings and sentence in all the local papers" (RGASPI, 558/11/57/55).

8 RGASPI, 558/11/71/29.

9 Lenin, *Polnoie sobranie socinenii*, Moscow: Politizdat, 1965, vol. 44, pp. 399–400.

10 APRF (Archives présidentielles de la Fédération de Russie), 3/60/25/3, published in *Politburo i tserkov'* (Politburo and the Church), Moscow: Rosspen, 1997, pp. 254–5.

11 APRF, 3/58/389/89–93.

12 On this particular *raion* show trial, see the materials published in V.P. Danilov et al. (eds), *Tragedia sovetskoi derevni, 1927–1939*, vol. V/1, Moscow: Rosspen, 2004, pp. 396–9, 454–71, 489–90; also I.V. Pavlova, "Pokazatelnye protsessy v Rossiiskoi glubinke v 1937 godu", *Gumanitarnye nauki v Sibiri*, 1998, vol. 2, 98–103.

13 Sheila Fitzpatrick, *op. cit*, p. 318.

14 Nicolas Werth, "Cher Kalinouchka . . .": Lettres paysannes à Kalinine, 1930", *Mélanges Marc Ferro, De Russie et d'ailleurs*, Paris: Institut d'Etudes slaves, 1995, pp. 223–43.

15 The Kady case was reported by Alexandr Soljenitsyn in *Arkhipelag Gulag*, Paris: YMCA-Press, 1973, pp. 420–1.

16 See Sarah Davies, *Popular Opinion in Stalin's Russia. Terror, Propaganda and Dissent, 1934–1941*, Cambridge: Cambridge University Press, 1997, pp. 124–33.

17 Peter Solomon, *Soviet Criminal Justice under Stalin*, Cambridge: Cambridge University Press, 1996, pp. 246–7.

18 The Uglitch case is reported in Michael Ellman, *op. cit.*

19 The Alechki trial is reported in V.P. Danilov et al., *op. cit*, pp. 439–43.

20 On the Sychevka show trial, see Roberta Manning, "Politiceskii terror kak politiceskii teatr" (Political Terror as Political Theatre), in V.P. Danilov et al., *op. cit*, pp. 51–70.

21 Nicolas Werth, *L'ivrogne et la marchande de fleurs*, *op. cit*, p. 214; François-Xavier Nérard, *Cinq pour cent de vérité. La dénonciation dans l'URSS de Staline (1928–1941)*, Paris: Tallandier, 2004.

22 English translation of this resolution in John Arch Getty & Oleg V. Naumov, *The Road to Terror: Stalin and the Self-Destruction of the Bolsheviks, 1932–1939*, New Haven: Yale University Press, 1999, pp. 533–5.

23 Neverthess, the scope of the "Beria purge" in the ranks of the NKVD remained limited: out of the 25,000 State Security operational agents on duty during the "Great Terror" only 1,364 were arrested, under the false accusation of "counter-revolutionary activities." See Nikita Petrov, "Le personnel des organes de sécurité soviétiques, 1922–1953", *Cahiers du monde russe*, vol. 42, 2–3–4, Avril–décembre 2001, 390.

CHAPTER 6

The trial of the "Gang of Four"

Visibility and invisibility of the Cultural Revolution

Anne Kerlan

Introduction

In October 1976, one month after the death of Chairman Mao, after an intense political struggle between different factions in power, the "Gang of Four" (Mao's former wife, Jiang Qing and three Party executives: Zhang Chunqiao, Yao Wenyuan and Wang Hongwen) were arrested under the authority of the new Prime Minister Hua Guofeng with the support of the Army. Most of the Chinese people were relieved by this capture: the Gang was hated and represented, in people's minds, the worst aspect of the Cultural Revolution ideology. In fact, and even if the exact responsibility of these Party leaders during the Cultural Revolution still needs to be thoroughly researched, they played, next to Chairman Mao, an important and negative role during the ten years of this troubled period.[1] The Gang of Four was known to support the most extreme leftist ideology; Jiang Qing in particular (Mao's wife since 1938) was a strong supporter of the Red Guards' activities and was very active in the violent campaign against artists that ended up with the death of several of them.

I will not discuss the complicated political environment that led to the capture and the trial of the Gang of Four, in the wake of the ascent of a new leader, Deng Xiaoping, who was keen to modernize China and had clearly chosen pragmatism as his ideology. The trial took place four years after the arrests, which occurred between November 1980 and January 1981. It was screened on television nationwide and received extensive media coverage.

However, today there are very few documents, archives or film footage still available in the public sphere. In neither the Chinese nor in the Western community could I find a significant body of literature on the subject.[2] Forty years after the trial, it seems nobody wants to remember it either in China or in the Western world. There might be various reasons for this silence. The fact that the records of the trial are still not available naturally prevents historians from carrying out research. In China, moreover, the silence around the trial is officially orchestrated, like everything else related to the Cultural Revolution. The trial was in Deng's mind the trial of the whole Cultural Revolution, a way for him to move on and open a new era. It was also a way to shut the door on troublesome questions about the political regime that had allowed such fury to arise. From this standpoint, the trial as we know it today – with all the silence and the lack of documents about it – is an excellent symbol of the way China deals with the memory of the Cultural Revolution.

This chapter does not aim at filling the gap and is not the result of research in the archives; it will rather expose some remarks about the few images we have of the trial and from there will go to the question of the visibility and invisibility of some past events in communist China. I will first analyze the images in order to understand the nature of a trial that has been defined as a show trial but was maybe a little bit more than that. I will then try to go behind the trial scene to understand its blind spots as well as the silence that has shrouded it since 1980. These are emblematic of the way the memory of the Cultural Revolution is officially blocked in China. I will finally expose how other strategies were developed, parallel to this official trial of the Cultural Revolution, to speak of and remember what was one of the bloodiest periods of Communist China.

The trial

A symbolic trial

The trial of the Gang of Four was in reality a trial of ten people: the Gang of Four plus six other Party executives who were close to Lin Biao, who had died in 1971 while escaping China after having been suspected of plotting against Mao. Organized by the Supreme Court of Justice and a Special Court of Justice, it opened on November 11, 1980, in Beijing, after four years of preparation, and lasted until January 25, 1981, with thirty-six magistrates appointed for it.

Portions of the indictment were printed in the press before the trial started; they accused the defendants of crimes that took place during the

Cultural Revolution. The charges specify that 727,420 Chinese were "persecuted" during that period, and that 34,274 died. The indictment also accused the "Counterrevolutionary Clique" of having attempted to seize power.

The trial was a public trial: 600 people were allowed into the courtroom and it was screened nationwide. Today, however, few of the images are still available. I worked here with images circulating on the internet; the sources are often not given, which is of course a problem. Looking at them, however, does give us some idea of the atmosphere of the trial. The setting and the staging of the trial are worth looking at, as they participate, I believe, in the message sent by those in power to the population: a message that the Cultural Revolution, including the practice of popular justice, is over. During the Cultural Revolution, popular trials would often put the defendant in the middle of the crowd or expose them to the crowd.[3] The spectators are also the judges. The setting of the Gang of Four trial reverses this dynamic by separating the judges from the public attending the trial. Moreover, the judges are exposed more than are the defendants, who are placed with their backs turned to the public. For Beijing's officials the trial was a way to assert the new legal system and specifically that the people were no longer making the law.

Figure 6.1 The courtroom of the trial of the "Gang of Four," Beijing, November 1980.

The nature of the trial: between Nuremberg and Moscow

Officials in Beijing did consider the Gang of Four trial as an important, seminal moment that would allow them to close the door on the Cultural Revolution period and to open a new era. For them, the trial had to be exemplary and as such was sometimes labeled as a "China's Nuremberg." With four years of preparation, the search for witnesses and evidence, the entire legal apparatus was supposed to testify to the seriousness and solidity of the charges that seemed to be "strongly rooted in fact."[4] For instance, when it was time to confront the defendants with their crimes, images that attest to the atrocities perpetrated against some victims were displayed.[5]

Despite the efforts of the authorities to organize a trial that had all the appearances of a real trial, grounded on solid proofs, foreign observers cast doubt on the success of the enterprise: for them, the trial was a political exercise.[6] The verdict was never in doubt. Legal defense was almost non-existent. Some procedural requirements of the new criminal legislation were not followed. To a certain extent, the Beijing trial was closer to the Moscow trial than to Nuremberg.

The theatricality of the trial

But many aspects of the Gang of Four trial differed from a Moscow trial: the reality of the crimes attributed to the Gang of Four, in particular to Jiang Qing, was not in doubt. For instance, Zhang Chunqiao decided to stay silent during the entire trial, refusing to participate. The most extraordinary attitude, however, was that of Jiang Qing, who put on a real show. Jiang Qing was a former actress and she certainly showed it.

First she smirked and yawned during the reading of the indictment. Then she refused to show any sign of repentance. On the contrary, she responded to the prosecutors or the witnesses, accusing them of forging evidence, and was expelled from the courtroom on several occasions.[7] As the trial got under way, Jiang Qing dismissed her assigned lawyers, deciding instead to represent herself. All this was filmed at length as if the trial of the Gang of Four was also an opportunity for her to perform one last role.

The pugnacity of Jiang Qing and the fact that this attitude was shown through the filmed footage to the Chinese population did not fit into the vision of a Moscow-style show trial. Nor did the final sentences: even if the death sentence was pronounced for Jiang Qing and Zhang Chunqiao, it was suspended for two years to allow them to repent. These death sentences were later commuted to life imprisonment, while Wang Hongwen and Yao Wenyuan were given life and twenty years in prison, respectively. They were all released later. The Beijing trial did not result in the physical elimination of the defendants.

Many questions are raised when one looks at the Gang of Four trial film clips. It was a show, but not exactly the same type of "show trial" that had happened earlier in Moscow: this time, the defendants, and Jiang Qing in particular, were part of the show and the show was broadcast as such. What was the idea behind such publicity? Why did Beijing officials authorize Jiang Qing's theatrical attitude? These are, among others, questions to ask of a trial where blind spots are numerous.

Silences and blind spots

In the absence of archives, it is difficult to believe that the broadcasting of the show and the visual impact of an unrepentant, pugnacious Jiang Qing was a mistake or a surprise. We must remember that what was at stake was twofold: to recognize the mistake that was the Cultural Revolution without endangering the very foundation of the political system and the Communist Party. By organizing the trial of the Gang of Four, the Beijing authorities were trying to attribute to this small group the entire responsibility for the Cultural Revolution. This meant, eventually, that one of the main blind spots of the trial was the question of Chairman Mao's real responsibility.

Mao: mistakes, not crimes

The trial of the Gang of Four never directly questions Mao's responsibility. However, as one observer noted it, Jiang Qing repeatedly invoked Mao to justify herself. She was, as she said, Mao's dog: "When he tells me to bite, I bite."

For some observers, the fact that Jiang Qing could speak about Mao the way she did proved that Deng Xiaoping was ready to allow a critique of Mao's role during the Cultural Revolution. Jiang Qing's attitude in the trial, her hints about Mao, would have been a way to bring indirect discredit upon Mao. This could be true to a certain extent; however, one could also find in Jiang Qing's words reasons to think that she was also (willingly or not) contributing to the building of the new status for Mao: after his death, he became a myth and untouchable as such.

For instance, after being shown the post mortem examination of Zhang Linzhi (minister of the coal industry), a victim of the Cultural Revolution, Jiang Qing made the following statement:

> This may be true. However, those "huge amounts of evidence," as claimed by you, are merely picking bones from an egg .... For

Figure 6.2 Jiang Qing, trial of the "Gang of Four," Beijing, November 1980.

> instance, a sound record from the National Beijing Opera Institution was played again and again. Also, having me repeatedly appear in court, six times so far, can reveal something too. I understand only too well what you said. What you are doing now is to uglify me, Chairman Mao Zedong, and the Great Proletarian Cultural Revolution, in which hundreds of millions of people participated. I was Chairman Mao's wife for 38 full years, not counting those years when we first knew each other. We have been through wars and hardships together. During the wartime I was the only woman who followed Chairman Mao to the frontier! Where were you hiding then?![8]

This speech of Jiang Qing's evokes the glorious past of Communist China, a past that cannot be, as she says, "made ugly." This is in line with the official vision of the time. According to this version of history, Chairman Mao had made mistakes while launching the Cultural Revolution, but these were only mistakes due to bad judgment, while the Gang of Four was accused of having turned these mistakes to their own advantage and committed crimes. Jiang Qing's defense – she was Mao's faithful wife – is coherent also with this vision of Chairman Mao, wrongly manipulated by those close to him.

Finally, the theatricality of Jiang Qing's attitude condemned her more than witnesses' accusation. In a courtroom that was set with formality and a sense of restored order, she acted as a wild, extravagant individual. I suspect then that if the officials in Beijing allowed Jiang Qing to speak so freely, it was more to show that she was an unfaithful person than to covertly start the trial of Mao. Mao was becoming a myth; Beijing officials needed this myth to stay in power; the trial and Jiang Qing's attitude were also part of the strategy that contributed to preventing people from questioning the real role Mao had played in the violence of the Cultural Revolution. Jiang Qing's show was also a diversion.

The absence of the ordinary victims

Jiang Qing's show also helped to frame the trial of the Cultural Revolution within a limited scope in terms of the real number of victims. Even now, the exact number of these victims is not known and estimates vary between 400,000 and one million[9]: many more than the indictment indicated, when it recognized that over 30,000 people died because of the Gang of Four's activities. For instance, the numerous crimes perpetrated in the summer of 1966 in Beijing against teachers and common Beijingers (1,772 people died in Beijing in two months) were not described or investigated during the trial.[10] At the trial, the crimes recognized were the ones committed against high-ranking officials and the crimes perpetrated by Jiang Qing against artists. In the first case, this allowed for the assimilation of these crimes into the political plots of the Gang of Four. In the second case, it was a way to hold Jiang Qing directly responsible. Jiang Qing was, in the 1930s, a minor film actress and later she decided to destroy whoever had a connection with her past: these crimes could then be explained for personal reasons. In both cases, the crimes did not question either the nature of the regime or the responsibility of Mao. By accusing the Gang of Four and only the Gang of Four, not only did the Beijing officials protect Mao, but they also denied the right of having existed, and a place in the official history of China, to the ordinary victims of the Cultural Revolution.

The trial of the Gang of Four and the official history of the Cultural Revolution

The real purpose of the trial was indeed to write the official history of the Cultural Revolution period in such a way that neither the Chinese

Communist Party and its executive nor Chairman Mao would be held responsible. The trial of the Gang of Four ended a few months before the publication of an important resolution of the 11th Central Committee 6th Plenary Meeting (June 1981) about "the history of our Party since the founding of the PRC." Not surprisingly, in this resolution, the crimes of the Cultural Revolution were attributed to the Gang of Four and Lin Biao. Chairman Mao's leadership was considered to be good "except for a few mistakes." If the Cultural Revolution was condemned as a moment of error, the political system built since 1949 by Mao was spared from criticism; the trial, in the end, legitimized the continuation of this system with its new leaders, notably Deng Xiaoping. In other words, the trial and the resolution that followed did not aim at doing justice to the numerous victims of Cultural Revolution or at questioning the nature of the political regime that produced it; it allowed on the contrary for the reassertion of the proper basis of the PRC.

This attitude is the one that has been adopted by the Chinese government since then. For instance, if many of the victims of the Cultural Revolution have been rehabilitated officially (the families received 420 yuan in compensation), their story, the story of how they were arrested, tortured or murdered, has never been made known, but rather has been kept from the public. Since 1986, only three books on the Cultural Revolution have been published with official authorization;[11] the most authorized one[12] does not give an exact account of the crimes perpetrated by the Red Guards but tends to minimize them. Even the official commemoration of the Cultural Revolution has been forbidden, as was the case in 2006 when Beijing's officials prevented some Chinese scholars from joining a conference in New York for the fortieth anniversary of the beginning of the Revolution.

The official history of the Cultural Revolution still follows the interpretation proposed during the trial of the Gang of Four. As a result, the deep reasons, the logic of power that produced the Cultural Revolution are never questioned. The trial set the Cultural Revolution apart as a tragic episode of Communist China. It did not allow for the questioning of the political or social origins of the violence that occurred during the Cultural Revolution. To do so would have meant questioning the principle of Mao's leadership, which was, and still is, something that it is impossible to do. Other deeply tragic episodes in the history of Communist China that could also help explain the Cultural Revolution are thus "forgotten." The Great Leap Forward, and the twenty million (or more) dead from starvation that it caused are forgotten as well. The trial of the Gang of Four acted, from this standpoint, like a mirage that allowed the leaders to erase many questions about the nature of the political regime, the leadership and the ideology that ruled and is still ruling China.

Where the past can be made visible

If the official history of Communist China is strictly controlled, a parallel history has started to develop since the end of the 1990s. It has developed in the margins of official history: in fiction writing, in overseas publications and, more and more, on video and on internet websites. Historians, working outside of their official occupation, are trying to gather, through interviews, the memory of their generation, a generation of Chinese who lived through the Cultural Revolution. Two aspects in particular are investigated, but not with the same degree of importance.

Most visible is the extensive research done in China to gather information on the Red Guards, those young people who devoted their youth to Mao and who were later sent away to the countryside for many years. Some of these ordinary Red Guards have published their memoirs, in books or even in films.[13] But even if they had a traumatic experience, the question of their implication in the murders of the Cultural Revolution is not raised in these memoirs. To some extent, those young people who were sent to the countryside instead of carrying on their education, feel that they are, themselves, victims of the Cultural Revolution. Their attitude, for some of them at least, is an attitude of pride; they claim they have no regrets about their youth and that they cannot be held responsible for the decisions made during that time.[14]

On the other side, and much more difficult, is the work of a few individuals who are trying to preserve the memory of the ordinary victims of the Cultural Revolution. There is, for instance, one website, launched in 2000 by an exiled Chinese historian, Wang Youqin, called "Chinese memorial" (www.chinese-memorial.org): the site is mainly a list of victims, with their biographies. It was blocked by the Chinese authorities and is not accessible from China. One must also mention the work of a filmmaker, Hu Jie, who, in three films, each one telling the story of a victim of the Cultural Revolution, has done a tremendous amount of work that goes a long way in gathering the details of one individual story.[15] The films are meant to be the courtroom of Communist China. This is a place where facts are established, where witnesses give their testimony, where evidence is shown, where one individual tragedy is put in connection with the political background that led to it, where, finally, the indictment is re-evaluated. In *Though I am Gone*, the husband of a victim (Bian Zhongyun, killed in Beijing by her students in August 1966) presents all the evidence he had gathered back then by taking photos of everything that happened from the dazibaos against his wife to her tormented body after she died. Looking at the camera and the spectator as if he was showing evidence in a court, he unpacked the bloody clothes she wore the day she was beaten to death by her students. Colleagues and witnesses come in front of the camera to reconstitute the facts. The film is the trial of Bian Zhongyun's murderers.

One thing, however, is missing in Hu Jie's films: the presence of the torturer, of the murderer of the victims. Not that Hu Jie did not try to have them face the camera, but because they refused. However, film footage of a mass meeting with Chairman Mao at Tiananmen square at the time Bian Zhongyun was killed provides the missing part. If Hu Jie does manage to establish some of the real political responsibility for the Cultural Revolution by showing Chairman Mao encouraging a young female student to perpetrate violence in Beijing in 1966, he does not succeed in confronting the actual murderers with their victims nor, more simply, does he manage to make them speak.

Hu Jie's films are a mirror of today's China both in what becomes visible and what is still veiled. In this country, the generation in power, the ones in charge of the country, the ones running businesses, the ones educating the young generations, writing books, doing research, belong to the generation of the Cultural Revolution. Some were victims, some were torturers, some were ordinary people. If the victims are barely starting to speak and still exist on the margins of official history, the torturers are still invisible and silent. The question of collective responsibility is still not raised. The trial of the Gang of Four was definitely a political act that allowed a semi-amnesia or a distortion of the historical reality. It had a twofold function: it opened a space for recrimination and criticism but drew a line so that the majority of ordinary Chinese people would be expelled from that space. Despite the effort of courageous people like Hu Jie, Wang Youqin and other individuals, who are trying to build a private sphere where other kinds of trials can take place, I suspect this will not be enough to give the Chinese nation what it needs to really move on: a public space where questions about the Cultural Revolution, its political origins, its victims and torturers can be raised.

Notes

1 On the Cultural Revolution see Roderick MacFarquhar and Michael Schoenhals, *Mao's Last Revolution*, Cambridge, MA and London: The Belknap Press of Harvard University Press, 2006 and Paul Clark, *The Chinese Cultural Revolution: A History*, Cambridge: Cambridge University Press, 2008.

2 One of the few books about the trial is David Bonavia, *Verdict in Peking: The Trial of the Gang of Four*, London: Burnett Books, 1984.

3 See for instance <http://www.youtube.com/watch?v=p63xt5AlahY&feature=related> at 1’51 to 2’46 and compare this with the arrival of the defendants during the Gang of Four Trial at <http://www.youtube.com/watch?v=91LEZxKlkrc> (both accessed 22 April 2011).

4 Bonavia, op. cit., p. 262.

5 See how the court showed slides of the dead body of Zhang Linzhi at <http://www.youtube.com/watch?v=YZ3-jrcHGEY&feature=related> (3’50 to 4’43) (accessed 22 April 2011).

6 See for instance Zafanolli Wojtek, “La signification politique du procès de Pékin,” *Politique étrangère* 1, 1981, 163–70.

7 See <http://www.youtube.com/watch?v=vzlEYFK89J8&feature=related> or almost the same with subtitles <http://www.youtube.com/watch?v=YZ3-jrcHGEY&feature=related> (3’12 to 3’49) (accessed 22 April 2011).

8 See <http://www.youtube.com/watch?v=YZ3-jrcHGEY&feature=related> (4’44 to 5’54) (accessed 22 April 2011).

9 See estimations by Wang Youqin, “Trouver une place pour les victimes,” *Perspectives chinoises* 4, 2007, 69.

10 Wang Youqin, op. cit, 70.

11 Gao Gao and Yan Jiaqi, *Wenhua da geming shinian shi* (A ten-year history of the Great Cultural Revolution), Tianjin: Tianjin renmin chubanshe, 1986; Wang Nianyi, *Da Dongluan de niandai* (A Time of Great Chaos), Zhengzhou: Henan renmin chubanshe, 1988; Jin Chunming, *Wenhua geming shigao* (An outline of the Cultural Revolution), Chengdu: Sichuan renmin chubanshe, 1995. On the context and content of these three official publications see Michel Bonin, “L’histoire de la Révolution culturelle et la mémoire de la ‘génération perdue’ sont-elles condamnées à l’oubli?” *Perspectives chinoises* 4, 2007, 54–8.

12 *Da dongluan de niandai*, the last reprint is 2005. On this publication, see Wang Youqin, “Student attacks against teacher: the revolution of 1966”, *Issues and Studies* 2, April 2001.

13 Wu Wenguang: *1966, My Time in the Red Guards*, 1993.

14 See Bonin, op. cit., 65.

15 *Xunzhao Lin Zhao de linghun* (“Looking for Lin Zhao’s soul”) (2004), *Wo sui siqu* (“Though I am gone”), 2005, *Wo de muqing Wang Peiying* (“My Mother, Wang Peiying”) (2010). This last film was for a long time available on the internet but as of April 2011 is not available anymore. One can see a trailer for a DVD version of the film at <http://www.youtube.com/watch?v=Pm4DO5Sx1Mw&feature=related> (accessed 22 April 2011).

CHAPTER 7

The Nazi People's Court (1944) or the failure of "total justice"

Johann Chapoutot

Between August 7 and October 10, 1944, Hitler's would-be murderers were tried by the "People's Court," the *Volksgerichtshof* in Berlin. With Goebbels' advocacy of "total war" and Hitler's countless speeches, the images of this trial have become the symbol of the Third Reich: when we think of it, we hear not only Goebbels or Hitler, but Freisler too: Dr. Roland Freisler, the President of the People's Court.

The story of this court began with yet another show trial, eleven years before, in Leipzig. (But was this trial of 1944 a show trial anyway? We will see.) Between September and December 1933, those assumed responsible for the Reichstag fire were tried by the *Reichsgericht*. But this propaganda event turned into a disaster for Goebbels: apart from van der Lubbe, the other defendants, communist leaders, were found not guilty and discharged. Worse, Goebbels had to interrupt the live broadcasting of the trial, because Dimitroff defended himself too well, and because judges as well as attorneys still played the game of justice, as if they had not understood that a new era had begun, or as if this was to be their last stand.

A few months later, on April 24, 1934,[1] a new law, the law against high treason (*Gesetz zur Aburteilung von Hoch- und Landesverrat*) created the *Volksgerichtshof*, composed of six senates, five judges for each senate, among whom there were only two professional lawyers. The other three judges were indeed laymen, representatives of the *Volk*: for the *Volksgerichtshof* – the People's Court – was to exert *Volksrecht* – People's Justice – not

Juristenrecht – a lawyer's Justice. The *Volksrecht* was the Nazis' proclaimed ideal: common sense (*gesunder Menschenverstand*) had to be the supreme norm, and was even introduced in German law as a source judges could refer to in their verdicts.[2] The "People's Law" was all sanity and reason, the true expression of the race, of the blood, far from the refined and incomprehensible abstractions of the *Juristenrecht*. Before this court, justice would at last be what it had to be, simple and swift: guilty, yes or no? If yes, the death penalty was to be executed right away; no appeal was possible. A play on words quickly nicknamed those curious judges, those *Strafrichter* (criminal judges), *Scharfrichter* (executioners, hangmen). Treason against the State would be handled in a military manner, the prime example, the archetype of Justice being, for the Nazis, the quick justice of the military. Roland Freisler wrote it in 1939: the *Sondergericht* was the drumhead court-martial (*Standgericht*) of the so-called "*inner front*."[3]

Still, to give it some legitimacy, some semblance of justice, the *Volksgerichtshof* was installed in the Berliner Kammergericht, a superb building (which still exists today, *am Kleistpark*, in Schöneberg) built during Kaiser Wilhelm's era, just before World War I. (The Allied Council would use it from 1948 until 1989 to house its activities).

And Roland Freisler, who became head of the *Volksgerichtshof* in August 1942, was a lawyer, after all, with a brillant career, intertwined with the history of the Nazi Party. Freisler, born in 1893, was a law student when he volunteered for the infantry in World War I. He came back with the rank of a lieutenant, and had been so changed by his war experience that he would always conceive of himself as a soldier. He could not conceal a certain fascination for the Bolshevik revolution which he had witnessed when he was held prisoner on the eastern front: the Bolsheviks had even made the scrupulous Freisler a *Lagerkommissar* – a camp commissioner, a representative of the inmates – from 1917 to 1918. Back in Germany, he became a doctor of law, passed the *Staatsexamen* and opened a law office with his brother in 1924. A member of the Nazi Party from 1925 on – that is: very early – he became one of the NSDAP's and SA's favorite lawyers when it came to defending brown-shirted stormtroopers who had broken too many communist jaws. "Raging Roland," as he was nicknamed, was valued by his *Gauleiter* as a fantastic orator, but not as an intellectual, although Freisler had already written much on legal doctrine and philosophy, and would go on to write even more after 1933.

The Nazi seizure of power was deeply satisfying for Freisler: in February 1933, along with other SA comrades, he took hold of some public buildings in Kassel and flew the swastika flag on them. From then on, his career took off and progressed at the level of the Reich: in June 1933, he became

Staatssekretär in Prussia's Ministry of Justice, and then, in May 1935, in the *Reichsjustizministerium*. Freisler was thrilled by the historical opportunity Germany and its lawyers were facing: for the first time since 1789, a revolution *of* and *in* the law was possible. Freisler wrote numerous essays and articles, collaborated in conferences, debates and publications of the *NS-Juristenbund* (National-socialist lawyers league), with Dr. Hans Frank (another successful ex-SA lawyer, and the future *Generalgouverneur* of Poland after 1940) and, until 1936, Professor Carl Schmitt. Dr. Freisler wrote what every other right-wing and nationalist lawyer wrote in those days out of conviction and/or opportunism, but Freisler was sincere and passionate when he proclaimed that it was time for a change. In his eyes, Germany had to abandon the individualist and liberal law inherited from the French Revolution, and should subsitute the *Gemeinschaft* (community) for the individual as the fundation of law.

The law for the Nazis was not an absolute value: it was relative, i.e. related to the *Gemeinschaft* and its interests. Hence the new and sound maxim: *Recht ist, was dem Volke frönt/nützt*: what is good for the *Volk* is legal. The law is not made out of abstract norms, but is a list of concrete, incarnated values. The law of the French Revolution and of the Weimar era was a weapon in the hands of the Reds (Communists) and the Blacks (Conservatives) to smash and destroy the Brown movement that had risen to save Germany. Now that the Nazis were in power, it was their turn to fight with their law, a law that would be the juridic transcription of the sole valid law: that of nature. The *Gesetz* had to be the transliteration of *Naturgesetz*. This law of nature commanded the erasure of anything that endangered the survival of the best. Hence the second maxim of Nazi law: *Recht ist Kampf, Recht ist Krieg* (law is war).

While the *deutsche Christen* (Nazi protestants), who pursued the dejewification of Christianity, said "We are the SA of Jesus Christ", Freisler said of the special courts (*Sondergerichte*): "We are the Panzer Divisions of the law (*die Panzertruppe der Rechtspflege*) . . . They must have the same energy and the same capacity to search, find and destroy the enemy."[4] This allegory speaks volumes: Freisler saw himself as a soldier. His weapon was the law.

And Freisler was happy to be sent to the front line: after years of duty as a legal intellectual, as a teacher and as a high-ranking official in the Ministry of Justice (as such, Freisler participated in the Wannsee meeting on January 20, 1942), Roland Freisler was appointed President of the *Volksgerichtshof* in August 1942. *Recht ist Krieg*: Freisler took these words seriously and intended to make war on the enemies of the true Germany. Under his presidency, in two-and-a-half years, the *Volksgerichtshof* condemned 5,000 people to death, among whom 2,600 were sentenced by his own First Senate alone.

Freisler conceived of his job as a *Verräterbekämpfung*, a war against traitors: the race and the Reich were at war. Anyone who attempted to resist the regime was henceforth a traitor. This concept (*Verräter*) was the central notion of the 1934 law that had created the *Volksgerichtshof*. Traitors were wrong (historically and biologically, and as a consequence politically too) and despicable. They had to be treated like the scum (*Gesindel*) they were: they were to be eliminated, *ausgerottet* in the Nazi language – destroyed from their very roots.

Forgive me if I have gone on too long, but it is necessary to understand Freisler's legal conceptions to understand what was at stake from August to October 1944 and what happened in the *Volksgerichtshof*.

When an attempt was made against Hitler's life, on July 20, 1944, the situation in the Reich was bleak: the Red Army had started a huge offensive that was to overwhelm the Heeresgruppe Mitte, the Wehrmacht's and SS's last hope to contain, as Goebbels said, the "Asian storm from the steppes."

There had been other assassination attempts against Hitler, but this one came from a circle of high-ranking Wehrmacht officers, members of the *Oberkommando des Heeres*, the general staff of the army, among whom was no less than a field-marshal; or two, if you count Rommel. Hitler decided he would take revenge on this "*Verräterclique*," this putsch of traitors, as he said on the evening of July 20, in a broadcast speech.

The head of the German Reich was changed by July 20: old comrades of the Führer, *alte und treue Parteikämpfer*, like Himmler and Goebbels, became more powerful than ever: Heinrich Himmler was appointed chief of the *Ersatzheer* and Joseph Goebbels became responsible for the total war (*Bevollmächtigter für den Totalen Kriegseinsatz*).

The old elites that had been part of the plot against Hitler's life had to be hunted down by the SS and tried by the *Volksgerichtshof*: Hitler did not want secret elimination, but public revenge, as public as his speech on July 20. One thing, which really went too far, was to be hidden from the public: the way they would be executed. Hitler wanted them hanged from meat hooks, *Fleischerhaken* – you can still see them today in Berlin's Plötzensee prison. Hitler ordered the executions to be filmed and shown to him. The rest, all the rest, had to be filmed and shown to the public: Hitler wanted a big show trial (*Schauprozess*), like the ones Stalin, whom he frequently mentioned and admired for his fierceness, had organized in Moscow between 1936 and 1938.

Goebbels agreed and noted in his diary: "They [the officers who took part in the plot against Hitler] will be cast out of the Wehrmacht and handed over to Freisler. I am sure he will find the right tone (*er wird schon die richtige Tonart finden*)."[5]

Freisler already had a brillant record as legal fighter, as the head of the "Panzer Divisions of the law": not only had he sent around 2,500 people to their deaths, but he had presided in masterly style over the Scholl Brothers' trial in February 1943, in Munich, where he had appeared in person. Apart from the *Weisse Rose*, Freisler had also crushed two other groups of "traitors": the *Rote Kapelle*, on the left, and the *Kreisauer Kreis*, on the right. Freisler had learned to lead show trials from the best of masters: at the end of 1938, when the USSR was thinking of switching alliances from the democracies to the Third Reich, Freisler had been permitted to attend Marshal Thoukhatchevski's trial in Moscow. The skills of Andreï Vichinsky, the prosecutor, impressed him. Some years later, he would imitate the master.

The *Volksgerichtshof* trial of the conspirators was indeed staged as a major propaganda event:

- There were visible cameras during the first session, for the newsreels, the *Wochenschau*.
- There were invisible cameras as well, behind Freisler, hidden behind the Nazi flag (you can see a little hole in the swastika when you look closely at the pictures) and behind a door, at the other end of the room. Nobody knew they were there, except for Freisler. These invisible cameras recorded images for the film Goebbels wanted to show to the Germans,

Figure 7.1 Berlin, *Volksgerichtshof*, trial of July 20, 1944: Hermann Reinecke, Roland Freisler and Heinrich Lautz. © Bundesarchiv.

Figures 7.2(a) and 7.2(b) Ulrich Wilhelm Schwerin von Schwanenfeld, in front of Roland Freisler, Berlin, *Volksgerichtshof*, trial of July 20, 1944. © NARA, Washington DC.

a documentary on the traitors called *Verräter vor dem Volksgerichtshof* (Traitors in front of the People's Court).

Freisler was incredibly skillful at staging this legal theater. First of all, he was the major character in the play: Freisler was formally the President of the court, but he was the state attorney too, leading the accusation in the name of the people, like Vichinsky. The real state attorneys sat quietly taking notes.

The lawyers for the defendants just sat there. They were too far from the defendants (five meters) to be able to speak with them, and were rudely interrupted when they dared try to do their job. The other judges listened to Freisler, went out and came in with him, saluted, arm raised, and sat down with him: they simply had no say, because Freisler was leading a squad, a judiciary stormtroop, he was not really presiding over a tribunal. The public were shown many uniforms: policemen (there were two policemen for each defendant, as was the procedure for a dangerous criminal, which they apparently were – interestingly, their uniforms had hardly been modified since the Weimar Republic, as if someone wanted to underline a continuity between the former police of a constitutional state and the new *Ordnungspolizei* of the Third Reich), numerous members of the Wehrmacht (looking at their former brothers in arms, and judging them), and members of the SS too.

Nobody but Freisler had a role in this theater, least of all the defendants who appeared before the court in civilian clothes (they had been thrown out of the Wehrmacht and could not wear their uniform), which were very often shabby (the jacket or the pants too large; somebody even had to wear a mere pullover, and was not allowed a shirt or a jacket). Everything was done to make the defendants feel ill at ease: no belt, no braces. General Hoeppner, the one who wore the pullover, was even forced to leave his false teeth in his cell.

With a profound feeling for dramaturgy, Freisler knew how to break the defendants or to play them against one another. Stage director Freisler created a dramatic moment in two episodes with officer Baron Leonrod and his confessor, the priest Hermann Wehrle. Leonrod having said that he had asked the clergyman if cognizance in a plot was a sin, Freisler called the priest to testify, and was pleased to confront the confessor and his penitent, who declared that Wehrle had told him that cognizance in a tyrannicide was not a sin, or less sinful than for a normal murder. As a consequence, Wehrle was indicted and, when he appeared again in front of the court, Freisler took a sadistic pleasure in quoting Leonrod's last appeal, in which the penitent wrote that he would have never have taken part in the plot against Hitler had his confessor told him tyrannicide was a sin. After that, he sentenced the priest to death.

Figure 7.3 Meeting of the NSDAP, Berliner Sportpalast, Berlin, February 18, 1943.

This example shows how Freisler enjoyed being the director of the movie, of which he, and he alone, would be the hero.

Freisler seemed to enjoy playing his role as well. He made grand gestures, behaving like an actor who could at last play the role of his life: Freisler enjoyed being Mr. Justice of the Third Reich, the great accuser, master of life and death, and he was aware of his power. Most of the time, he did not speak in the proper sense of the word: Freisler literally yelled at the defendants, to humiliate them; he shrieked. His tone, even his accent (the way he lengthened some vowels[6]) reminded the spectators unmistakably of Joseph Goebbels. He resorted to the same tone, he had the same accent – out of mimicry, it seems – and he even had nearly the same physical appearance: thin, dry, nervous. Joseph Goebbels, indeed, valued Freisler highly, contrary to Hitler, who sometimes scorned this "old Bolshevik," as he called him. Goebbels and Freisler had much in common: they both had been inclined to the left wing of the NSDAP, they both had a horrified fascination for Stalinism, they were both willing to push the Nazi experience to the very end. And they both were at war, in this Fall of 1944.

In fact, it appears that Freisler and Goebbels were doing exactly the same thing: total warfare – the first one on a judicial level, the second one on a broad social and political level.

The scenery of the theater confirms this interpretation of the 1944 trials. The main room of the Berlin Kammergericht was redesigned to be the scene of Nazi *Volksjustiz* (People's Justice). When we look at the bench, at what the public and the defendants saw, we see three Nazi flags hanging over the judges, who sat under the bust of Hitler (another bust was on the left, over a fireplace). This scenery reminds us of another public event, 17 months before: Goebbels' proclamation of total war in Berlin's Sportpalast, on February 18, 1943. The scene is strikingly similar: Goebbels' rostrum (which looks like Nuremberg) is dominated by three flags and one giant eagle (and a long flag saying "*Totaler Krieg, kürzester Krieg*": Total war, shortest war).

When you see the pictures, when you hear the protagonists of the two events, you cannot but observe the similarities, even if the scale of Goebbels' speech is different.

Total war, total justice? It seems the time was ripe for both in the fall of 1944. As I said before, Goebbels was proclaimed the Führer's commissioner for total war on July 25, 1944. His speech from February 1943 had had little practical effect. In the autumn of 1944, with the eastern front collapsing, total war had to become reality. On September 25, 1944, Hitler signed a decree to mobilize all men able to bear weapons, from age 16 to 70: total war was real now, with this so-called *Volkssturm*. There was no difference between soldiers and civilians anymore. The *Volkssturm* was somehow a success: the mobilization was effective, people fought, and would fight on until Berlin was burned to ashes, in May 1945.

But what of "total justice," this legal and judicial equivalent to total war? World War I Lieutenant Freisler saw himself as a *Kämpfer* too: a lawyer was a warrior for the race and for the Reich. He was a total warrior now. But this total legal and judicial war, this total justice, turned out to be a total failure.

Goebbels wanted to expose the plotters, he wanted to show their moral ignominy to the whole population of Germany. But the film *Verräter vor dem Volksgerichtshof* would in the end not be shown. Goebbels forbade it. Worse: what should have been the jewel of a propaganda treasure was not only hidden, but destroyed. One copy survived, but was classified under § 88 of the Reich's criminal code (RStGB), which meant a strict prohibition on showing it, on seeing it, or even mentioning it, under a penalty of fifteen years in prison. The exact opposite of publicity and propaganda.

Why such a failure? Why prohibit it, if Freisler was so good an imitation of the Propaganda Minister? Freisler simply went too far. The defendants were already weakened: they had been beaten and deprived of sleep by the Gestapo, they were fearing for their families. Some were psychologically annihilated when they appeared in front of the court. They knew their death was certain: there is simply no other possible verdict for an officer who tries to kill his head of state in a time of war. And still, Freisler yelled at and insulted the defendants. To Ulrich Wilhelm von Schwanenfeld, who, on August 21, 1944, had dared to mention the "murders" committed by the Nazi Regime, Freisler shouted: "Murders? Murders? You are such a despicable scoundrel!" ("*Morde? Morde? Sie sind ja ein schmälicher Lump!*"). The insults "pigs," "murderers" and "rotten traitors" ("*Schweine,*" "*Mordbuben,*" "*gemeine, miese Verräter*") were shouted over and over again in the faces of the helpless defendants. Freisler did not hesitate to trespass on every limit, not only of humanity, but of vulgarity too: when Field Marshal von Witzleben tried to prevent his trousers from falling down, Freisler yelled: "You dirty old man, why are you always fumbling with your trousers?"

Freisler was so despicable that he was openly despised by some defendants, who made it clear they did not acknowledge his authority. When he tried to humiliate, he was rebuked more than once. On August 30, 1944, officer Cäsar von Hofacker interrupted him: "Shut up now, Herr Freisler. Today, my head is at stake. In one year, yours will be." Another defendant, Joseph Wirmer, sent to hell by a raging Freisler, coldly retorted: "It will be my pleasure to welcome you there, Herr Präsident" (September 8, 1944). More than once, the defendants openly said they were standing by what they had done: when Freisler asked Ulrich Wilhelm Freiherr von Schwanenfeld if he was not devastated by the meanness of his action, he simply and loudly answered: "No." This left Freisler dumbfounded. He could not but repeat "No . . ." out of sheer perplexity in the face of such courage.

It soon appeared that a film that was to show the moral corruption of the defendants showed the exact opposite: the stunning dignity and noble behaviour of the accused, their courage and moral strength. The "scoundrel" (*Lump*) is clearly Freisler, and behind him – right behind him in fact – the regime, symbolized by Hitler's bust and by the Nazi flags. What should have been an indictment of the traitors turned into a plea for the resistance. It seemed, too often, that it was not the defendants but the accusers who were on trial.

The comparison between "total war" and what I call "total justice" opens new ways of looking not only at the end of the Third Reich, but at its very historical and cultural significance. I am currently working on Nazi legal doctrine. Working on the 1944 trials fueled this research. Allow me to suggest my interpretation.

The *Volkssturm* was a success (more out of fear of Bolshevism than out of anything else), and its cinematic expression, Veit Harlan's masterwork *Kolberg*, was not only produced with millions of Reichsmarks, but also released in the worst possible conditions. It had to succeed, because, in the eyes of Goebbels, the movie *Kolberg* was the propaganda miracle weapon (*Wunderwaffe*), the *Durchhaltefilm* per se.

Verräter vor dem Volksgerichtshof was not. The second show trial of the Reich, after that of 1933, was yet another failure: looking at the reels that had been shot during the hearings, Goebbels knew this trial was a disgrace. He knew too well that these pictures would never be acknowledged as justice by anyone in the Reich. The first and, as far as I know, only time the trial is mentioned in the newsreels, Freisler does not speak. Even the verdict is read by the commentator: not only are these films invisible, but Freisler is inaudible as well.

This "total justice" could neither be seen as justice, nor could it be seen at all: with the prohibition of the movie,[7] we have a show trial that was neither a trial, nor shown . . .

Maybe because Freisler had not "found the right tone" after all. Maybe, also, because Nazi acculturation was not completed after twelve short years of power. Nazi culture was a plan for generations, not for one, or half of one. Goebbels knew that, in the eyes of the public, *Recht* was not yet *Krieg*, and that a courtroom was still the sacred arena of norms and normative behaviour, not a scene for a yelling warhorse like the Nazi judge Roland Freisler. The "renewal of Justice" (*Erneuerung des Rechts*) and the normative revolution of national socialism had occurred in many writings, and had effects on many soldiers, but had not totally changed the minds of the German people. It simply had not had enough time to bring about such a transformation.

Epilogue

In the very same room where the Berlin People's Court headed by Roland Freisler had held its hearings, the first session of the so-called Nuremberg Trials took place: symbolically, the Allies wanted to make sure the lawlessness of the Third Reich would give way to the rule of law, in the same building where Freisler had raged and died.

In fact, Freisler, who had been such a bad actor for the role of his life, died on the stage – or on his own field of honor, on his front line, on February 3, 1945, when the Berlin Kammergericht[8] was hit by a bomb during an air raid that killed some 20,000 people in Berlin.

He rests today in Dahlem Cemetery, in Berlin, with his wife Marion, who joined him in 1997. One last word: Marion Freisler became famous in 1985 when it was made public that her widow's pension was high, because the State had assumed that her husband, had he survived the war, would have led a brilliant career in the judicial system or would have been a high-ranking civil servant. One third of the judges of the *Volksgerichtshof* indeed enjoyed the bliss of brilliant careers after the war.

Notes

1 In the year 1934, Hitler and other Nazi leaders showed what they understood by "law," "judge" and "trial": on July 13, 1934, Hitler made a speech in front of the Reichstag to justify and legalize what had happened 14 days before, i.e. the assassination of the SA leaders instead of trials: "In this moment, I was the Supreme Judge of the German People" ("*In dieser Stunde war ich oberster Gerichtsherr des deutschen Volkes*"). Leading lawyers were all too happy to justify the event for him, such as Carl Schmitt in his famous article, "Der Führer schützt das Recht".

2 See paragraph 2 of the law reforming the Reich's Criminal Code, June 28, 1935.

3 "*Sondergerichte sind die Standgerichte der inneren Front*", in Roland Freisler, "Gedanken zum Kriegsstrafrecht und zur Gewaltverbrecherverordnung", in *Deutsche Justiz*, 101, 1939, no. 50, pp. 1849–56, p. 1851.

4 Roland Freisler, "Die Volksschädlingsverordnung", Tagung des Reichsjustizministeriums, October 24, 1939, BABL, R 22/ 4158.

5 Joseph Goebbels, *Tagebücher*, Munich: Institut für Zeitgeschichte, Teil II-Band 13, Juli–September 1944, July 23, 1941, p. 141.

6 The way he pronounced the past participle "*geloooogen*" (lied), the infinitive "*haaaben*" (to have) remind one undoubtedly of Goebbels.

7 Christian Delage was kind enough to remind me that only two other films were prohibited by Goebbels although they had been meant to be propaganda masterpieces: the images of the burning books of May 10, 1933's auto-da-fé, and Fritz Hippler's *Der ewige Jude*, some scenes of which, shot in the Warsaw ghetto, were deemed too shocking for the audience and, in the end, counter-effective. Still, both the autos-da-fé and Hippler's movie were shown before they were prohibited: the film on the 1944 trials was never shown.

8 It was not completely destroyed, though, and could host the Allied Council for the whole duration of the Cold War. Today, this superb building, located in the western part of Berlin, is the seat of the Berlin administrative courts.

CHAPTER 8

The Majdanek trial: the Holocaust on trial on film

Kazimierz Czyński's *Swastyka i Szubienica* (1945)

Stuart Liebman

Scholarly study of the range of films about the concentration camps and the Holocaust made during the first five years after World War II is still very much in its earliest stages. Quite a large number of these films were produced in a variety of genres – newsreels, documentaries, propaganda and re-education films, fundraising vehicles on behalf of survivors, and even feature-length fiction films. Most originated in several East European countries – what Timothy Snyder has recently termed "the bloodlands"[1] – where of course, the populations were most directly affected and the killing fields had been primarily located; important examples, however, also emerged from Allied nations in the West. Within this large corpus, films about the post-war trials of the perpetrators of war crimes and crimes against humanity constitute a small, but significant, sub-genre, encompassing major works like Roman Karmen and Elizaveta Svilova's *Sud Narodov*, released in Europe in April 1947,[2] and *Nuremberg: Its Lessons for Today* by Stuart Schulberg, which was produced for the United States Office of Military Government in occupied Germany (OMGUS) in 1947, but only shown in the Western occupied sections of Germany from November 21, 1948 onward.[3] Many shorter accounts of other, similar trials – the *Nachfolgeprozessen* at Nuremberg; the Lüneberg proceedings for Bergen-Belsen camp officials; the Krakow sessions trying Auschwitz leaders and guards; and the Dachau trial held for Buchenwald camp personnel – were also released in episodes mounted by Gaumont British News, Universal, and British Pathé, among many other newsreel companies.[4]

All but forgotten in the scholarly literature about the trial film genre – as, indeed, in historical studies of Polish documentary cinema – is the 25-minute compilation short, *Swastyka i Szubienica* (*Swastika and Gallows*), by the little-known Polish director, Kazimierz Czyński.[5] To the best of my knowledge, it has never been discussed in depth by any scholar studying filmed Holocaust trials and the representations of justice they meted – or failed to mete – out.[6] Recent consultations at the Muzeum Panstwowe na Majdanka in Poland revealed that its archivists were only barely aware of the film's existence. Indeed, although the museum was established 65 years ago on the very site of the liberated concentration camp while the war against the Nazis was still raging in the west of Poland, it has evidently never acquired a copy for its collection, even though the film was shot only a few miles away in the city of Lublin. Yet the trial it portrays was very important. It was the first trial of German concentration camp personnel – four SS guards and two kapos – held on liberated Polish soil, and it commenced at a date, November 27, 1944, far earlier than the more well-known ones mentioned above. The trial may thus certainly be said to anticipate the first attempts by any of the Allied forces to keep their promise of holding *German* concentration camp personnel accountable for their multifarious crimes. Therefore, *Swastyka i Szubienica* arguably has the distinction of being the first cinematic portrayal of a trial concerning what we would call today the Holocaust or Shoah.[7] The film, moreover, incorporated vivid images of the first concentration/death camp, Majdanek, ever captured virtually intact by Allied forces. Many were taken on the very day Red Army units overran the camp – July 24, 1944. Moreover, the filming continued for weeks thereafter, capturing for posterity indelible pictures, re-used many times subsequently, of the infamous camp's electrified barbed wire fences and guard towers; its "baths," crematorium ovens and chimney; the whitened bones and still smoking piles of ashes of the last victims; and the mountains of shoes and other objects stolen from the helpless men and women the Nazis destroyed in the Operation Reinhard death camps.[8] This imagery has constituted a virtually complete iconography for the representation of such camps ever since.

What is more, *Swastyka i Szubienica* included some of the first detailed accounts by survivors about the heinous crimes committed against Polish citizens, Russian POWs and, above all, against Jews, and it did so at a historical moment when such public candor about the Nazis' concerted effort to murder Jews was not the norm. This is striking and unusual, as is the inclusion of damning testimony elicited from some of the perpetrators

Figure 8.1 Caption from the film *Swastyka I Szubienica*

themselves. Yet *Swastyka i Szubienica* remains virtually unknown even to specialists in Holocaust cinema. Examining it in the context of the circumstances of its production and distribution opens a window onto the early cinematic construction of Holocaust memory amid the rapidly changing political environment of Soviet-occupied Eastern Europe.

All the cinematic material used for *Swastyka i Szubienica* was shot by December 3, 1944, the date at which the four German guards and one of the kapos who had been on trial were hung before a large crowd of onlookers near the crematorium at Majdanek.[9] Starting in late July, a team of Polish filmmakers under the leadership of the Polish-Jewish director Aleksander Ford, the head of the Polish Army's Film Unit, aided, at least initially, by a group from the Moscow-based Central Documentary Film Studio led by Roman Karmen, recorded startling images of a concentration and death camp for the first time. Most of those working for the Polish unit were Polish Jews who, like Ford, had escaped to the Soviet Union at the outset of the war.[10] During August, their cameras followed the important hearings of the Polono-Soviet Extraordinary Commission as it surveyed the camp's environs, exhuming victims' bodies from mass graves and autopsying the remains, interrogating survivors and deposing perpetrators. And they also

Figure 8.2 "Report about the Criminal Trial at Majdanek"

recorded the huge Catholic funeral mass conducted on August 6 for the nearly four hundred prisoners in Lublin Castle who had been murdered by the Germans before they retreated from the city on July 23. From this footage, Ford and his team composed *Vernichtungslager Majdanek, Cmentarzysko Europy – Majdanek Extermination Camp, the Cemetery of Europe.*[11] The film was completed and screened at the Apollo and Baltyk movie houses in Lublin during the week prior to the start of the trial of the guards recounted in Czyński's film.[12] By screening this ostensibly documentary film with its sensational, unprecedented images as the trial was about to begin, the Communists clearly demonstrated their desire to stir up anger in audiences and to stimulate demands for vengeance during the proceedings. But, made more than six months later, *Swastyka i Szubienica* had, it would seem, other purposes: its narrative of just punishments judiciously arrived at clearly aimed to build confidence in the newly established Polish regime's ability to deliver fair and swift justice.[13]

In fact, *Swastyka i Szubienica* borrowed a significant number of iconic images from Ford's film in order to deftly fill in the crucial background to the trial and to underscore the enormous and systematically engineered crimes and the moral stakes at issue in the trial. Pre-eminent among these images were shots of the victims murdered at Lublin Castle as the German Army retreated; multiple layers of electrified fences; the watchtowers; threatening signs in Polish and German; the crematorium complex itself; the smoking bones of victims in the ovens; the array of shoes and other clothing items looted primarily from the Jewish victims; and, most ominously, canisters of Zyklon-B crystals ostensibly used in the gassing process.[14] The one-minute-long montage of such images at the beginning of the film served as a kind of précis of the German crimes that would be exposed in the legal hearings that followed.[15] Cameramen from Ford's team were also employed to film the trial from its opening on November 27 in the cramped conditions of the former Nazi Party headquarters on Horst Wesselstrasse (today *ulica* Racławickie) in Lublin until it ended on December 2; they also filmed the hanging on the next day. These images, however, were not included in *Vernichtungslager Majdanek*. They instead became the central core of *Swastyka i Szubienica*, which may therefore be said to be a kind of pendant to Ford's film. After the latter film's editing resumes Ford's account of the unspeakable crimes, it then continues to pursue the implicit crime and punishment trajectory of Ford's narrative by summarizing the legal determination of the guards' guilt and then observing the dispensation of stern but appropriate justice.

I have not yet found any documentation in the archives about precisely when work on *Swastyka i Szubienica* began, though we can reasonably infer that production would have started sometime at least by the late spring so that the work could be finished in time for the one-year anniversary of the liberation of the camp when the film's premiere apparently took place. No new footage appears to have been shot for the film; none, in any case, was used. It is thus entirely appropriate that the credits identify its principal author, Kazimierz Czyński, as its director of montage, rather than according him the larger responsibilities as the film's director. Czyński was, in fact, a rather minor figure in Polish film history who is rarely remembered today even in his native Poland. Born in 1891, Czyński directed several feature films during the silent period; most prominent among them was his 1930 adaptation for the screen of one of the late works – *Wiatr od Morza* (in English: *Wind from the Sea*) by the distinguished, recently deceased Polish writer, Stefan Żeromski. The novel and film celebrated the post-World War I corridor to the Baltic Sea that newly independent Poland had obtained from Germany as a result of the Treaty of Versailles. We can reasonably infer from this choice of topic that Czyński was a proud Polish patriot. In any case, after the Żeromski adaptation, for reasons that are not clear, Czyński apparently ceased to direct films himself and instead became the production head of a small Polish film company until World War II erupted.

During the occupation, the fifty-year-old Czyński, who was not Jewish, was not permitted to make films and could only find work as a manual laborer. The war's end, however, changed his situation for the better, if only momentarily. Aleksander Ford, soon to become head of the newly nationalized Film Polski company, may himself have been instrumental in recommending Czyński to edit the accumulated footage his team had shot. Despite his own communist convictions, a dearth of trained film cadres and the somewhat relaxed political circumstances in early 1945 allowed Ford to make such a choice. Czyński was in any case called out of retirement and assigned the somewhat delicate responsibility of crafting the new regime's first compilation film[16] that would develop a telling moral lesson about judicial probity in the new Poland.

A cinematic model did exist for Czyński's work, although it is not clear that he had ever seen it; nor do existing records suggest that the political powers in control of liberated Poland imposed such a model on him, although that remains entirely possible. In February 1943, the Red Army reconquered the city of Krasnodar and five months later put on trial eleven Soviet citizens who had aided the Germans in their massacres by shooting and gas vans of 6,700 civilians, about half of whom were virtually the entire Jewish population of the town. Soviet authorities at the highest levels of the regime – possibly including Stalin himself – decided to produce a propaganda film about the trial of those they regarded as traitors to the fatherland. Its aim was above all to broadcast the determination of Soviet authorities to deter any further collaboration by Soviet ethnic minorities with an enemy still dangerous, if now on the run. But they were also obviously interested in convincing doubting Western Allies of the probity and fairness of Soviet judicial procedures, a belief that had been seriously damaged by the dismal spectacles of the notorious show trials, several of which were filmed, during the 1930s.[17] The film produced was called *Prigobor Naroda* (*The Verdict of the People*) and it was released in Moscow on August 19, 1943, only a month after the conclusion of the trial; it would be nearly two years before *Swastyka i Szubienica* was completed and shown in Poland.

The Verdict of the People established many of the typical features of the films aiming to represent Soviet justice, and many parallels exist with the film Czyński was asked to compose. Both contain verbal descriptions in voiceover and gruesome images of the prisoners massacred by the Germans as they retreated from Krasnodar and Lublin respectively. Both offered digests of the carefully staged courtroom rituals and proceedings, though neither can be said to be simply the unvarnished representation of the legal proceedings. Some of the narration and testimony were clearly chosen for maximum propaganda effect, and evidently some license was taken in the order in which they presented the testimonies.[18] That is, both film accounts represented a carefully tailored image of due process, Soviet style. Both also aimed to make the charges clear and vivid through dramatic revelations by witnesses of the unprecedented atrocities. Such testimony was highly valued.[19] In both films, too, key players in these legal theaters played similar roles. The judges actively questioned witnesses in order to bring out incriminating statements about what had happened. The prosecutors often resorted to emotional hyperbole, accusing the entire German nation of the crimes.[20]

Witnesses provided details that are damning to the defendants, and in both works the perpetrators themselves confessed to criminal acts. Throughout, the defense attorneys were utterly marginalized; they are only glimpsed in Czyński's film and do not speak on camera at all. In court, they had been utterly abject and compromised their clients' defense by making devastating comments.[21] All such features are quite familiar from the annals of Soviet jurisprudence.[22]

On the other hand, one should not underestimate how much interest the newly empowered Polish Communists had in presenting the appearance of just, independent and traditional values of the court as a representation of

Figure 8.3 Defendants Anton Thernes and Wilhelm Gerstenmeier

Figure 8.4 The Polish presiding judge

Figure 8.5 Defendant Heinz Stalp testifies

the fair-mindedness of the new regime. They seem to have been particularly concerned to reassure their highly suspicious fellow Poles, whose animosity toward the anti-religious and historically predatory Soviet Union was well known. The court, in fact, had been empowered by the nominally independent (though in fact created by the USSR) new Polish Committee of National Liberation (*Polski Komitet Wyzwolenia Narodowego*; the PKWN, for short), proclaimed as the new government in Chelm at the end of July 1944.[23] To suggest that this truly was a *Polish* court, however, an enlarged crucifix seen in closeup sits prominently in front of the judges as a key symbolic statement inscribed in the *mise-en-scène* at the very moment the judges enter the courtroom as well as at several other points. Such a religious icon would almost never have appeared, of course, in any Soviet film; its presence was certainly a calculated gesture to reassure Catholic Poles.[24] And, compared to Soviet show trials of the 1930s, or even to the Krasnodar proceedings, *Swastyka i Szubienica* seems considerably more than a mere exercise in judicial rhetoric, despite the intense emotionality of Prosecutor Sawicki's final summation to the court.[25] The evidence brought to bear in it includes, as already noted above, images of the camp installations shot, it must be admitted, for maximum sinister impact.[26] On the other hand, we are shown the solemn swearing-in of the witnesses, a procedure well established as part of the legal rituals in the West. And the testimony we watch and hear in extended, uncut excerpts seems quite un-coerced and authentic, though it is true that the defense attorneys do not cross-examine key assertions or challenge the connection of their clients to the crimes, either in the film or, indeed, at the trial itself.[27] For example, a Mrs. Dora Minc, identified pointedly by the voiceover narration as a Jewess who had escaped the camp, speaks about the murder of Jewish children taken from their mothers by SS women guards who offered false promises about their safety.

> I saw guards attempt to separate children from their mothers. When they resisted, they beat them until they were nearly unrecognizable. I saw four women with children between the ages of three and four years who clung to their mothers' clothing. A female guard grabbed them and threw them as if they were packages. The female SS guards tried to reassure the women that their children would be sent to nurseries where they would have everything they needed.[28]

Equally moving are the remarks by a pharmacist and Polish army officer named Tadeusz Budzin, a former inmate in the camp, who had already been filmed while offering evidence during the investigations of the Polono-Soviet Extraordinary Commission. Czyński used the section of his testimony when Budzin amplifies his remarks from his earlier testimony and speaks about the lethal injections of Evipan and perhydrol administered by SS guards and doctors. His earlier recorded remarks, though ultimately unseen in Ford's film, clearly pointed to Greek intellectuals – clearly they were Jews – as the principal victims of these procedures.

Most impressive is the kapo Heinz Stalp,[29] who speaks astonishingly calmly about how he watched the machine-gunning of some of the 18,400 Jews murdered during the so-called *Erntefest*, or "Harvest Festival" on November 3 and 4, 1943. This is the first occasion I know of in which a German spoke directly on camera about the enormous scale of such mass crimes against the Jews.[30] His testimony was preceded in the film by the remarks of an unidentified former Polish prisoner who provided corroborating evidence in advance for Stalp's testimony.

> I remember a Tuesday at Majdanek that was called "Bloody Tuesday." They woke us up at an earlier time than was usual. After an assembly on the Appelplatz surrounded by armed Germans – the SS, police and the S[icherheits] D[ienst] – we could hear their orders: "Kill them with machine guns. All Jews out!"[31]

Stalp's testimony, which appears to have been presented on the first day of the trial, November 27, follows this candid statement focusing on Jewish victims and builds upon it. It deserves to be quoted *in extenso*.

> Later, on the third of September . . . no! . . . it was November, an "action" took place during the course of which approximately 18,000 Jews were shot. I remember this very precisely because I was sick at the time and I was hospitalized in zone five. They had cleared a large site near the crematorium and installed four large loudspeakers through which they broadcast music – waltzes, popular or well-known songs. And one could see how from one of the barracks, naked Jews – men, women and children all together – how they came from the barrack, and in groups of fifty they were brought before a large open pit – four large pits, thirty meters in length, four meters deep and three meters wide, had been dug earlier – and these prisoners, these Jews, these Jews who had been selected, stood on the edge of the pit and were shot from behind by two machine guns.

Figure 8.6 December 3, 1944: The sentence is carried out

By the end of the trial and the film, in the light of such revealed facts, the prosecutor Henryk Ciesluk's call for the death penalty[32] and the sentence pronounced by the court certainly are made to seem utterly appropriate because all of the defendants, despite their denials, had been directly linked by witnesses to criminal acts. Indeed, the crimes some of the perpetrators admit to were so heinous as to make the justice meted out to the perpetrators on the very next day at the foot of the Majdanek crematorium chimney seem fair indeed. Their hanging was attended by a large crowd of people, an index of popular sentiments Stalin is said to have appreciated.[33]

One must also keep in mind, therefore, that *Swastyka i Szubienica* substantially differed from its Soviet model in the way it used stunningly candid accounts of actions taken *against the Jews*. Soviet ideology and the well-known, widespread anti-Semitism of the leadership generally dictated that individual victims should not be differentiated on the basis of ethnicity; except in the Soviet Yiddish press, Jews and others were usually named only as "peaceful Soviet citizens," and specifying the massive crimes against Jews was never a prominent feature of early Soviet propaganda films about the war.[34] As illustrated above, *Swastyka i Szubienica* pulled no punches in this regard. For this alone, it should be valued more generously in the annals of Holocaust cinema, for such candor – perhaps surprisingly from today's perspective, as more and more facts have become and are still being made available – becomes increasingly rare in the spate of Holocaust films released in the first half-decade after the war.[35] In 1945, the provision of such facts was quite limited in nearly all films, and *Swastyka i Szubienica*'s inclusion of them tends to confirm – *pace* prominent skeptics – Michael Marrus's modest claim that Holocaust trials ultimately served the long-term goals of memory by establishing publicly the Holocaust as a fact while making vital evidence more widely available.[36] And, I would add, when such statements were included in a film, the principal mass visual medium of its day, the evidence became more widely known. *Swastyka i Szubienica* was released toward the end of July 1945, more than six months after the trial and execution of the defendants.[37] The release date, that is, was apparently timed to correspond with the first anniversary of the liberation of Majdanek. Clearly, the authorities, who were proceeding with other trials of collaborators and smaller Nazi criminals, hoped to reconfirm the fairness of Communist justice to a population growing ever more fearful of local Communist and Soviet intentions. As of now, the extent and duration of the film's distribution are uncertain and its effect on the Polish population is at this point difficult to assess. Given the relative paucity of references to it in newspaper articles at the time, however, the film seems to have come out at an untimely moment. This may be because a sentiment of revulsion against the graphic depiction of executions was beginning to take hold. In both the USSR and Poland, the authorities soon decided to limit such scenes.[38] The film's stress on the suffering of the Jews, moreover, was also unpopular with traditionally anti-Semitic home audiences obsessed with the idea that a highly mythologized *żydokommune*, a Jewish-inspired Communist takeover of Poland, was at hand.[39] It is fair to say, therefore, that the very features that make *Swastyka i Szubienica* of interest to Holocaust scholars today may have made the film less useful to the authorities when it was made and that for that reason they decided to limit screenings or even to remove it from distribution. This, in fact, may be the reason why the film has remained buried and largely unknown in the archives for so many decades.[40] In my opinion, however, it deserves to be recovered at the very least as an instructive moment in the earliest history of Holocaust trials and Holocaust cinema.

Notes

1 Timothy Snyder, *Bloodlands: Europe Between Hitler and Stalin*, New York: Basic Books, 2010.

2 In the United States, *Sud Narodov* – which literally means "judgment of the people" – was released under the title *Nuremberg Trials* on May 24, 1947.

3 The making of Schulberg's film and the assistance provided by Pare Lorentz, as well as her recent effort to restore the film, is described by Schulberg's daughter, Sandra, in her articles "Filmmakers for the Prosecution" and "Restoration and Preservation of One of the Most Important Films Never Seen: *Nuremberg: Its Lessons for Today* (1948)", *National Archief Magazine* [The Hague, Netherlands] (November 2009): 6–51 and 54–9.

4 Some of these segments are available through the website of the Steven Spielberg Archive of the United States Holocaust Memorial Museum, while others are accessible on DVDs, most of variable visual quality. See, for example, *Classic Nuremberg Trial Newsreels, 1945–1946* (Quality Information Publishers, 2007).

5 For example, the distinguished scholar of Polish documentary films, Stanisław Ozimek, devotes little more than half a page to the film in the chapter "Film Dokumentalny," in *Historia Filmu Polskiego*, Vol. 3, Warsaw: WAiF, 1974, p. 108. I thank Professor Monika Adamczyk-Garbowska of Marie Curie-Skłodowska University in Lublin for this reference.

6 I have previously discussed the film briefly in my articles, "La libération des camps vue par le cinéma: l'exemple de *Vernichtungslager Majdanek*", *Cahiers du judaïsme* No. 15 (2003): 49–60; "Documenting the Liberation of the Camps: The Case of Aleksander Ford's *Vernichtungslager Majdanek – Cmentarzysko Europy* (1944)", in Dagmar Herzog (ed.), *Lessons & Legacies*, Vol. VII, Evanston: Northwestern University Press, 2006, pp. 333–51; and "Obraz Obozu w Pierwszych Filmach Dokumentalnych", *Dialog* [Łódz, Poland] (January 2010), 91–99.

7 In July 1943, the USSR conducted a trial of Soviet, principally Ukrainian, collaborators in atrocities against Jews and others at Krasnodar in 1943, and a contemporary film was made about it. None of the accused were German, and though some were accused of participating in gassing victims in mobile vans, none worked in a death camp per se. Excerpts of this film are available in German director Irmgard von zur Mühlen's *Krasnodar: Trial of 1943* (1987). Jeremy Hicks's forthcoming book on Soviet films about the Holocaust may very well provide more ample documentation about and insights into the Krasnodar film: J. Hicks, *First Films of the Holocaust: Soviet Cinema and the Genocide of the Jews, 1938–46*, Pittsburgh: University of Pittsburgh Press, 2012.

8 These victims were above all Jews. See Yitzhak Arad's study, *Belzec, Sobibor, Treblinka. The Operation Reinhard Death Camp*, Bloomington, IN: Indiana University Press, 1987.

9 The second kapo on trial, Edmund Pohlmann, committed suicide in his cell on the night of November 28.

10 In addition to Ford, the brothers Adolf and Władysław Forbert, Stanisław Wohl, Olga Mińska (Ford's wife), the scriptwriter Jerzy Bossak as well as Roman Karmen, among others on the Russian team, were of Jewish origin. For more on Russian Jewish photographers' contribution to the war effort, see David Schneer, *Through Soviet Jewish Eyes. Photography, War, and the Holocaust*, New Brunswick, NJ: Rutgers University Press, 2011.

11 A Soviet filmmaker, Irina Setkina, who was also associated with the Central Documentary Film Studio, also later made a somewhat shorter film about the camp from the same corpus. It was widely distributed in the Soviet zone of occupation in Germany as well as in France; many of its images also ended up in the archives of other Western countries.

12 See Władysław Jewsiewicki, *Polscy Filmowcy na Frontach Drugiej Wojny Swiatowej*, Warsaw: Wydawnictwa Artystyczne i Filmowe, 1972, p. 177. Jolanta Lemann-Zajiček lists

the date of the premiere at the Apollo Cinema as November 26. See her *Kino i Polityka. Polski Film Dokumentalny 1945–1949*, Łódź: PWSFTviT, 2003, p. 11.

13 It is noteworthy that two other documentary/propaganda films about camps from Russia or the Russian occupation zones in Eastern Europe were released shortly before or during other war crimes trials. Roman Karmen's *Oświęcim* (1945) was released near the beginning of the Nuremberg Trial of major war criminals. In what would become the Deutsche Demokratische Republik, Richard Brandt, a former colleague at Erwin Piscator's "Freie Bühne" in Berlin, produced *Todeslager Sachsenhausen* (1947) before some of the individuals it portrayed were put on trial between October 23 and 31, 1947. And just as Roman Karmen produced (with Elizaveta Svilova) a cinematic follow-up to the Nuremberg trial (*Sud Narodov*, 1947), so a German director, Bruno Kleberg, produced a film, *Sachsenhausen Prozess* (1947), after the Sachsenhausen trial. See Günter Agde, "Bilder von Schuldigen. Das Konzentrationslager Sachsenhausen im Film," *Filmblatt* 32 (Winter 2006), 19–40.

14 Note, however, that many – perhaps most – of the victims gassed at Majdanek were executed using carbon monoxide.

15 Other images of the Lublin Castle massacre victims and the looted clothing tellingly reappear midway through the film to buttress the prosecution's assertions of German culpability.

16 For the history of compilation films, see Jay Leyda, *Films Beget Films*, New York: Hill & Wang, 1964).

17 See Chapter 5 by Professor Nicholas Werth in this volume.

18 We can compare, in fact, the scenes we are shown with transcripts of the trial that were published: *Majdanek. Rosprawa przed specyalnym są dem Karynym w Lublinie*, Kraków: Spółdzielnia Wydawnica "Czytelnik," 1945. In fact, there are considerable discrepancies between the published version of the Lublin trial, a typescript account held at the Majdanek camp museum and the testimonies recorded during the trial. No single version appears to be complete.

19 See Alexander Prusin, "Poland's Nuremberg: The Seven Court Cases of the Supreme National Tribunal, 1946–1948", *Holocaust and Genocide Studies*, Vol. 24, No.1 (Spring 2010), 8.

20 Leonid Ivanovich Iachenin (alternatively: Yachenin) led the Soviet prosecution of the Krasnodar defendants and the histrionic Jerzy Sawicki was, with the more sober Henryk Ciesluk, one of two principal prosecutors at the Lublin trial. An American radical journalist, Anna Louise Strong, reports on her conversations with Ciesluk in her *I Saw the New Poland*, Boston: Little, Brown, 1946, pp. 62 ff.

21 Jaroslawski, the court-appointed defense attorney for the defendants Gerstenmeier and Vogel, requested on the very first day of the trial to be released from his duties because "in the course of a thousand years Germany has systematically committed crimes against all its neighbors . . . because Germany, obeying its Führer Adolf Hitler, attacked the Polish state in September 1939 and brought about a horrible world war . . .". And Kazimierz Krzymanski, who defended Anton Thernes, also asked to be removed because "the misdeeds that are to be judged here in this courtroom are so absolutely gruesome and were planned and committed in such a satanic way that we, who have lost our loved ones in Majdanek . . . cannot be expected to defend those who are accused of having committed these atrocities." J. Graf and C. Mattogno, *Concentration Camp Majdanek* (http://www.vho.org/GB/Books/ccm/11.html; accessed September 10, 2010). This source should be used with extreme care since its authors are Holocaust revisionists, but some of the documents they provide are useful.

22 The Krasnodar trial was conducted under Soviet military tribunal rules. See Ilya Bourtman, "'Blood for Blood, Death for Death': The Soviet Military Tribunal in Krasnodar, 1943", *Holocaust and Genocide Studies*, Vol. 22, No. 2 (Fall 2008), 246–65. For a more general overview of the Soviet's investigation of wartime atrocities see M.A. Sorokina, "People and Procedures. Toward a History of the Investigation of Nazi Crimes in the USSR", *Kritika*, Vol. 6, No. 4 (Fall 2005), 797–831. For further discussion of Soviet war crimes trials, see Alexander Prusin, "'Fascist Criminals to the Gallows!': The Holocaust and Soviet War Crimes Trials, December 1945 – February 1946", *Holocaust and Genocide Studies*, Vol. 17, No. 1 (Spring 2003), 1–30.

23 As of August 1, the government was seated in Lublin.

24 Note, too, the extent to which Ford stressed the Catholic identities of the victims murdered at Lublin Castle, especially in the account of the funeral ceremonies held on August 6, 1944. Large crosses, nuns in habits and icons are shown many times; the Prelate of Lublin, Kruszyński, dressed in his ceremonial robes, also conducted the service. We now know that there were also many Jewish victims whose presence was ignored. See Tadeusz Radzik, *Zagłada Lubelskiego Getta*, Lublin: Wydawnictwo Uniwersytetu Marii Curie-Skłodowskiej, 2007, p. 71.

25 Curiously, Sawicki's concluding statement is not included in the typed summary of the trial.

26 These images do not seem to have been shown at the trial itself. Perhaps since the camp was so near Lublin, there was no need to introduce such images during the trial.

27 The typed transcript also shows that few objections by defense attorneys were made to the claims made by witnesses.

28 This and the next two quotations are taken from the testimony presented on screen.

29 In various published accounts, Stalp's last name is given variously as Stahl (see *the New York Times*, December 4, 1944, 18) or as Salp (see *The Daily Worker*, September 1, 1944, 8). The typed transcript of some of the preliminary interrogations initially spelled Stalp's name as Stalke. Sometimes, too, his first name is given as Hans. In general, there is a great inconsistency in the spelling of the perpetrators' names.

30 He also directly implicated two war criminals, Erich Mühsfeldt and Anton Thumann, who were later caught, tried and executed by the Allies. Stalp's testimony does not appear coerced. However, he may well have been promised leniency on the basis of his testimony about crimes he claims he merely observed and did not commit. However, he was also found guilty and hung on December 3, 1944.

31 These remarks do not appear in the typed transcript.

32 Ciesluk interestingly refers to the extermination of the Łódz Ghetto inhabitants that had only recently taken place in August 1944, as well as to the ongoing horrors at Auschwitz, liberated only two months later, on January 27, 1945, by the Red Army.

33 Bourtman, citing E. Epifanov, *Otvetstvennost' gitlerovskikh voennykh prestupnikov i ikh posobnikov v SSSR*, Volgograd: Volgograd Judicial Institute, 1997, p. 2, reports that Stalin received daily reports on the progress of the trials as well as estimates of the number of Soviet citizens attending the public executions. See Bourtman, *op. cit.*, 256–7. American audiences enjoyed these hanging scenes when they were distributed in the United States in late April of 1945. See *The Daily Worker*, April 28, 1945, 12, and the advertisement for the film *Nazi Death Factory; Execution of Nazi S.S. Guards* in *The Daily Worker*, April 29, 1945, 17. When such scenes were banned, loud protests followed. See *The Daily Worker*, May 3, 4 and 7, 1945, passim.

34 For more on the rhetoric of Soviet statements about the Jews, see Amir Wiener, *Making Sense of War: The Second World War and the Fate of the Bolshevik Revolution*, Princeton:

Princeton University Press, 2001; and Yitzhak Arad, *The Holocaust in the Soviet Union*, Lincoln, NE: University of Nebraska Press, 2009.

35 See my "Documenting the Liberation of the Camps," *op. cit.*, passim.

36 Michael R. Marrus, "The Holocaust at Nuremberg," *Yad Vashem Studies* 26 (1998), 5–41. Questions about Marrus's and others' optimistic conclusions include Donald Bloxham, *Genocide on Trial. War Crimes Trials and the Formation of Holocaust History and Memory*, New York: Oxford University Press, 2001.

37 See "Kronika Filmowa," *Rzeczpospolita* No. 202 (July 29, 1945), 4. I again thank Professor Adamczyk-Garbowska for this reference.

38 See Prusin, "Poland's Nuremberg", 15–16. The course of *Swastyka i Szubienica*'s career in Polish cinemas, in any case, remains to be mapped.

39 See Bozena Szaynok, "The Role of Anti-Semitism in Post-war Polish-Jewish Relations", in Robert Blobaum (ed.), *Anti-Semitism and its Opponents in Modern Poland*, Ithaca, NY: Cornell University Press, 2005, pp. 265–83. For an even longer perspective, see Joanna Michlic, *Poland's Threatening Other: The Image of the Jew from 1880 to the Present*, Lincoln, NE: University of Nebraska Press, 2008.

40 The film's stress on such politically dubious gestures, moreover, may also explain why Czyński's career was soon eclipsed once again. He had never been identified as socialist, let alone communist, in his sympathies, and the new rulers of Poland, under pressure from Stalin and his henchmen, who were both politically adroit though increasingly illiberal, paranoid and anti-Semitic, would certainly have been wary of employing artistic talents with such sympathies. As far as I know, Czyński made only one more film – in 1947 – before his death on November 15, 1956.

PART 3

Khmer Rouge on trial

CHAPTER 9

The psychological evaluation of Duch, a criminal against humanity in Cambodia

Françoise Sironi

Figure 9.1 Senior Khmer Rouge regime member Kaing Guek Eav, also known as Duch, during the court session announcing the verdict of his trial at the Extraordinary Chambers in the Courts of Cambodia on the outskirts of Phnom Penh on July 26, 2010. © Chor Sokunthea/Reuters.

Introduction

In January 2007, I was appointed by the co-investigating judges of the Extraordinary Chambers in the Court of Cambodia (ECCC), Mr. You Bunleng, for the Cambodian side, and Mr. Marcel Lemonde, for the international side, to perform a psychological examination of Duch. This responsibility requires a specific expertise in clinical psychology.

What probably legitimized my participation, as an expert witness, in the trial of a former Khmer Rouge official is that I have twenty years of clinical practice, as a psychotherapist and a clinical researcher, with torture victims, and victims of other types of collective violence (genocides, massacres, rapes, wars, displacement of populations). I founded, together with other colleagues, a treatment center for torture victims in Paris, the Primo Levi Center.

Besides this, I also have fifteen years of clinical experience with former perpetrators of collective violence. In 1995, I opened, with other French and Russian health practitioners, and also with the war veterans themselves, a rehabilitation center for Russian veterans of the Afghanistan war, in the city of Perm (Russia).

In Paris, I treated French soldiers who were traumatized years after their participation in the war in Algeria (before the independence of this former French colony), Harkis (Algerian combatants in the French Army) as well as former combatants in the Foreign Legion. Now, because of the transgenerational transmission of traumatic memories, I also treat, by psychotherapy, some of the children of former participants in the war in Algeria. At the Paris Court of Appeal, I perform psychological examinations of victims of violence, as well as of perpetrators of crimes, rapes and mental manipulation.

Finally, I am also a specialist in ethnopsychiatry and in transcultural clinical practice and psychotherapy. I directed the Georges Devereux Center, at University of Paris 8. This center specializes in the psychological treatment of migrants, and socially, culturally or sexually marginalized persons in France.

General principles guiding the making of psychological evaluations of criminals against humanity

Before being appointed by the co-investigating judges and the ECCC, I was asked to send them a report explaining how I would conceive of such a mission, in terms of methodology and encounters with the accused.

One of the most important points for me was that the psychological investigation had to be done by sticking to the general principles shared by all parties who participated in the ECCC. Those principles were unique, and very innovative in the history of international trials as regards crimes against humanity. Both categories of participants, international as well as local officials (lawyers, judges, prosecutors, etc.) were equally present. Also very innovative was the presence of two kinds of Law, Civil Law and Common Law, inside the same criminal trial.

In order to conform with the multicultural configuration of the Court, I asked to work with a Cambodian co-expert, whether a psychologist or a psychiatrist. I also required the presence of a Cambodian interpreter, although Duch spoke very good French, since he was educated in the French language at the time of the French Protectorate in Cambodia. This way, the plurality of his inner cultural references and mental representations was taken into account in the methodological framework itself.

In January 2007 I was officially appointed to undertake this mission, and to play the leading role. The time was extremely short, since I had to deliver the final report on March 31. Between the end of January and the middle of March I went twice to Phnom Penh, where each time I spent ten days, seeing Duch twice a day in detention with the co-expert, Mr. Ka Sunbaunat, and the interpreter, Mr. Ouch Channorah.

Mr. Ka Sunbaunat is a Cambodian psychiatrist. He is in charge of mental health in all Cambodia, inside the Ministry of Health, and the dean of the Faculty of Medicine in Phnom Penh. He is one of the local specialists in psychotraumas due to the former Khmer Rouge regime. He also knows the history, religion and anthropology of his country very well. Mr. Ka Sunbaunat was himself a victim of the Khmer Rouge regime, as well as his whole family and that of his wife. At that time, he had been deported from Phnom Penh to the work camps, where he had to hide that he was a student in medicine. His life was in danger, because of the sociocultural hatred the Khmer Rouge directed at intellectuals.

Mr. Ouch Channorah is an interpreter in French-Khmer language. He was officially appointed by the ECCC, and had to respect the secrecy concerning what he was hearing during our clinical interviews in detention, with Duch. Mr. Ouch Channorah was 30 years old at the time of our psychological mission. He never knew his father, since he disappeared at the time of the Khmer Rouge, while his mother was pregnant with him.

I was born in Alsace, a French region located near the German and Swiss borders, of an Alsatian mother and an Italian father. The family history on both sides is marked by the imprints of a collective history linked to the Second World War, to Mussolini's fascist regime, and to the invasion of Alsace by Hitler and the Nazis.

Mr. Ka Sunbaunat, Mr. Ouch Channorah and myself spoke together about our past, our motivations and our commitment to participate in this psychological investigation of a criminal against humanity. My strong desire to do so was guided by the idea of avoiding any uncontrolled possible counter-transferential reactions which might then create possible cognitive impairments or blank spots, and influence our thoughts while doing this psychological investigation of a political murderer.

The first time we met Duch, we introduced ourselves by mentioning also our personal relations to collective history and specifically the consequences of political violence. We did so in order to avoid the risk of developing "dead angles," secret questionings and other events that could have caused interferences in the process.

We also worked via the internet with Mr. Ka Sunbaunat, in order to finalize the report of the psychological investigation. Before starting the clinical interviews, we read all the information contained in Duch's case-file. I had also read all the necessary and significant literature on Cambodia, in order to contextualize the psychological investigation: anthropological and historical books, literature concerning the Khmer Rouge period, as well as the period just before and just after this totalitarian regime. I also studied psychological and psychiatric literature concerning victims and perpetrators of the Cambodian genocide. What also helped me is that I had an extensive clinical experience of victims of torture and victims of the Cambodian genocide, by virtue of treating traumatized Cambodian persons living in exile in Paris.

The need for a specific approach and methodology: geopolitical clinical psychology

An adequate methodological approach is the key to success when undertaking psychological examinations of criminals against humanity. An appropriate approach avoids the creation of dead angles, as we have already seen. It also allows significant facts to emerge. Methodology is actually like a key that permits the opening of a specific door, which is the understanding (not the justification) of a criminal against humanity.

During twenty years of clinical work with victims and perpetrators of collective violence, I have had to adapt my clinical practice to the specific psychological impact of severe political traumatization. This led me to create a new approach called *geopolitical clinical psychology*.

Geopolitical clinical psychology gives a visible existence to all the different components that constitute the psychology of each person: personal factors, and political, cultural, historical, social and spiritual ones. This approach brings into light the articulation, the joint between collective history and personal stories. All of us are influenced by collective, political history. How, for each of us? It is not only the determining events and life in childhood that have to be investigated, when we have to explain how such a person became a criminal against humanity. We also have to analyze the impact of collective history upon his personal story, and to deconstruct, with him, the process of becoming a torturer, a collective murderer.

Collective events and history have the same weight, in our approach, as private life. Both collective and individual events are thoroughly analyzed. We know how easily they can be manipulated and how easily they can be transformed (consciously or unconsciously) into what I call *political emotions*. Political emotions are very common and concern each of us. They constitute the point of articulation, the bridge between individual and collective history, in all of us.

Political emotions are the result of two types of experiences:

- Either they stem from emotions linked to personal life that were denied and displaced, and which turned, later on, into collective, political emotions. This may lead to violent needs of revenge, to a pathological need for power, or to a paranoiac vision of collective life. But these private emotions which turn into political emotions may also possibly lead to non-violence, to surpassing oneself in benevolent actions or creations. They also lead to a strong need for political repair, and to a constant optimism as regards political collective life.
- Or they are emotions produced by collective history, with a great impact on private life. The link can be conscious or unconscious. The visible part of this influence will be depression, psychosomatic or organic diseases (cancers, heart problems, etc.), paranoiac reactions, isolation, hiding, social withdrawal . . .

The main events and emotions that can possibly turn into political emotions are the following: humiliation, separation, early affective deficiency, traumas due to violence (mistreatment, rape, incest . . .), migrations, deculturization and loss of any inner cultural framework, fright, unexpressed anger, powerlessness, feelings of inferiority, etc.

The general characteristic of these types of emotions is that they can be manipulated very easily, on a collective level. This is what all dictators do, all over the world, as well as demagogues in democratic countries when they manipulate information. So, in political criminality, different causes can lead to similar effects and political behavior.

The geopolitical approach in psychology and psychopathology is first of all a *clinical approach*. It is a praxeology, which means that the theory stems from the practice. This approach is necessarily a multifactorial one. The geopolitical factor – that is to say the impact of history, geography, culture and politics on our single psychological lives – has as much importance as events linked to intra-psychical life events or feelings. Usually, in clinical psychology, we consider these collective, cultural or social factors as being secondary ones, factors that give a "specific color" to our lives. But their determining influences are denied. I do the contrary. My clinical experience with traumatized persons, with victims and perpetrators of collective violence, has taught me that those factors linked to collective political life are as important, as determining, as factors stemming from our private life (early interactions, childhood, etc.).

One of the goals of the geopolitical clinical approach is to apply psychology to political criminality. It is to define and describe, in each particular case of a criminal against humanity, what are the collective and individual events that produced political criminality in this specific man, and not in his neighbor?

The final report of the psychological investigation of a criminal against humanity has to bring to light the effect, case by case, of the interactions between the three following main factors:

1. The articulation between individual story and collective history. This axis is called "factorial axis A."
2. The deconstruction of the mechanisms of making a criminal against humanity. This axis is called "factorial axis B."
3. The analysis of the intentionality of the accused. Did he know what he did when he did it? What about his consciousness? Was he aware of the impact of his decisions and actions? This axis is called "factorial axis C."

Intentionality is, historically, a philosophical concept. It represents the capacity to mentally order objects, and subjects, so as to have a design. Intentionality has also to do with empathy. In a clinical perspective, empathy means the capacity of the subject to think the thoughts of others, and the capacity to feel the feelings of others.

When analyzing political criminality from a psychological perspective we also take into account the question of intentionality, case by case. This leads us to consider the following questions: What does it mean to think? Is it possible to analyze thinking and cognitive activities outside their context? Under what conditions is a subject conscious of his actions?

I asked Hanna Arendt's question to Duch: "What happened to your conscience?" Duch didn't understand my question, despite my repeating it, and having it translated into Khmer language, and even checking, with the co-expert, after our session in detention, that the cultural factor couldn't hinder understanding. This question could not be understood by Duch.

Below are some examples of items that are investigated within the different factorial axes.

Factorial axis A: articulation between collective history and individual story

- Course of life.
- Childhood, adolescence, adult life, in their conscious and unconscious dimensions.
- Family group, taking into account the cultural specificities of family life.
- Striking or possibly traumatic or disorganizing life events.
- Love affairs and affective life.
- Existence, or not, of structuring friendships.
- Illusions and disillusions linked to personal life as well as to collective or political life.
- Illnesses (both physical and psychological), and the psychosomatic dimension of life.
- Groups of belonging or affiliation: family, cultural, political, spiritual groups, etc.
- Evolution and changes of groups of affiliations.
- Ancient and contemporary history of the country, and its possible impact on the subject.

This investigation will be done in a geopolitical clinical perspective. Therefore, it is highly recommended to work with an interpreter, a cultural mediator, that is to say with a person who knows the country from a political, anthropological and historical point of view.

Factorial axis B: the deconstruction of the mechanisms of making a criminal against humanity

The following items will be investigated:

- The role of political emotions: shame, humiliation, fear, rancor, grief, anger, guilt (survivor's guilt, or induced guilt . . .).

- The possible experience of deculturization processes: experience of subjection, of destruction of identity, attacks against cultural objects and values, systematic rapes in political and war contexts (as a victim, or as a perpetrator).
- The techniques of influence possibly used upon the accused. Has he been trained, and how, in methods of torture? Has torture been used on him for training purposes?
- The impact of acculturization (if it is relevant): traumatic contact, positive or negative contact with other cultural groups, or with social or spiritual, or economic groups that are very different from that of the accused.
- The initiatory methods or techniques possibly used with the accused, when making a torturer out of him, or during his military life for example.
- The content of educational manuals used in training.
- What did a criminal against humanity learn during his career (according to his point of view).
- The personal links and point of view as regards a specific ideology; his possible doubts . . .
- The impact of the passage of time between the commission of the crimes and the time when the psychological investigation takes place.
- The impact of the evolution of international history on his life, and his possible ideology, beliefs. As an example, the end of communism, namely in Poland, had a great impact upon the conversion of Duch to Christianity, in 1996: "I made the statement that the Christians were the winners in Poland," said Duch in order to explain his conversion.

Factorial axis C: the analysis of the intentionality of the accused

- The process of obedience: genesis, type of educational methods used on the accused when he was a child, in the army, police, or political group . . . Obedience by terror, learned attachment to a person by fear, by perverse pleasure . . .
- The making of disempathy (undoing empathy, the capacity of feeling the feelings of others, and of thinking the thoughts of others), and the actual state of this art of induced dehumanization.
- The way otherness is lived: otherness in himself, and otherness as regards the others.
- The influence of the political or military system upon the accused.
- The making through forced acting, and thinking through actions.

- The experience of power and the exercise of power: fascination, renunciation of his own identity, in favor of a collective one, psychological changes induced by the exercise of power . . .
- The Ideal Self, the process of idealization, the need and causes for it.
- Mimetism, and identification with the figure of the master.
- The existence, or not, of factors of resistance against dehumanization: strong attachment to a religious group, for example, or a group fighting for respect of human rights . . . or with a political group (as for example the increased psychological resistance of the deported communists who belonged to the French Resistance during World War II).
- The figure of disobedience: how did doubts occur, what did the accused do with them, the presence of ambivalence, the possibilities for resistance, escape, the risks taken by the accused.
- The psychological evolution of the accused, the impact, on him, of the psychological evaluation, of the criminal process, of the trial.

After having collected the different items corresponding to the content of the three factorial axes, we do a lateral analysis. We also bring to light the correlations between the different factorial axes, and the links of causality. The result of this type of analysis is a combination of factors that renders possible the making of a psychological geopolitical portrait, which corresponds precisely to that specific criminal against humanity. We use the draft table shown in Table 9.1, when establishing the psycho-geopolitical portrait, as an intermediate step before presenting the final results.

Analysis of the results

Table 9.1 Draft table of analysis of the results

Articulation between collective history and individual story	Deconstruction of the making of criminals against humanity	Analysis of intentionality
Items	Items	Items

We didn't use any psychological tests, like measuring intelligence, using scales of aggressiveness, of anxiety, of depression, or projective tests like the Rorschach or the TAT (Thematic Apperception Test) because all of them are pre-established tools that are absolutely not culture-free, and not adapted to a psychological examination corresponding to each unique criminal against humanity that we have in front of us. We would have made an important methodological mistake, since these tools have never been standardized according to a Cambodian and a Chinese population, in the very peculiar case of Duch. Yet some psychologists or psychiatrists nevertheless use such tests and scales in cross-cultural psychological evaluation, pretending to be scientific.

Application: geopolitical clinical psychology and the case of Duch

The role of a psychological investigation in a criminal trial in a Civil Law jurisdiction is to help the Court in understanding the psychology of perpetrators, and the psychology of victims. The investigating judges are the ones who deliver the official order of commission. This document contains a number of questions the expert (the witness in Common Law) has to answer, according to his own knowledge and experience, and according to the contemporaneous state of the art of the knowledge that exists on the matter, in psychology. The final report is then delivered to all the parties participating in the trial, that is to say the prosecutors, the judges, the general attorney, the defense attorneys, etc.

Usually, in a legal system governed by Civil Law, the report of a psychological investigation is secret. It is not a public document. It is the property of the different parties. But since the deposition (the oral presentation of the statement) made by the experts has been published online, in English, French and Cambodian languages on the ECCC website, I authorize myself to communicate publicly on this case, by presenting, here below, only the biographic elements and elements of analysis that stem directly from the public deposition presented in front of the court.

The questions of the co-investigating judges

The questions mentioned in the order of mission delivered by the co-investigating judges at the ECCC were the following:

1. Describe the psychological functioning of the accused, by clarifying:
   - the aspects of his personality; and
   - his degree of intelligence, his capacities of reasoning and intellectual construction.
   - Report on whether the accused is easily influenced and impressionable.
   - Analyze his capacities of empathy.
   - Determine if the evaluation reveals weaknesses, dysfunctions, or the presence of a psychopathology. In this case, describe them, and explain the possible impact and effects on the actions of the accused.

2. Proceed to the analysis of the detainee's life course, by taking into account the cultural, political and sociological context, at the time of the facts (from April 17, 1975 to January 6, 1979), and also today.
3. Make any observations that may help the Court. Advise on whether the accused can be rehabilitated and reintegrated into society.

As we usually do in a system of Civil Law when proceeding to a psychological investigation for the Court, I also asked the co-investigating judges for access to all the documents contained in the file of Duch's case (i.e. the statements of Duch's interrogations, the video documents of the reconstitution of the facts, etc.) that I considered as necessary in order to answer the questions of the co-investigating judges.

The proceeding of the psychological investigation

We had thirteen psychological interviews with Duch, in the detention center in Phnom Penh. Each interview lasted for more or less three hours. There were three of us: the co-expert, Ka Sunbaunat, who was 51 years old in 2007 and is a psychiatrist in charge of Mental Health at the Ministry of Health of Cambodia; the interpreter, Ouch Channorah, 30 years old in 2007, and myself, 49 years old in 2007. We saw Duch all together, except for one interview where Duch was alone with Ka Sunbaunat, and another interview where I saw him alone. We wanted to give him the possibility of saying, either to a man or to a woman, what he possibly may not say to all three.

We met him three other times, in August 2009, just before our deposition, according to a request made by Duch's defense attorneys to the Court. We were asked to evaluate whether there had been a change in the psychology of the accused since the beginning of the trial, in February 2009, and what impact the trial had upon him.

Methodology is a key point when doing psychological investigations of criminals against humanity. Therefore we proceeded to a permanent analysis of the counter-transference of the three of us. Being responsible for this mission, I had to keep this important factor under control, since we couldn't know, in advance, how the psychological investigation of this criminal against humanity would impact on us, and mainly on the two Cambodian participants. Mr. Ka Sunbaunat lost a lot of members of his family during the Khmer Rouge regime. He lived as a deportee in the fields for four years. The interpreter, Mr. Ouch Channorah, never knew his father. His mother was pregnant with him when her husband disappeared, due to the persecution of the Khmer Rouge.

How Duch mastered torture

During the Khmer Rouge regime, Duch was the chief of the S-21 security center, located in Phnom Penh. This was a center of torture and of execution where about sixteen thousand children, women and men were tortured and killed between April 1975 and January 1979. The Khmer Rouge regime caused two million deaths in a population of seven million Cambodian citizens at the time, in a very short period of time, since the regime lasted only three-and-a-half years. This political regime of terror was inspired by both the French Revolution and the Stalinist methodology, according the ECCC political expert, Raoul Jennar.

After the Khmer Rouge took power and marched into Phnom Penh, the city was completely evacuated by the following day. The inhabitants of the cities were considered as "bourgeois," and they were called "the recent people." They were accused of being totally contaminated by capitalistic values and had to go to the fields and work camps, in order to be re-educated by the "ancient people," that is to say the farmers in the countryside.

All over the country of Democratic Kampuchea, two hundred other centers of torture and death like S-21 existed. The specificity of S-21 was that this center specialized in treating political leaders and local leaders of the party, accused of being enemies of the people, CIA agents or KGB spies.

The difference between Duch and the four other accused who are actually in the ECCC detention center (Nun Chea, Ieng Thirith, Yeng Sary and Khieu Sampan) and whose trial began in 2011, is that Duch pleaded guilty. He recognized his responsibility regarding 80 percent of the charges against him.

During the Khmer Rouge period, Duch was totally convinced by the revolutionary project, and this justified, in his eyes, the high number of killings. It is Duch who elaborated the methods of torture used at S-21. He was also training and advising his staff, at S-21, in techniques of torture and interrogation. He became a theoretician of torture, elaborating a meticulous system of classification of the methods of torture. He did it by applying a mathematical model. Duch was actually a teacher in mathematics before joining the Khmer Rouge resistance, in the early 1970s.

His passion was teaching: he was a teacher in secondary school, then in S-21, where he taught his subordinates how to perform interrogations and how to torture. Later, after the fall of the Khmer Rouge regime, he went to China where he worked as a teacher, from 1986 to 1989. Later again, he worked as a teacher in a refugee camp close to the Thai border, where he was discovered by the journalist and photographer Nick Dunlop.

Duch elaborated a scientific system of torture, composed of a "cold method" and a "warm method." He never told us either his methodological influences or who trained him. Anyhow, Duch became a skilled master in the art of dissecting the so-called "confessions," that is to say the famous avowals obtained under torture. As usual, the use of torture was not to obtain information. Duch knew perfectly well that only 20 percent, at a maximum, of these confessions were true, as he said. So, the role of these confessions was to feed the paranoia of the Khmer Rouge leader, Pol Pot, who succeeded in transforming the whole country into a galloping, paranoiac system. As is usually the case, totalitarian regimes that are produced by paranoiac leaders can only result in absolute, total and rapid self-destruction, unless there is an action from outside.

The analysis of the confessions shows that they were organized according to a perpetual logical system. Duch conceived his system of interrogating, torturing and killing according to a system of perpetual destruction. Each autobiography that the detainees in S-21 had to write, and write again, had only one aim: the denunciation of eight to eleven persons per confession. Consequently the prisoners invented or gave names to stop the torture. And when they weren't any longer useful for this perpetual system, they were sent to the killing fields. So, the ratio, per prisoner, was eight to eleven new persons who were then arrested and tortured. They too had then to write their own autobiography, denounce eight to eleven persons, and so on. This mathematical model, called a perpetual system, was intended to feed the paranoia of Pol Pot with perpetually renewed human sacrifices.

A short biography of Duch and key elements of his life story

In order to understand the making of a criminal against humanity, we have to analyze the correlation between a man and the machine of death (S-21) he created. Therefore, we have to examine the significant events in the life of Duch, starting with his childhood.

The name given to Duch at birth by his parents was Kaing Guek Eav. He comes from a Chinese family who migrated to Cambodia in his father's generation. In Cambodia, the Chinese were traditionally despised by the Cambodian population. The first notable fact is that since his childhood, his name has been changed many times. When he was two or three months old, an astrologer told his parents that they had to change the birth name of the baby, in order to protect him against evil spirits. Otherwise, he would have serious problems in his life. The parents of Duch did so and changed his name to Yim Cheav. He kept this name until he was fifteen years old. But he didn't like this name at all, since it meant "slow, poor, old-fashioned" and "straggler."

So, when he was fifteen, he asked his father for permission to change his name again, and to take his previous name. His father agreed. When I asked him, in detention, what it means – Duch – he stood up from his chair, very straight. With his arms along his thighs, he declared, as if he were at school: "Duch means the scholar who stands up straight when his master asks him to stand up." So the name of Duch means, in itself, "obeying a master."

A connection has to be made with the image and aim of communism, at that time, in the 1950s, and in this part of the world. The communist culture and way of life, which he joined a few years later, meant evolution, quick progress, fighting against poverty, and modernity. All that he wanted to be was contained in his name.

During the Khmer Rouge regime and even after, Duch spent his life disguising his identities within different names. Actually, it was Pol Pot who advised the main leaders of Democratic Kampuchea to change their name very often: "This makes you elusive," he said. Changing names many times is like having successive or parallel identities. Later, when Duch was arrested, he openly took his name, Duch, once again. The name is important in Chinese culture. He therefore gave his name to his grandson, and what is really significant is that he added the Chinese name, Yun, to this name.

Duch has a very negative image of his father, although he was a self-taught man, like him. His father was actually under the control of a Chinese uncle, who was a usurer. Duch felt humiliated by this situation, by having such a dominated and powerless father. During his whole life, he was looking to rehabilitate the image of his father, for it to be displaced by idealized masculine models of fathers who were in the position of masters, and whom he obeyed without question. And when one of his immediate superiors, Vorn Vet, considered by Duch as an ideal master, was, in his turn, brought to S-21, he couldn't prevent his "erasure": in the vocabulary of the camp, it meant elimination by torture and death, after collecting the "confessions."

According to what he said, Duch wasn't a victim of mistreatment, although he had been beaten several times by his mother, and beaten at school by his French teachers at the time of the French protectorate. "But this is normal in our culture," said Duch, in chorus with the co-expert and the interpreter. All three of them considered child beating to be normal, in Cambodian society. Nevertheless, pain and humiliation have always had the same psychological consequences, all over the world.

Duch was always very impressionable. He was first very impressed by, and full of admiration for his French teachers and masters. These teachers transmitted to him a specific philosophical doctrine and way of life: stoicism. It structured his identity very strongly and lastingly. When he himself became a teacher of mathematics, he transmitted the values of stoicism, of self-control and self-denial of pain and feelings to his students.

A hypothesis can be raised: since Duch said everyone (at least Duch's teachers) was teaching and behaving according to this doctrine he learnt from the French, these teachers could have been former supporters of Pétain. They could possibly have been fascists who went to the French colonies after World War II and the defeat of fascism, in order to hide far away from their native cities. They may have feared feelings of revenge among the population. They recycled, in the colonies and French protectorate, banished principles of life. We can think, again, only as a hypothesis, that they recycled their political ideas into a pedagogic system.

Duch was fifteen years old when he discovered communism. He was very positively impressed by the visit of a Chinese communist leader to Phnom Penh. Since the Chinese were ostracized in Cambodia, the Chinese revolution took on a personal meaning in the mind of Duch. The victory of the communists in China itself acted, for Duch, like a restoration of the narcissistic wound caused by humiliation (seeing the misdeeds of Chinese profiteers, the usurers, and the poverty of his parents). A strong desire grew in Duch: to join the attractive movement for a collective, political restoration, namely communism. First he found stoicism, as a possible unconscious restoration. Then communism seems to have been a better proposition for turning his political emotions into a collective life project. The rehabilitated Chinese people, through the communist system, signified also the possibility of re-affiliation to his ancestors.

For Duch, individual identity is very difficult to conceive. He only lives for collective identity. This is why group belonging and affiliations are so important to him. The feeling of having an individual identity probably never existed in his mind.

Four notable events had a great importance in the psychology of Duch, although their impact was not conscious for him. All of them occurred in a short period of his lifetime, between fifteen and eighteen years old. They had a cumulative impact, and transformed his wounds into what I have called and already described above as *political emotions.*

- When he was fifteen years old, first, he asked the permission of his father to take his birth name, again, even though the astrologer considered it dangerous for him. Duch himself, as a Cartesian mind, was reluctant, at first, to be reminded of these facts and traditional beliefs during our clinical interviews. But they are part of his culture, and recalling them during our interviews had a "therapeutic effect." It weakened the ongoing and unconscious action of different psychological mechanisms of defense such as the splitting between the different parts of himself, like repression and denial. At that period of our psychological investigation, he also started to dream again during the night, and to think of all his life during daytime in detention. We later analyzed all these psychological productions with him.

- The second important event was that Duch had a disappointing love life when he was a student. As a consequence, he consciously developed the repression of all emotions linked to personal inner life, especially in relation to those who hurt or humiliate. They were sublimated into a passionate political involvement. The disappointment was not due to the withdrawal of his lover, but to the shock when his beloved told him that she hadn't chosen the same course of study as him, that is to say Science. She chose Literature.
- The third event was the theft of his bicycle. Duch, who had placed a great intellectual investment in his studies, couldn't go to school anymore, since there were no buses and no cars at that time in the place where he lived.
- The fourth event was the arrest of ten of his friends, whereas he had already joined the clandestine communist party. One of his friends was considered by him as a brother.

So he lost the protection of an appropriate name, and he lost his fiancée, a brother and the possibility of studying during the same period of his life (between fifteen and eighteen).

Collective events are also important, during this period of his life. There was a disastrous political situation in Cambodia at that time, during the Lon Nol regime, mainly due to corruption. American bombs never stopped falling on Cambodia, due to their military operations all along the Ho Chi Minh path, on the Vietnamese border. All these collective and individual events made Duch join the clandestine communist party and turn into a zealous Khmer Rouge.

Duch was detained from 1968 to 1970 for his communist sympathies. Then he joined the resistance and stayed with them for five years, until the victory of the Khmer Rouge regime. Later, when he was in a position of power, his sleeping wounds, as well as the need for recognition by a paternal figure, burst into the light of day: "My chiefs always fed my energy, they stimulated me," explained Duch during our clinical interviews.

He was proud to be able to anticipate the changing and secret political guidelines of Pol Pot, in order to always adjust his reports based on the forced and false confessions obtained in S-21 to Pol Pot's pathological and paranoiac needs. But his increasing paranoia made him become extremely unpredictable. Duch was scared, from 1976, because he was losing the ability to predict Pol Pot's behavior, strategy and political line. As a cognitive consequence of this unpredictability, Duch developed a nervous breakdown (sleep impairment, doubts, anxiety, apathy). It was at first rather well contained, since Duch developed a great capacity for repressing all inner feelings. The depression burst out into the open in 1978. He knew perfectly well that the politics of elimination in the perpetual system that was implemented in order to feed Pol Pot's paranoia with sacrificial victims would also catch up with him very soon. Duch was nevertheless very proud of the perpetual system he created in S-21. This is probably why he didn't destroy the files and the pictures at the end of the Khmer Rouge regime.

When the regime fell, he joined the zone controlled by the Khmer Rouge at the Thai border, where he worked as a teacher of mathematics. He made a religious conversion to Christianity in 1996. But it wasn't for religious purposes, as he told me, but because the Christians were the winners, over communism, at that time.

During our interviews, the analysis of his private life showed that it was always rather "poor" and stereotyped. The disappointment that occurred when he was eighteen is still present today, covered by strong sublimation into political life. Like a knight's way of loving, he kept the image of this young lady in his mind, as an idealized figure of love. Emotions must be kept at distance and turned into abstraction. Duch is a pragmatic man. He married a comrade, a communist woman, after having asked the permission of his chief. He had four children while he was working in S-21. His wife was killed in 1995, in a mysterious way. She was killed during an attack on their house, said Duch, who was the only witness and who was only slightly hurt. He suspected Pol Pot of being behind it. Duch never showed any emotions when he spoke about his wife or his children. He was always perfectly stoical. We should not forget that one of the mottos of the Khmer Rouge was "Extinguish your heart."

Geopolitical clinical analysis

If we refer to the usual categories of classification of mental disorders, we can say that we have not found any psychopathology, any mental illness, in the case of Duch. The concept of perversity can be evoked, because of the denial, denegation, and manipulation when he was a chief at S-21 and also after, during his trial. The relationship of ascendancy over the members of his former staff in S-21, and his arrogance sometimes in front of the victims attending the trial, were notable. Duch still inspired fear among them. This perversity is the result of the articulation between some individual psychological characteristics (narcissistic wound, humiliation, need to obey, to be recognized) and the Khmer Rouge model of making a new category of men.

The diagnosis of "typical disorder" (**"désordre type"**)

Actually it is another diagnosis, an ethnopsychiatric one, that best characterizes the psychological functioning of Duch. It is the category of "typical disorders" as elaborated by the psychoanalyst Georges Devereux. It is a category of multifactorial disorders which are both psychologically and sociopolitically determined. It is "sociopolitical psychopathology" at an individual level, or "sociopathology" at a collective level. In both cases, individuals and society as a whole are impacted.

In each totalitarian society, there are individuals who are what I call "system-men." Duch is a system-man. These "system-men" are, think and behave, at an individual level, in a perfect isomorphism with the shape and formal structure of the political and collective life of the country. These "system-men" are, in each society, the point of articulation, the bridge, the link, between the collective, political, ideological level and the individual idealized way of thinking. A paranoiac leader creates a paranoiac regime, and induces peculiar psychological behaviors among the population, which tries to adapt in order to survive: fear, obedience, obsessional behaviors, splitting, denial of reality, etc.

This sociopolitical psychopathology called "typical disorder" shows that there exists an isomorphism between individual psychology and collective history. Individual psychology is impacted by collective history. But this category of sociopsychopolitical diagnosis doesn't at all avoid individual responsibility in political criminality. This sociopsychopolitical category of troubles shows how the individual level of responsibility is expressed in a criminal joint undertaking ("*entreprise criminelle commune*").

In the case of Duch, the man as well as the country, Cambodia, have gone through several experiences of radical acculturization between different cultural systems, such as French culture and the Cambodian one, and at an individual level for Duch, also between Chinese and Cambodian culture. The psychological mechanism of adaptation, in this case, is splitting between two systems of value which continue to co-exist, on their own, in a man's mind. This can lead to obsessional behavior. The need to keep different and non integrated parts of the Self under control is a constant unconscious mechanism. What can't be accepted as being a part of the Self will be projected onto a designated "enemy." Denial will than take place: denial of what can't be understood from a logical point of view, or denial of what can't be accepted in one's Self, in the others, or in society.

After several experiences of acculturation, the country, as well as the man Duch, has experienced a brutal deculturation: the inculcation of Khmer Rouge ideology. Singular identity was willingly uprooted in the case of Duch, and a new man, a new psychology was implemented, an identity formed which was purely collective. The renunciation of personal identity was an adequate psychological system of adaptation to a deculturalizing ideology, which takes away any singularity. Each totalitarian system reduces the range of possible behaviors in a society. This is why a Cambodian torturer and criminal against humanity is psychologically closer to a Nazi German or a Rwandese criminal against humanity than to a Cambodian, a German or a Rwandese non-criminal individual.

At the opposite extreme, each democratic society contains the possibility to widen and diversify the range of possible behaviors. Democracy allows the expression of multiplicity inside the individual psychology, and outside, in society.

A specific behavior emerged, at the collective level as well as at the individual level. It was a traumatic model of existence based on terror, general fear, fantasies of being totally transparent, suspicion, denunciation considered as a positive value, and the eradication of personal emotions and personal thinking. The whole of Democratic Kampuchea, as well as each single citizen, was dehumanized. They had to adapt, or to perish.

An obsessional personality

The concept of "personality" is unsatisfactory to me, since there is never a pre-existing structure of the mind. A symptom, a trend of personality is always an articulation between society and individual potentialities. Besides, the concept of personality is not culture-free. It is a psychological, historical and sociocultural entity. Each cultural group, each political society, each period of history, has a preferential model of what is considered as a "normal" personality. The Khmer Rouge too had such a model. Duch's personality was perfectly matched to it. He was perfectly adapted to that model of personality produced by a totalitarian society.

Duch could not build unity out of the multiplicity inside him: being Chinese for the Cambodians, admiring French culture, which is at the same time also the culture of a colonial power, and defending communist values .... Multiplicity makes him ambivalent. One thing and its possible contrary co-exist in each of us. But Duch fought strongly against this psychological reality. He fought against what makes complexity in each human being. He denied the existence of what cannot be understood, resolved, controlled. Duch eradicated what is complicated, what cannot be reduced into a rational, mathematical model, like feelings for example. His psychological life was a co-existence of compartments without any links between them. Any link, any mixing, would herald the danger of disintegration, of personality collapse, of depression.

The obsessional personality, in the case of Duch, is a co-construction between individual psychology and the making of a system where dehumanized humans were an idealized model of society. Duch purified himself by eradicating any expression of humanity, and he contributed to purify the country by eliminating, erasing, any "otherness": the "recent" people, the traitors. Denial, splitting, isolation, putting distance between himself and reality, rationalization, avoidance are typical defense mechanisms in obsessional psychological functioning.

The strong need for affiliation and collective belonging

This is the consequence of experiences of acculturization and deculturization, and of eradicating one's own identity. The need for group identity in spite of personal identity is constant: he belonged to communism, then to Christianity, then he adapted to the world, culture and values of the ECCC, and more recently he reconnected, inside himself, with the two strongest groups of affiliation in his case: the Chinese and the communist ones.

The feeling of possessing a personal identity is not culture-free. It is not universal. Yet when it doesn't exist, or when it has been intentionally eradicated, it may lead to a totalitarian psychological functioning. To be able to accept multiplicity in itself, as well as in society, is a long process. First, the subject has to experiment with re-affiliation within his different groups of belonging. Only later is he able to be conscious one day, or perhaps never, of having his own specific, unique identity. This also opens, or re-opens, the path to empathy.

Presence of remorse, yet absence of guilt

We consider the feeling of guilt from a psychological point of view, not from a legal one. The feeling of guilt is not culture-free. No feeling exists by being only and totally "natural". Feelings are induced by culture. Guiltiness is consequently induced by the moral and intellectual influence of Christianity. So is it with the concept of individualism, which means to believe that we exist on our own. The culture of human rights has developed this concept, which is actually and originally a Christian one. How could the Christians conquer the Romans? By taking into account the weak points of Roman hegemonic culture. In this collective culture, individualism was an absolutely "dead angle." Guiltiness is an inner, individual feeling, that has a chance to be considered as interesting by a culture, or not. It is so in a Christian culture, but not in an Asian culture. Whereas the concept of remorse opens access to a more significant possibility, from a cultural point of view, to express the link that exists between the existence of feelings and their expressions in a local culture. Remorse is a better candidate. It is a painful feeling, accompanied by shame, and caused by the conscience of having acted badly. It is a point of junction between the individual and collective expression of "guilt." Remorse is simultaneously linked to the consciousness of having committed a crime, and to fear of punishment. When feeling remorse, the misdeed, and responsibility for the crimes, is not taken on individually, but collectively. There can only be a recognition of shared responsibility. Remember that Duch cannot have access, in his very deep psychological functioning, to a real individual sense of identity: because of cultural factors, because of repression (a mechanism of defense existing since early in his life), and because of the Khmer Rouge conception of a new man, dehumanized and reduced to a collective pattern of identity.

Duch obviously experiences remorse, but not as a feeling of guilt. Being able to feel guilty supposes here, too, full access to the feeling of having an identity of one's own. The misdeed is accepted, at an individual level. Full access to the concept of guilt means feeling oneself personally responsible, and accepting individual responsibility. Duch was reluctant. Although Christian, he always refused to pay the price, alone, in the name of all the others, the former leaders of Democratic Kampuchea, and in the name of other criminals against humanity that are still living in the open all over Cambodia. So Duch is not a Christlike figure, who takes on his shoulders all the misdeed and guilt of the others.

The impact of the trial upon him is that it brought him to remorse, and to a wider and culturally learned sense of identity, thanks to the multicultural frame of the ECCC, and thanks to the mandated participation of the different actors in court. But inner, psychological time doesn't correspond to the agenda of the ECCC. Duch is nevertheless a living person. That means he is in process, he is moving, when conditions around him bring him to move. He has also his strategies of existence, his pragmatic choices. Yet he remains split. Conscience supposes an individual sense of identity, supposes the possibility of making a personal choice. For now, Duch is probably in resistance against the idea of having a single identity, although he has started to experiment with it, more than ever before in his life. There will be a next step . . .

Conclusion

To the question: "Did the trial have an impact on Duch's psychology?" I answer: "Yes." The case of Duch perfectly illustrates the articulation in each of us, between collective and individual history. A new psychological approach is necessary to understand and describe the effect of it. Therefore I had to develop a new field in psychology: geopolitical clinical psychology. This approach is very efficient when evaluating criminals against humanity, as well as the victims.

What the court proposed to Duch was a universal proposal stemming from our collective (and not only western) conscience of worldliness. But worldliness, the sense of universality, is a process; it is hardly given at birth. International trials are a tool of rehumanization of the perpetrators as well as the victims, a tool among others, like the *gacacas*, the Commissions of Justice and Reconciliation, and also, at an individual level, psychotherapy, for example. They are new tools. We are still learning from the various practices. All together, these tools create the possibility of building a real conscience of togetherness. It is not given by nature; it is not given by culture. It represents an optimistic, contemporaneous and strong belief, that international justice is an appropriate tool for building a humanistic worldliness.

As Yehudi Menuhin wrote in his book *A Violin for Peace*, published in 2004: "The world is at a dangerous crossroads. For the first time, we have to follow two roads at the same time: One leads us towards unity, always wider, towards the community of nations, towards the global. The other road leads to the human beings in their own culture, their daily needs, their dignity, hopes and fears . . . Living together, although respecting the differences, is one of the major challenges, today, for all the countries in the world."

Integration of both local and global dimensions in every single aspect of our lives is becoming a new form of humanism, a humanism that, I really hope, will be able to victoriously repel all the various forms of contemporaneous fanaticisms and resistance, for a new coming world.

Bibliography

Accoce, P. and Rentchnick P. (1988) *Ces nouveaux malades qui nous gouvernent*, Paris: Stock.

Arendt, H. (1966, 1991) *Eichmann à Jérusalem: rapport sur la banalité du mal*, Paris: Gallimard.

Arendt, H. (2005) *Responsabilité et jugement*, Paris: Payot.
Bar On, D. (1989) "Holocaust perpetrators and their children: a paradoxical morality", *Journal of humanistic psychology*, 29 (4), 424–43.
Chandler, D. (2002) *S-21 ou le crime impuni des khmers rouges*, Paris: Autrement.
Devereux, G. (1967) "La renonciation à l'identité comme défense contre l'anéantissement", *Revue Française de Psychanalyse*, Tome 31, No. 1, 101–142.
Devereux, G. (1985) *Ethnopsychanalyse complémentariste*, Paris: Flammarion.
Ferenczi, S. (1913, 1970) "Dressage d'un cheval sauvage", *Psychanalyse II. Oeuvres complètes*, Paris: Payot, 27–31.
Fromm, E. (1983) *De la désobéissance*, Paris: Laffont.
Goldensohn, L. (2005) *Les entretiens de Nüremberg, présentés par Robert Gellately*, Paris: Flammarion.
Milgram, S. (1974) *Soumission à l'autorité. Un point de vue expérimental*, Paris: Calmann-Lévy.
Semelin, J. (2005) *Purifier et détruire. Usages politiques des massacres et génocides*, Paris: Seuil.
Sereny, G. (1975) *Au fond des ténèbres*, Paris: Denoël.
Sironi, F. (1999) *Bourreaux et victimes. Psychologie de la torture*, Paris: Odile Jacob.
Sironi, F. (2004) "Comment devient-on un bourreau?", in Berthoz A., Jorland G. et al., *L'empathie*, Paris: Odile Jacob.
Sironi, F. (2007) *Psychopathologie des violences collectives. Essai de Psychologie géopolitique clinique*, Paris: Odile Jacob.
Sironi, F. (2010) "Les apports de la méthode géopolitique clinique dans les expertises psychologiques des criminels contre l'humanité", *Revue Francophone du Stress et du Trauma*, 10(1), 39–50.
Sironi, F. (2011) "L'expertise psychologique des criminels contre l'humanité. Le cas de Duch", *Les Cahiers de la Justice*, 1, 65–81.

CHAPTER 10

Pleading guilty before the international criminal courts

The case of Duch before the Khmer Rouge tribunal

François Roux

Introduction

Most international criminal jurisdictions allow for the possibility that the accused will plead guilty, with the proviso that such pleas are preceded by discussions with the prosecution that evidence a recognition of guilt. The conclusion of these discussions results in a "plea agreement," in which the parties agree on the main charges to which the accused will plead guilty, as well as on those which the prosecutor will drop for lack of sufficient proof, and finally the parties propose the length of sentence to the judges.

This is the current practice before the International Criminal Tribunal for Yugoslavia (ICTY) and the International Criminal Tribunal for Rwanda (ICTR). I have myself, with my defense team, led two negotiations of guilty pleas before the ICTR (the cases of Vincent Rutaganira and of Joseph Nzabirinda), after having pleaded and obtained an acquittal (the case of Bagilishema) before the same Tribunal. I found the practice of the "plea agreement" very instructive and quite interesting.

The situation before the International Criminal Court, and before the most recently conceived international tribunal, the Special Tribunal for Lebanon, is more complicated by virtue of the rule that, in these jurisdictions, the victims are entitled to participate in the process. No guilty plea has yet been lodged in front of the International Criminal Court, nor, for even stronger reasons, before the Special Tribunal for Lebanon, and so no one can yet say what role the victims will ask for or be allowed to play in these proceedings. Here, however, I will address the guilty plea in the specific context of the Extraordinary Chambers in the Court of Cambodia (ECCC) and the rules developed before the Special Tribunal for Lebanon where the defense bar was charged with helping and counselling future defense teams, and most notably with aiding an accused who wished to plead guilty. This resulted in the development of some specific special procedures organized by the bar and the defense attorneys in Lebanon.

The context of the Duch affair before the ECCC

- The Law: The rules of procedure (or internal rules) before the Extraordinary Chamber within the Cambodian Tribunal did not foresee the possibility of an accused pleading guilty. In practice, the procedural rules applicable in the Tribunal are from the Romano-German rules of civil law, incorporated into the ECCC by virtue of Rule 87 (5) of the internal regulations of the Tribunal, which stipulate that "The Chamber shall give the same consideration to confessions as to other forms of evidence."
- Being a mixed Tribunal, the ECCC could always refer to the jurisprudence of other international criminal tribunals. They tend to recognize mitigating circumstances: the cooperation of the accused, a guilty plea, the expression of sincere remorse. One of the objectives of the Tribunal, according to the Preamble to the agreement reached between the United Nations and the Royal Cambodian Government in 2003, is that now, more than 30 years after the events, the Tribunal "should work towards national reconciliation."

In these circumstances it was legitimate for the defense to try to take account of the accused's recognition of his responsibility for the crimes committed in S-21.

The facts as known to the public at the opening of the investigation

Duch was the Director of the sadly infamous Cambodian detention center S-21, located in Phnom Penh, and now the Tuol Sleng Museum. Starting from 1995, numerous documents have been recovered from this detention center and have been classified and archived by the Documentation center of Cambodia with a specific view to future trials of the Khmer Rouge responsible for these atrocities.

In 1999, shortly before his arrest, Duch admitted that a number of crimes were committed at S-21, while other elderly Khmer Rouge officials, such as

Pol Pot, refused to make any such confession. Duch also acknowledged that he was the Director of S-21 and so was responsible for the commission of these crimes. Even though Duch cannot be regarded as a high-level Khmer Rouge official, he was arrested in May 1999 and was detained by the Cambodian authorities for many years pending the creation of the ECCC. In 2001, the ECCC was established to pursue the leading officials of Democratic Kampuchea, and so to apprehend "those most responsible for the crimes and serious violations of Cambodian penal law, the rules and customs of international humanitarian law, as well as the international conventions recognized by Cambodia, committed between 17 April 1975 and 6 January 1979" (Articles 1 and 2 of the law creating the ECCC).

Duch's acknowledgement of responsibility before the ECCC

From the beginning of the proceedings, Duch had decided that he would cooperate and admit his guilt. The trial would not have been the same if Duch had determined to keep silent. He gave detailed information about the functioning of the Democratic Kampuchean regime and the crimes committed at S-21. Asked by the investigating judge to comment on David Chandler's book, he confirmed its description of the criminal system in place in S-21. More than that, he agreed to take part in a judicial reconstruction of the crimes at the site where they had actually been committed. As has often been said, this reconstruction was a major and unique judicial act never before seen in the history of international criminal justice. Thirty years after the event, the Director of S-21, accompanied by two policemen, the judges and lawyers, returned to the site of his crimes. Here he expressed his remorse and apologized to three of the victims who were also present at the reconstruction. Two of them, like many of the others present at the reconstruction, were taken aback and addressed the judges as follows: "Your Honours, I have now heard the words that I have waited thirty years to hear. I am at peace."

On the first day of the trial, March 31, 2009, Duch reiterated his admission of guilt:

> The crimes committed during this period were extreme. More than that, the loss of human lives rose to 1,700,000 persons, and as a member of the Kampuchean Communist Party (KCP), I admit that I am responsible for these crimes committed by the KCP during this period.
>
> Secondly, I would like to return to the crimes committed at S-21 and recognize my legal responsibility for these violations. I would

> like to stress that I am responsible for the crimes committed at S-21, and in particular for the torture and the executions that took place there.

Duch continued to recognize his responsibility throughout the trial:

> Yes, I was the Chief of M.13. I was equally the Chief of S-21 and was the architect of all of the crimes committed there, including the detention and the inhumane conditions of detention meted out upon men, women and children, including the execution of women and children, acts for which I must claim responsibility.
>
> I am also responsible for all the crimes committed at S-21. I was at the same time a member of the Party and I was moved by the thought that more than one million Cambodians were dead. I was emotionally responsible for the death of more than a million of the people killed.

It was consequently something of a surprise to the general public that on the last day of the trial, Duch's Cambodian attorney, himself a former prisoner of the Khmer Rouge, asked the Chamber to accept Duch's admission of guilt, and also to acquit him, because according to him, Duch simply followed orders (which, according to Cambodian law, is your duty). Duch could not, therefore, be considered a principal responsible for the commission of the crimes.

The admissions of guilt have been analyzed by psychological experts. Paragraph 171 of the investigating judge's report reads as follows:

> The experts found that, despite the presence of a certain disempathy, since 1999 Duch constantly expressed his regrets. They indicated that the question that remained was that of whether these regrets were sincere or the result of his circumstances "was one that could not be answered, the reality of his situation was one which existed far beyond any such simple proposition as sincerity or deceit"...

In front of the court, Françoise Sironi, a psychological expert witness, stated:

> we think that there is a real question facing the accused. It is true that he has recognized his crimes, but it is also the case that he has to ask himself what he can do to make amends and that this question of reparation is still in fact an open one for him. My colleagues and I have concluded that this is not a pragmatic question. It is

> not a strategic question. It is a real question and I want to say, and especially in connection with the victims, he is psychologically open to this issue.
>
> Yes, Mr. Roux ... he is sincere, to borrow your term, in this process ...
>
> But as we were mandated as experts, it was always our role and our duty to constantly keep in mind that we are not in a therapeutic dialogue about his health; that we are in a judicial proceeding in which different factors have to be evaluated and, in spite of it all, we need to know that as experts we are not being manipulated by the subject. And here we can respond that we are not; in support of this we can report that at no moment did we have any such impression of manipulation. We developed a strong bond with the subject, that was not the issue. As a result of this we can speak to his sincerity and his sincerity in the course of the trial.

These recollections were often understood by the victims but were also often rejected. Thus Robert Hamill, a civil party, declared before the Chamber on August 17, 2009:

> I recognize the fact that Duch has pleaded guilty. I am angry beyond words, but at the same time I also recognize and respect the accused's plea of guilty. It is a small contribution, but nonetheless an important one in redressing the wrong that the accused has done. Those who did not plead guilty and who refuse to recognize the harm they caused deserve twice the degree of condemnation and hate.

David Chandler, a historian expert witness, after his session before the Chamber of first instance on August 6, 2009, was asked the following question posed by the defense: "Do you think that the fact that the accused recognizes his guilt is in the service of history?" He replied:

> Yes. The reply is, I believe, fairly easy. I was very struck and very moved by the accused's recognition of his guilt. It is something unique amongst the surviving members of the Khmer Rouge government. I am not speaking of the surviving victims, I am talking of the surviving Khmer Rouge actors.
>
> The accused today said – and he had the right to say it, he chose to make this confession and I admire him for that – that he was an actor in and hostage of a criminal regime.

Unfortunately the positive impact of this cooperation and recognition of responsibility was belittled by the co-prosecutors throughout the initial investigation and throughout the trial. It is this which reappears, for example, in the extract below from the final written statement of the co-prosecutors, submitted on November 11, 2009:

> 427. The cooperation of the accused did not facilitate the judicial economy of the trial except in a very limited manner. The information that he furnished had only a slight impact on the main issue at trial, namely eliciting the broadest possible understanding of the crimes committed at S-21 and the role that he played in them. A variety of factors should help minimize the attenuating effect of the accused's cooperation. The accused cannot, on the one hand, pretend to be fully cooperating and hope that in return he will receive a significant reduction in sentence, while at the same time refusing to cooperate and challenging significant aspects of the factual details presented by those making accusations against him.

Such a position feeds the dissatisfaction of the victims with the criminal process and is a matter of serious regret. This dissatisfaction can often be ameliorated by the criminal process even if the victims' expectations exceed what justice can offer: Justice can never return their vanished loved ones to them. This is what Robert Badinter wrote in an edition of *Le Monde*: "Justice should not be therapy for the suffering of the victims"; and I would add "and cannot be."

This position of discrediting the admission of guilt was even more unfortunate because of the extraordinarily large number of Cambodians who were able to follow the trial, either by attending the Tribunal (more than 30,000 came) or by watching on television.

From the perspective of a trial aimed at reconciliation, it would have been beneficial for everyone to affirm and valorize Duch's recognition of his guilt rather than to discredit it. This attitude of the prosecutor was even more incomprehensible in light of the fact that he intended to use Duch as a witness in the next trial of four high-level directors of the Khmer Rouge administration and policy. How can he maintain that Duch's testimony is credible on one occasion when he has declared the opposite the day before?

The judges, by contrast, at several points took full account of Duch's acknowledgment of his responsibility. This emerges clearly from the referral ruling given by the investigating co-judges on August 8, 2009:

> 167. Duch, as Head of S-21, has always acknowledged his responsibility for the crimes committed there. He has explained that he was moved to abandon his silence in 1999, believing that "one cannot not tell the truth about S-21" after having heard that Pol Pot "denied the existence of S-21 and claimed that it was an invention of the Vietnamese." Duch has frequently expressed his remorse to the victims and their families, as well as to the former employees of S-21 who were under his command. He has confirmed that none of his employees willingly undertook the tasks that he ordered done, and none was proud of what they had done, but that, thrown into a climate of terror in which one risked one's life every day, they had no choice but to carry out his orders.
>
> 168. Furthermore, Duch cooperated voluntarily in the investigation, refusing at all points to implicate his subordinates in any way while refusing to exonerate himself in any way by placing the blame upon his superiors in the Party. Faced with certain incoherences in his depositions before the co-investigating judges, he indicated that these could be explained by "the fear and shame" that he felt upon being reminded of "this extremely sad history of crimes."

In its judgment of July 26, 2010, the Chamber of first instance notes:

> 609. The Chamber thinks that, notwithstanding his request for acquittal presented on the last day of the trial, the accused's cooperation with the ECCC can be treated as a mitigating circumstance. The accused has exhibited throughout a willingness to cooperate with the ECCC, both during the investigation and throughout the trial. He has provided valuable information on his role in and the functioning of S-21 and on the crimes committed there. In cooperating in this manner with the ECCC, the accused has indubitably facilitated the hearing before the Chamber. More than that, the Chamber believes that this attitude has contributed significantly and positively to the effort of national reconciliation, one of the objectives pursued throughout the work of the ECCC.
>
> 610. The expression of remorse is one of the factors that can be taken into account as a mitigating circumstance in hearings before international tribunals. When offered the chance, the accused repeatedly presented his excuses and expressed remorse for his crimes. The Chamber always addresses the fact that the effect of mitigating circumstances such as remorse should be reduced by the fact that in the last moments of the trial he did not fully and

> categorically recognize his responsibility. In particular, his request for acquittal, presented to the court after the pleadings were complete, even if it does not entirely erase his previous manifestations of remorse, does limit the weight that the Chamber is able to give to this remorse in terms of reduction of sentence.

To recognize one's responsibility does not mean abandoning all defense

As relayed by the Chamber of first instance in its judgment, at paragraph 47: "The accused has in general admitted to or not challenged many of the most significant facts expressed in the modified ruling." Meanwhile, throughout the trial, the defense was careful to ensure that the Chamber did not view Duch as a scapegoat for all of the crimes committed by the regime in Democratic Kampuchea. We were also careful to make sure that Duch was not held responsible for crimes he claimed not to have committed or for which there was insufficient evidence as, for example, he denied having ever himself carried out acts of torture on prisoners at S-21. The defense thus contested a number of issues of proof put forward by the co-prosecutors ahead of time. On the other hand, the defense did plead mitigating circumstances and did ask the Chamber to take into consideration in this regard the notion of a "crime of obedience."

In his book entitled *S-21 ou le crime impuni des Khmers rouges* (published in 1999 in English under the title *Voices from S-21: Terror and History in Pol Pot's Secret Prison*), David Chandler, after having described in minute detail the system of terror in place at S-21, tries in the final chapter to understand why such a criminal enterprise was put into effect. He speaks of the crime of obedience and, recalling Milgram's experiment, he concludes his book with the words: "To find the source of the evil daily practised at S-21, we need look no further than ourselves." Questioned by the defense on the crime of obedience, David Chandler responded after the trial in the following fashion: "Cambodia had no culture of questioning orders given by people in authority . . . I used Milgram's experiment to show how, in a situation such as that at S-21, obedience was a factor that augmented the horror," and he adds, "This does not explain everything, but it is, I think, useful for understanding the point at which people such as us accept the fact that if those responsible say it is good, then it must be good. And this was the culture at S-21."

In 2000, François Bizot, a former hostage of Duch's (in 1971), in his book titled *The Gate*, asked himself the question: Who is "the man –

who looks like me – sitting behind the executioner?". In his testimony before the Chamber in the session of April 9, he said: "I fear, sadly, that when we take stock of the humanity of the executioner we understand him terrifyingly well."

Taking account of all of these factors the Trial Chamber condemned Duch to 35 years in prison, from which they deducted five years for the violation of his rights that took the form of his provisional imprisonment for more than ten years prior to the trial.

The Special Tribunal for Lebanon: relevant rulings

In the absence of any relevant experiences to date before the Special Tribunal for Lebanon, we will content ourselves with citing some written rulings on the subject of guilty pleas.

The possibility of pleading guilty and of negotiating a plea agreement with the Prosecutor is foreseen in Rules 98, 99 and 100 of the Rules of Procedure and Evidence (RPE):

> Rule 98
> Initial appearance of the accused
> A) In the execution of a summons to appear or arrest warrant or upon transfer to the seat of the Tribunal, an accused shall be brought before the Trial Chamber or a Judge designated by the President, as appropriate, without delay and shall be formally charged. The Trial Chamber or the Judge shall:
> i) satisfy itself or himself that the right of the accused to counsel is respected;
> ii) read or have the indictment read to the accused in a language the accused understands and satisfy itself that the accused understands the indictment;
> iii) inform the accused that, within seven days of the initial appearance, he will be called upon to enter a plea of guilty or not guilty on each count, but that should he so request, he may immediately enter a plea of guilty or not guilty on one or more counts;
> iv) if the accused fails to enter a plea at the initial or any further appearance, decide whether to enter a plea of not guilty on the accused's behalf;
> v) in case of a plea of not guilty, set a date for trial or for a status conference, as appropriate;

vi) in case of a plea of guilty, act in accordance with Rule 100; and
vii) set other dates as appropriate.
(amended October 30, 2009)

B) Where the accused has not chosen a counsel, the Head of the Defence Office may assign a counsel available at short notice to act temporarily for the accused pursuant to Rule 57(D) (ii) to represent the accused at the initial appearance and at any further appearance as may be necessary for entering a plea. (amended 8 February 2012)

Rule 99
Plea agreement

A) The Prosecutor and the Defence may agree that the accused will enter a plea of guilty to one or more counts of the indictment, and the Prosecutor shall do one or more of the following before the Trial Chamber:
   i) apply to amend the indictment accordingly;
   ii) submit that a specific sentence or sentencing range is appropriate;
   iii) not oppose a submission by the accused for a particular sentence or sentencing range.
B) The Trial Chamber shall not be bound by any agreement specified in paragraph (A).
C) If a plea agreement has been reached by the Parties, the Trial Chamber shall require the disclosure of the agreement in open session or, on a showing of good cause, in closed session, at the time the accused pleads guilty in accordance with Rule 98.

Rule 100
Guilty pleas

A) If an accused pleads guilty in accordance with Rule 98, or requests to change his plea to guilty, and the Trial Chamber is satisfied that:
   i) the guilty plea has been made voluntarily;
   ii) the guilty plea is informed;
   iii) the guilty plea is unequivocal; and
   iv) there is a sufficient factual basis for the crime and the accused's participation in it, either on the basis of

independent indicia or lack of any material disagreement between the Parties about the facts of the case, the Trial Chamber may enter a finding of guilt and set a date for the sentencing hearing.

B) If an accused enters a plea of guilty pursuant to a plea agreement under Rule 99, the Trial Chamber shall, prior to entry of a finding of guilt, satisfy itself that the accused:
   i) understands the terms of the plea agreement;
   ii) has discussed the terms of the plea agreement with his counsel;
   iii) understands the consequences of a plea of guilty;
   iv) has not been threatened or coerced in any way to enter into the plea agreement; and
   v) has entered into the plea agreement voluntarily.

(added November 10, 2010)

Mitigating circumstances: substantial cooperation: Article 172 (B) (ii) of the RPE

Rule 172
Penalties

A) A convicted person may be sentenced to imprisonment for a term up to and including the remainder of the convicted person's life.

B) In determining the sentence, the Trial Chamber shall take into account the factors mentioned in Article 24(2), of the Statute, as well as factors such as:
   i) any aggravating circumstances;
   ii) any mitigating circumstances, including substantial cooperation with the Prosecutor by the convicted person before or after conviction;
   iii) the general practice regarding prison sentences in Lebanon;
   iv) the extent to which any penalty imposed by a court of any State on the convicted person for the same act has already been served.

C) Credit shall be given to the convicted person for the period, if any, during which the convicted person was detained for the investigation of crimes within the jurisdiction of the Tribunal, any custody pending surrender to the Tribunal or custody pending trial or appeal. (amended 30 October 2009)

Participation of victims in the STL

The relevant rulings concerning the participation of victims in the proceedings before the Special Tribunal for Lebanon are Article 17 of the Statute, as well as Article 86 of the RPE (on the conferment of participant status upon victims) and Article 87 of the RPE (on the modes of victims' participation in the trial).

Only experience can say how these trials will take place before this Tribunal, with everything that such implies, including the question of what role the victims should or should not play in cases of a guilty plea.

CHAPTER 11

The place and participation of the victims in Duch's trial

Brice Poirier

Introduction

The images on the next page were filmed on January 10, 1979 in Phnom Penh, just one day after revolutionary Vietnamese forces entered the city. The Vietnamese Revolutionary Republic and Cambodia were at war at this time, a conflict which had been particularly intensified in 1978. The Khmer Rouge had been defeated, and had to flee Phnom Penh. Therefore the Vietnamese took Cambodia out of the Khmer Rouge regime, and discovered the horror of the former Tuol Sleng high school, which became the S-21 detention center during the Democratic Kampuchea era.

This liberation by the Vietnamese authorities was followed by one trial *in absentia* in August 1979 of the Khmer Rouge leaders Pol Pot and Ieng Sary, in order to legitimize the power of the new occupants of Cambodia. Ieng Sary, sentenced to death by the Vietnamese Revolutionary Tribunal (a sentence which will never be carried out[1]) is one of the currently charged persons at the Extraordinary Chambers within the Courts of Cambodia (ECCC) in case 002. The Khmer Rouge leader, "brother no. 1," Pol Pot died in 1998.

What do we see in these images? The detention and interrogatory system, the practice of torture, and the deaths of the last detainees who were abandoned. When you watch it in its totality, we are able to gather evidence of how S-21 functioned and what forms of torture were used there. We can see bodies tied to their deathbeds. Certain bodies have been opened up and

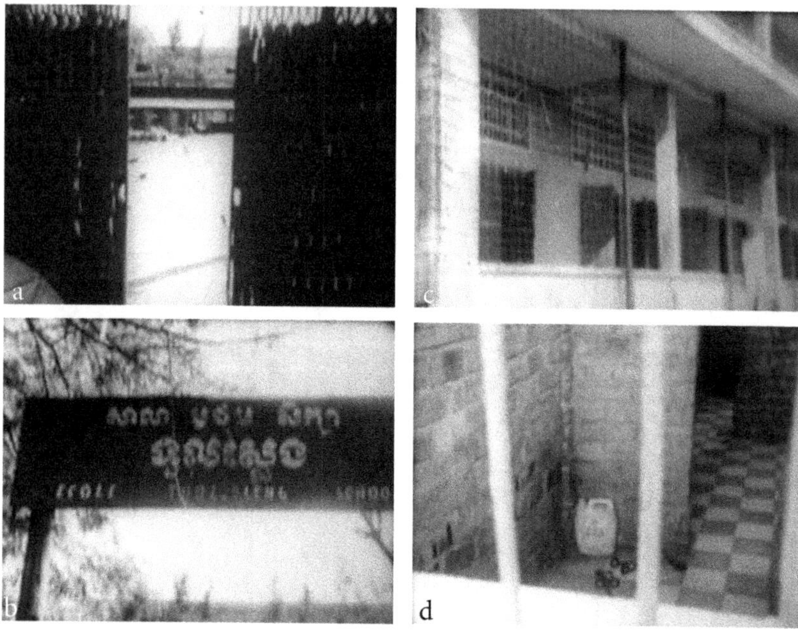

Figures 11.1 (a)-(d) Opening of Tuol Sleng Prison by Vietnam's People Army, Phnom Penh, 1979. Source: Documentation Center of Cambodia/HTV.

laid out to make the observer believe that they might have been subject to ongoing medical experiments. The cells, the chains and locks that secured the detainees are other elements that shed light on how the torture center operated. In total, 12,800 people who died there have been officially recognized; however, more than 15,000 actually perished there.

The Vietnamese authorities gave this document to the Document Center of Cambodia (DC-Cam) in 2008, the organization which collects and archives the history of Cambodia, and, more particularly, that of the Khmer Rouge period. This is of enormous assistance to the co-prosecutors and to the ECCC in its judicial work.

Also, the judgment in August 1979 of the "Pol Pot and Ieng Sary clique," which was organized by the Vietnamese Revolutionary Tribunal, mentioned the name of one child survivor of S-21, Norng Champal, in the testimony of young "Phal." According to the historian David Chandler, only seven people survived S-21, among whom Vann Nath, Chum Mey and Bou Meng have already testified in Rithy Panh's documentary film *S-21*.[2] The case of Norng Champal brought into question the theories[3] and the thoughts that have been presented up to now and Duch's assertions that no one came out of S-21 alive.

Norng Champal, victim of S-21, victim of Duch, asked to join the action as a civil party but his application was late. The co-prosecutors therefore called him to testify as a witness. Only a very short extract was finally broadcast in the courtroom, enough to allow the witness to identify himself and to authenticate the video footage.

One of the peculiarities of the "Khmer Rouge tribunal" is that the victims have the possibility of joining as a civil party. That is also the reason why I have been in Cambodia and I currently work for the NGO named Avocats Sans Frontières France, whose mission is to defend and assist the civil parties throughout the trials at the ECCC.

In case 001 90 civil parties were acknowledged. In comparison to the 12,800 detainees who perished in S-21, this number might seem very small. However, these civil parties know that they are only a few, but they have taken an active part in the proceedings and were symbolic of many Cambodian lives. They have in a way humanized this trial and have had an effect on public opinion.

The participation of the victims: an original system for an international criminal trial

The first international criminal trial of its kind: the Extraordinary Chambers within the Courts of Cambodia (ECCC)

This tribunal, this court, is unusual in international criminal law. Unlike the International Criminal Court for former Yugoslavia (ICTY) or the International Criminal Court for Rwanda (ICTR), the "Khmer Rouge Tribunal" was based on a Cambodian law issued in 2001 and was not set up as a result of a United Nations (UN) Security Council decision. These Cambodian courts established by the 2001 law are specialized chambers within the existing judicial hierarchy.[4] This is a national tribunal with UN support; the "ECCC" with the "assistance of the United Nations." In the same way as the Special Tribunal for Sierra Leone or the Special Court for East Timor, these chambers constitute a mixed or hybrid court.

The personnel are also mixed; most of the staff are Cambodian. The judges, no matter the stage of the proceedings, whether it is the pre-trial phase, the trial phase or the appeal phase, are for the most part Cambodian. In order to guarantee the impartiality of the chambers, and to avoid any decision being made on the basis of a Khmer majority, the UN has advanced the idea of a "super majority," which means any decision is subject to a minimal agreement of the international bench. The co-prosecutors, the co-investigating judges and the co-lawyers work as pairs, on an international footing as well as on a Cambodian footing.

The ECCC law, which was approved in an agreement of 2003 between the Cambodian Government and the UN, settled the question of international cooperation and adherence to international standards. The court's status depends entirely on Cambodian law. On the basis of the application of this internal law, two remarkable peculiarities in international criminal justice result: the investigation phase, and the existence of civil parties that may take part at trial. Consequently, the victims, by virtue of the Cambodian law, are entitled to take part in the criminal proceedings as a full party.

The ECCC: the first international criminal trial to allow the participation of civil parties at trial

This may simply be progress in relation to the status of witness that has been granted to victims in the past in international courts. But contrary to being simply a witness, the victim is free to participate; the victim is free to present his case with the assistance of a lawyer of his choice; the victim has access to the case files; the victim may ask for investigative measures, may appeal a decision, and can obtain reparation for the harm he has suffered. This is a remarkable form of progress in terms of increasing victims' participation in international courts.

International judicial texts acknowledge that the victims:[5]

a) are entitled to an active judicial voice including the right to have access to the proceedings and to participate in them when their interests are at stake;
b) are entitled to be treated on an equal footing, with equal respect and dignity during the entire proceedings including protective measures against potential threats, measures to address new trauma, and are entitled to be supported and respected in their intimate memories as victims;
c) are entitled to adequate and effective reparation.

A civil party is a victim when it is proven that he or she has been harmed, and this is linked to crimes that have been prosecuted.[6]

Under Rule 23.1 of the Internal Rules, "the purpose of Civil Party action before the ECCC" is to:

a) participate in criminal proceedings against those responsible for crimes within the jurisdiction of the ECCC by supporting the prosecution; and
b) allow victims to seek collective and moral reparations.

For the first time, the awarding of reparations was specified in the mandate of an international tribunal, thus confirming this as a principle of international criminal justice. These reparations before the ECCC, therefore, cannot be individual or material.

The results of the victims' participation in Duch's trial

During the verdict on July 26, 2010, victims expressed their disappointment, or at least many of them did, at the sentence that was handed down, and at the reparations. Indeed, although it was acknowledged,[7] the participation of civil parties in the trial and the recognition of their rights was, in more than one way, limited.

Victims' participation: a significant form of progress

Civil parties have taken part in the proceedings before the ECCC in a significant manner. The following figures reflect this effective participation:[8]

- A total of 90 civil parties, represented by four teams of lawyers, participated in case 001.
- 22 of them testified before the Trial Chamber.
- 9 percent of the time of the hearing was reserved for questions relating to civil parties.
- 24 percent of the total speech time at the trial was awarded to the civil party lawyers.

Civil parties contributed to this work of justice by aiding in the ascertainment of the truth, and by changing the perception of the role of the accused. They have humanized this trial; they have fostered a phenomenon of identification on the part of the Cambodian population.

There is, first of all, the case of what we call "survivors," the direct victims of S-21, who, at least some of them, had already testified in Rithy Panh's documentary film.

Vann Nath, the artist, who survived thanks to his portrait of Pol Pot, survived S-21 and came to testify as a witness and as someone who represents the memory of the killings to young Cambodians.[9]

Mr. Chum Mey, a civil party since the very beginning, was one of the people most involved in the victims' presence in the trial. During the first weeks of trial, he became the victims' spokesperson and strongly contributed to the echoing of this story in Cambodian society. His testimony was one of the strongest during the hearings. When he spoke in the dock, and when he showed the scars from his detention, it became symbolic of the trial.[10]

Finally, Mr. Bou Meng, also a survivor of S-21 and a painter like Vann Nath, who wished to express his desire for justice for victims, and his will to have these crimes not fall into oblivion, and to obtain from the accused the truth of what happened to his wife, from whom he was separated the day they arrived at S-21.[11]

Then there are the indirect victims, those who joined as civil parties because of the disappearance of family members. These civil parties, beyond being motivated by the desire to see justice done, are especially keen to establish the truth about what happened to their relatives.

Madam Phung Guth Sunthary[12] and her mother, Madam Im Sunthy, who were present every day of the trial, from the preliminary hearing to the day of the verdict, joined as civil parties because of the death of their father and husband respectively. They were seeking the truth about what happened to Mr. Phung Ton, former dean of the Royal University of Law of Phnom Penh. Their testimonies were given with a great intensity, and in themselves showed us the demand for truth that most of the civil parties expected. The accused showed a great amount of consideration for this intellectual because Mr. Phung Ton was one of his professors; he was troubled to hear their testimony and therefore refused to express himself clearly on the fate of Mr. Phung Ton.

Ms. Martine Lefeuvre and Ouk Neary spoke about the death of their husband and father, Ouk Ket. This former Cambodian diplomat returned to Cambodia in 1975 following the Khmer Rouge call to all intellectuals to come and rebuild the country. The testimony of a wife and daughter looking for truth and justice illustrates, in the same way as the case of Phung Ton, the systematic elimination of the former intellectual elite of the time.

And finally, Mr. Chum Sirath,[13] civil party in the trial, whose presence and revolt, broke the accused down, and underlined the inconsistency in what he was saying, and stressed the lack of sincerity in his apologies.

Presence was crucial for showing, particularly to jurists who are not trained in the civil law tradition, that victims can contribute to the trial and participate in the proceedings. This is essential because, so far, the victims have not been allowed to be heard in the courtroom and proceedings remain more of a technical discussion between jurists, witnesses, or experts, who are all qualified as professionals.

Having the voices of the victims, their presence, and their suffering, in the courtroom, however, provides balance in the trial, makes the trial more human, and introduces a real-life element, an element of truth that forces the accused to face another reality, as well as the concrete consequences of his criminal policy, his acts of torture, the orders that he gave, and the confessions that he forced out of the prisoners he tortured.

The civil parties' participation: a progress that still needs improvement

Beyond the lack of funds for civil parties to guarantee their participation and their legal representation, several elements led to a "backward step" in the recognition of their rights.

The right of free voice before the court

The opportunity given to the victims to participate actively in the trial and to speak during the hearings was challenged in May 2008 when a civil party wished to express herself before the Court, and directly to the person charged.[14] In response the court confirmed the prohibition on civil parties expressing themselves freely in the trial. They had to be represented by a lawyer if they were to be heard.[15] The civil party in question believed that this was a form of violation of her fundamental rights as a civil party to be heard.

A limited right to participation

During the hearing on August 29, 2009, the Trial Chamber considered the issue of whether civil parties are not allowed to question the accused about his character or to ask questions to the experts and witnesses on this subject.[16] This decision did not seem to fall in line with Rule 23 1.(a) of the Internal Rules, which states that the aim of civil party action is to participate in support of the prosecution of the person responsible for crimes under the jurisdiction of the ECCC.

Furthermore, as Judge Lavergne underlined in his dissenting opinion,[17] this is obviously one of the interests, one of the aims of civil party participation: to be able to contribute through their questions, and through their comments, to the effort to ascertain the truth by studying the personality of the accused, his eventual motivations, as well as his character traits or his psychological features, to facilitate the understanding of what happened in the case.

Obstacles to the admissibility of civil parties

Several victims have seen their civil party applications rejected by the Trial Chamber.

Two key difficulties have led to the dismissal of civil party applications. The first is the difficulty in providing evidence that the people in question have family members who were imprisoned or that they themselves were detained in S-21. Second is the difficulty in providing the kinship link between the applicant and the person who died in S-21. The role of archives is therefore essential here. The lawyers and the judge are linked to the historian, whose work determines the granting or not of civil party status.

Also, it might seem incredible, when we understand the Cambodian context – which implied destruction of archives, and the absence of identification documents during the past decades – that the Chamber would reject the applications because the victims cannot provide any kinship link with the person who was detained in S-21. The Chamber did not refer to international custom that takes into consideration the difficulties in producing such evidence in times of armed conflict.

These cases obviously give rise to controversy. Is this a form of confusion? Is this a problem of memory on the part of the civil parties? Is this due to a flaw in the administrative system of S-21, which was well organized? Or is this certitude due to the loss and destruction of archives? This point that was illustrated by the dismissal of several civil party applications will have to be ruled on by the Supreme Court on appeal.

The absence of reparation

Generally speaking, it is notable that there is a lack of proportionality between the elements required to obtain civil party status, in which the notion of a civil party is fully applied, and the rights linked to this. In particular, there was a total absence of reparation granted in the judgment of July 26, 2010.[18]

No reparation measures were ultimately granted in case 001, because the accused was indigent, or because they said that there were no financial means to implement reparation measures, on the part of the ECCC or on the part of the Cambodian Government. The issue of reparation is a great disappointment to the victims. Nothing was provided as a result of the judgment of July 26, 2010, only the publication on the website of Duch's public apologies; the sincerity of which is of course, very much in question. The question of financing these reparations and of having the State or an organization in charge of these reparations still remains open today.

Prospects and conclusions

Case 001 represented 90 civil parties. Due to the broad scope of investigation in case 002 (which covers all the crimes committed during the period of

Democratic Kampuchea and aims at prosecuting the senior leaders who are still alive: Nuon Chea, Ieng Sary, Ieng Thirith and Khieu Samphan), more than 4,000 victims joined as civil parties in this case. This leads the court to new challenges: to adapt the procedure, to create one new scheme of legal representation, or to think again about reparation measures.

The ECCC therefore has to adapt itself to such a flow of victims who wish to contribute to the judicial process. A distinct judicial regime from the one that was in place in case 001 is therefore progressively taking form. The challenge for the tribunal is to reconcile the victims' rights without being overwhelmed at the same time. Thus, these applications were only admissible up to a certain deadline and the question of the admissibility was referred to the co-investigating judges and the pre-trial stage in order to avoid being overwhelmed during the trial phase. The redesign of civil party legal representation is also in process. Two lead co-lawyers will be appointed and will have the mission of coordinating civil party actions and setting up a common strategy during the pleadings.

Regarding the issue of reparation, the absence of project or reparation measures leads us to believe that this is a field in which a lot still has to be done, and that the law still has to envisage what reparation measures could be workable. Therefore, and in conclusion, through the experience of case 001 the civil parties in the trial symbolically represent a much higher number of real victims. This has allowed Cambodian people to identify with the suffering, torture or execution which Cambodian families have suffered, and from which they are still suffering. Their word is a word redolent with history, and they make history appear to those for whom the opportunity to speak was never granted.

The mission of the ECCC constitutes a unique opportunity for the Cambodian people to turn this dark page of their history. They have the chance to ensure both that the drama of the Khmer Rouge does not fall into oblivion, and to bring the guilty who are still alive to trial. Then, in retrospect, the ECCC may be seen to have contributed to the restoration of justice and the rule of law in Cambodia.

Notes

1 By virtue of a royal decree of 1996, a pardon was granted to Ieng Sary for the 1979 death sentence.

2 *S21, la machine de mort Khmère rouge*, documentary film directed by Rithy Panh, 2003.

3 *Cambodia Daily*, August 28, 2008: "177 released from S-21, DC Cam records show".

4 Article 2 of the law of establishment of the ECCC.

5 Article 68 §3 of the Rome Statute for the International Criminal Court: "Where the personal interests of the victims are affected, the Court shall permit their views and concerns to be presented and considered at stages of the proceedings determined to be

appropriate by the Court and in a manner which is not prejudicial to or inconsistent with the rights of the accused and a fair and impartial trial"; and the basic principles and guidelines on the right to a remedy and reparation for victims of gross violations of international human rights law and serious violations of international humanitarian law (Human Rights Resolution 2005/35).

6 Rule 23 2 of the Internal Rules: "The right to take civil action may be exercised by victims of a crime coming within the jurisdiction of the ECCC, without any distinction based on criteria such as current residence or nationality. In order for Civil Party action to be admissible, the injury must be: a) physical, material or psychological; and b) the direct consequence of the offence, personal and have actually come into being."

7 Press release of Redress, the International Federation for Human Rights (FIDH) and Avocats Sans Frontières (ASF) of March 2008.

8 Victims Support Section Progress Report June 25, 2010.

9 Transcript of Proceedings – "Duch" Trial (Trial Day 35), June 29, 2009.

10 Transcript of Proceedings – "Duch" Trial (Trial Day 36), June 20, 2009.

11 Transcript of Proceedings – "Duch" Trial (Trial Day 37), July 1, 2009.

12 Transcript of Proceedings – "Duch" Trial (Trial Day 61), August 19, 2009.

13 Transcript of Proceedings – "Duch" Trial (Trial Day 62) August 20, 2009.

14 Newspaper "*Le Monde*: "L'ex-dirigeant Khmer rouge face à ses victimes" by Francis Déron, February 10, 2008.

15 Newspaper *Cambodge Soir*: "Une partie civile estime que les juges violent son droit à être entendue," July 4, 2008.

16 *Ka-Set*: "Procès Duch: Un jour noir pour la participation des victims," August 28, 2009.

17 Dissenting opinions of Judge Lavergne, judge of the Trial Chamber, Decision on civil party co-lawyers' joint request for a ruling on the standing of civil party lawyers to make submissions on sentencing and directions concerning the questioning of the accused, experts and witnesses on testifying on character, Trial Chamber, October 9, 2009.

18 Judgment case 001, § 675: "Although victim needs in these areas are undisputed, they are inherently incapable of satisfaction through an order against the Accused, and the requests in their current form cannot provide the basis of enforceable orders against Kaing Guek Eav. They are consequently rejected."

PART 4

Visual memory

CHAPTER 12

Visualizing "the other 9/11": memory of the Chilean coup

Constance Ortuzar

A long time before 9/11, the 11th of September was a very meaningful date in Chile. It was the day in 1973 on which Chilean military forces overthrew Salvador Allende – who chose to commit suicide rather than surrender[1] – in a *coup d'état* carried out by bombing the Moneda Palace in Santiago.

As early as 1974, the 11th of September became a bank holiday in Chile and was celebrated by supporters of Pinochet's regime as a "second independence day"[2] and the day the *Junta* saved the country from what they considered a communist threat. The regime's opponents, on the contrary, refused to celebrate the day and held clandestine commemoration ceremonies. As noted by sociologist Alfredo Joignant,[3] the struggles around the memories triggered by the day can be observed first in the contradictory vocabulary used by the opposing sides. Those in favor of Pinochet wanted to *celebrate* the "*pronunciamento*," while those hostile to his regime wanted to *commemorate* the coup, the "*golpe de estado.*"[4]

It was not only during the seventeen years of the dictatorship that this day was a contested issue. Even after the dictatorship, the bank holiday status of September 11 remained until 1998, and so to a considerable extent prevented a genuine process of commemoration from developing.

It was only in 1998, while Chile was beginning to engage in what was intended to be a healing process, that the country finally came to commemorate rather than celebrate the "11th of September." That is, until an extraordinary historical coincidence came to interfere with the plans. In 2001, the terrorist attack of 9/11 on the World Trade Center and other US targets came to totally eclipse the Chilean 11th of September. From then on, the 11th of September in Chile became – because of the greater importance of the United States on the international stage – "*el otro 11 de Septiembre.*"[5]

The fact that both events share the same date resulted in a great change in how "*el 11 de Septiembre*" is remembered, perceived and represented. After 9/11, a series of books and articles about September 11, 1973, were published in Chile, such as *El otro 11 de Septiembre*, a compilation of texts, poems and analyses by Chileans recalling this traumatic event.[6]

Further, although these two events are radically distinct in nature – one being a political coup, the other a terrorist attack – their memory, and specifically their visual memory shares some important features. Both involve the spectacular destruction of a symbolic building as well as featuring "smoke" and "planes." But has this specific visual memory of the Chilean coup always been the prevalent one? Hypothetically, the construction of this representation may have been influenced by the images of 9/11.

In January 2010, a Museum of Memory and Human Rights opened in Santiago de Chile, dedicated to the memory of the human rights violations committed under the dictatorship. This museum belongs to the category of memorial-museum of the type which has blossomed throughout Europe and the world in the last forty years, alongside what historians have called the "memory craze" (Allan Megill, 1998) or the "flot mémoriel" (François Hartog, 1993). These memorial-museums present a collection of archives and images and in doing so subscribe to an educational purpose transmitted through an interpretive plan and a scenography. They therefore have to reconcile sensory and didactic goals. The Chilean institution begins its display with a room called "11 de Septiembre" entirely focused on the day of the military coup. This room presents the event through three different types of visual displays: six individual kiosks showing edited archival films, a triptych of screens presenting images of the bombing of the Moneda Palace, and then a live transmission of the Palace in the present day. I will be analyzing the representation of the events of this particular day as constructed by the Museum of Memory and Human Rights, and venture the hypothesis that the iconic motifs of 9/11 have had a profound influence on the manner in which the Chilean 11th of September is represented and commemorated.

The turning point in 2003

The year 2003 marked a turning point in the history of the commemoration of the "Chilean 9/11." The left-wing parties in Chile organize a remembrance march every September 11, but the governing alliance La Concertación (to which the four presidents who succeeded Pinochet belonged), although left-wing, has most often remained neutral with respect to the politics of memory, preferring a conciliatory approach, driven by the desire to reach social peace. Indeed, Chile is far from settled on a peaceful memorial process, even today. Despite the fact that the return to democracy was achieved by means of a referendum, a large proportion of the Chilean people continued to affirm their support for Pinochet, and kept on defending the success and achievements of the military regime. In today's Chile, a part of the right wing still associates itself with Pinochetism. Alfredo Joignant observes that the day itself has seen violent confrontations over the subject of memory in Chilean public spaces. He deduces from this fact that it was politically expedient for the governing Concertación to take up a neutral position.[7]

But in the year 2003 the government definitively marked the thirtieth anniversary of the Coup with a symbolic gesture. The then President of the Republic, Ricardo Lagos, held a commemorative ceremony, the highlight of which was the re-opening of Morandé 80, the side door of the Moneda Palace, through which the dead body of Salvador Allende had been carried out on September 11, 1973. Closed ever since, its re-opening in 2003 marked an important step taken by the Chilean government.

Furthermore, as noted by researchers Alfredo Joignant[8] and Roberto Fernandez Droguett,[9] in 2003, the commemoration of September 11 in Chile reached its historical peak. Both writers employ the word "saturation" to characterize the numerous cultural and political manifestations which occurred on that day. Chilean television in particular broadcast many shows dedicated to the event and its memory, and scholars as well as newspapers published many articles on the topic. I understand this remarkable mobilization as the consequence of two factors: on the one hand, 2003 is the year of the thirtieth anniversary of the coup; on the other hand, in a contradictory movement, after first having overshadowed the Chilean date, 9/11 probably shed light on it. As a result, Chile has experienced a sudden flow of images of the coup.

Early non-visual memory of the coup

It seems, surprisingly, that the memory of the coup did not have any strong visual representation until 2003. Some photographs from the day had quite a wide circulation and were closely associated with the day. These became what we might term iconic images of the coup.

Those were not, however, the main supports of the memory of the coup. An oral and poetic memory existed. The famous poet Pablo Neruda, and

(a)

(b)

(c)

Figure 12.1 (a) Firemen carrying Allende's body out of the Palace in a traditional poncho (November 9, 1973); (b) Soldiers watching the burning Palace of La Moneda (November 11, 1973); (c) Salvador Allende walking out of La Moneda in June 1973, surrounded by GAP members, during an unsuccessful putsch attempt. This award-winning picture has been famously mistaken for the last picture of Allende and wrongly associated with the day of the coup.

the singer Victor Jara (who was executed in the national stadium on that very day) each left a final poem in testimony of the coup. Traditional bands of politically engaged musicians such as Quilapayun composed songs based on Allende's last speech, which, incidentally, has also been an important item in the memorial process, a speech learned by heart by schoolchildren and used as a basis and inspiration for poems and songs.

We could further say that, before the events of 9/11 and, later, the thirtieth anniversary of the coup, its memory in Chile was more incarnated in emblematic figures than it was visualized. First, it was the figures of Allende, Jara and Miguel Enriquez, General Secretary of the MIR (the Movement of the Revolutionary Left), who dominated the field of Chilean memory. As for the conflict over memory, its manifestations were built around the opposing figures of Allende and Pinochet. Clandestine commemorative ceremonies were held at the anonymous grave of Allende in the Viña del Mar cemetery, while honorific ceremonies thanking Pinochet for his actions took place as well. Even later, after the return to democracy, both figures still appeared as figureheads of the conflicting viewpoints of opposed parties.

In Chile, it was in this context of conflicting memories that, in 2001, the events of 9/11 were widely broadcast. Televisions across the entire world showed the event almost live. This event, and its media coverage, radically changed the way we see present time represented. The almost live broadcast of images of such violence may have established a new paradigm for the visualization of contemporary history. Chilean memory, therefore – all the more so since it shared the date as a mark of a traumatic memory – was bound to be affected and was always likely to change.

Visual representation of the Chilean 9/11 in the Museum of Memory

In May 2007, in front of Congress, President Michele Bachelet announced the project of the Museum of Memory and Human Rights that was to open in 2010 on the occasion of the bicentenary of independence. It is the influence of 9/11 on the visual representation of the Chilean 11th of September at this museum that I wish to analyze.

While much of the exhibition revolves around its open and central space, the first room is dedicated to the "11 de Septiembre." The events of the day are portrayed in films in three distinct displays. Six individual kiosks show edited archival films. A tryptich of screens portrays the Palace bombing and a live screen shows the Palace as it is today.

First it should be noted that, contrary to the representations that preceded the establishment of the museum, here the figure of Allende is almost absent, or at least his death is not once evoked. His last speech can be heard in one of the individual kiosks, illustrated by images filmed by an amateur on September 11 and 12.[10] Physically he is almost nowhere to be seen with the exception of a very brief shot in a montage of archival images picturing the years preceding the coup and the social context of the years 1970 to 1973 (under the governance of the Unidad Popular). Only those familiar with his figure and paying close attention to the video will notice this brief appearance. Pinochet, similarly, appears only once in the images shown in the room. Nonetheless, Pinochet joined the putschists on that very day. His leading role was only later determined, and his relative absence is thus more understandable.

As for the victims of the day, they are not specifically represented but are present in the great wall of photographs among all the other victims of the 17 years of dictatorship. In a way, it seems the museum has made the choice to display a disembodied memory.

If we put in parallel the great importance given to the material aspect of the coup and the lesser importance accorded to its human aspect, we may venture that the interpretive plan of the museum is more one of national

Figure 12.2 Visitors in front of the triptych, taken at the public opening of the Memory and Human Rights Museum, Chile, January 2010. Source: Photo archive of the Museum of Memory and Human Rights, Chile.

reconciliation than mere commemoration of the victims. Indeed, we can consider the triptych to be the centerpiece of the room. It is the only piece in the exhibit in front of which visitors find a bench to sit on, inviting them to stay for longer. As seen in Figure 12.2, a photograph taken on the opening day of the museum, it is also the piece that attracts the most visitors.

The three screens show archival footage of the bombing of the Moneda Palace alternately synchronized and unsynchronized following an aleatory pattern. The plasticity of the display helps to give it a central role in this part of the exhibition.

These images, in a way, share many characteristics with 9/11: the planes and the smoke inevitably seem similar to what everyone saw on television in 2001. But mostly, I would observe that the intention of the museum has been to highlight the destruction of a building, hence the material and symbolic impact of the coup. Before 2001, we saw that the memory of that day had been mostly incarnated in emblematic figures. It seems the events of 9/11 have had an influence on the representation of the other September 11th, creating a model of visualization centered on physical destruction and the symbolic impact it implies.

Another notable element in the room is the large-screen live broadcasting of the Moneda. If we continue with the juxtaposition of this visualization in parallel with that of 9/11, we might think of Ground Zero. But if Ground Zero is a memorial site constantly reminding us of what happened there, and occupying the function of "lieu de mémoire," in French historian Pierre Nora's words,[11] thereby being a spatial mark of a past event that enables the reactivation of memory, the Moneda Palace does not strictly speaking occupy the same function. Rebuilt identically and still in use as the Presidential Palace, rather than "constantly reminding" us of the tragic 11th of September 1973, it seems to be a sign of national reconciliation, and maybe of the desire to forget the past (an attitude much criticized in Chile). President Lagos, who presided over the important commemorative ceremony of 2003, said in a famous speech made the same year that "many have thought of turning the page to overcome the trauma of the past, but there is no tomorrow without yesterday." This live transmission of the Moneda purports to show that the past has been overcome, even though the arrival at a consensual historical memory in Chile is still a long way off.

Notes

1 An autopsy performed on Allende's body in May 2011 confirmed his suicide.

2 Chilean independence day being very close in time, on September 18, the two dates came to be celebrated together throughout a whole week of national holiday called *Fiestas Patrias*.

3 Alfredo Joignant, "De la fête nationale aux luttes commemoratives autour du 11 septembre chilien (1973–2003)," in Micheline Labelle, Georges Leroux et al., *Le Devoir de mémoire et politiques du pardon*, Quebec: Presses de l'Université du Quebec, 2005.
4 The *pronunciamento* ("declaration" in Spanish) is the military rebellion in which officers declare themselves publicly against the existing government whereas in a *golpe de estado* (*coup d'état*) the armed forces seize control of the state in a sudden and organized movement.
5 "The other 11th September" in Spanish.
6 Ariel Dorfman et al., *El otro 11 de Septiembre: una antología acerca del golpe de estado en 1973,* Melbourne: Ocean Press, 2003.
7 Joignant, *op. cit.*
8 *Ibid.*
9 Fernando Droguett, "The memory locations; about the strike and the military dictatorship in Chile. A self-ethnographic analysis of the September 11th march," *Cuadernos de neuropsicologia*, v.1, n.2, Santiago, 2007.
10 Amateur images shot by Juan Angel Torti, who gave them to the museum.
11 Pierre Nora (ed.) *Les lieux de mémoire*, Paris: Gallimard, 1984.

CHAPTER 13

Hollywood: pre-visualization and post-9/11 style?

Vincent Dozol

In the aftermath of 9/11, *MASH*'s director Robert Altman linked Hollywood directly to the attacks. He told the Associated Press: "The movies set the pattern, and these people have copied the movies . . . Nobody would have thought to commit an atrocity like this unless they'd seen it in a movie." He was also quoted in the same article as saying: "How dare we continue to show this kind of mass destruction in movies? . . . I just believe we created this atmosphere and taught them how to do it."

Beyond the old debate on how movies could impact people's behavior, to what extent can we blame violence on films, or do films only reflect the violence of society? We could, however, analyze the connection between the film industry and 9/11 through a different lens.

How does Hollywood deal with this "national nightmare"? I would answer: Not only by trying to re-create this day through cinematic images.

Did the attacks create something that goes further than basic representation?

How has fiction writing been transformed by this trauma?

How did the American film industry react to 9/11 and the claim of a resemblance between the attacks and fiction films?

In this chapter, I will not discuss the movies that directly address the events of September 11, 2001, such as Oliver Stone's *World Trade Center* or *United 93* by Paul Greengrass. The subjects of the films do not really matter, as I will not discuss movies that are factual, but rather those that are, at first glance, pure fiction and meant as entertainment, where the influence of 9/11 is more diffuse.

By "post-9/11 style," I mean formal cinematic elements (e.g. lighting, editing, camerawork) as well as the manner of creating movies (from the basic story to the general ideas), something characteristic of this event in cinema.

This chapter will try to frame an analysis of the influence and the transformative effects of 9/11. I will also endeavor to sketch the outline of a possible shift in the film industry system, and so we need to start with movies produced before the terrorist attacks, such as *The Siege* (Edward Zwick, 1998), which anticipated them. Then we will move on to films that are responses to the attacks, such as *War of the Worlds*, directed by Steven Spielberg in 2005, and *Cloverfield*, directed by Matt Reeves in 2008.

When people were asked to describe their reactions to the attacks, the first thing that came to their minds was to describe them as something "like a movie." In fact, New York City (NYC) has been destroyed several times before in films, as also in comic books and in other graphical arts, as Max Page has discussed in his book *The City's End: two centuries of fantasies, fears and premonitions of New York's destruction*. *Planet of the Apes* (Franklin J. Schaffner, 1968), *Meteor* (Ronald Neame, 1979) and *Independence Day* (Roland Emmerich, 1996), for instance, all depicted the spectacle of chaos and the destruction of American institutions. In 1998, three major box-office hits were *Armageddon* (Michael Bay), *Godzilla* (Roland Emmerich) and *Deep Impact* (Mimi Leder), all showing the destruction of NYC skyscrapers and other recognizable buildings, a destruction that mostly came from the air. This trend was already challenging the idea of US territory as a sanctuary.

An anticipation film: pre-visualization of 9/11

In 1998, the film that most directly foreshadowed 9/11 was *The Siege*, a terrorist-action thriller directed and released by Edward Zwick. *The Siege* is the story of FBI agent Anthony "Hub" Hubbard, played by Denzel Washington, investigating a wave of terrorist attacks in NYC. He is helped or obstructed by CIA agent Kraft (Annette Bening). The plot reveals quickly that the terrorists are Palestinian groups out for revenge after their leader, Sheik Bin Talal, is captured by US forces. The terrorist operations eventually lead to the declaration of martial law and the occupation of Manhattan by the US army.

The film follows the reaction of several authorities to the attacks. To stop the explosions, the Arab population of New York is deposited in camps in sport stadiums. General Devereaux (Bruce Willis) violates the Geneva

Convention by torturing and killing a supposed terrorist in order to get information. This sequence is a reference to the past, to Chile under Pinochet (a regime discussed by Constance Ortuzar in Chapter 12 of this volume) or to the treatment of the Japanese population in America by the US Government during World War II. But this sequence also anticipates the violation of civil liberties after 9/11, the controversial Patriot Act, the Abu Ghraib scandal, the treatment of suspects at Guantanamo Bay, and the waterboarding excesses.

A warning call

In an interview, Edward Zwick mentions the kind of research he did when developing *The Siege*. He reports that he spent a good deal of time with the Justice Department and the Department of Defense and with many people from the Joint Terrorism Taskforce, "who looked upon these events [the devastating attacks by Muslim extremists on American soil] with a certain tragic inevitability. They believed that it was not a question of if it would happen, but when and on what scale."[1]

The movie is indeed framed very seriously, as a warning call to the new world order, where the figure of the enemy and the nature of the threat is not as clear as it was before.

Another terrorist action film

That said, this film is shot like all other terrorist-action blockbusters. In terms of formal cinematic elements, *The Siege* does not differ from previous films, does not innovate at all.

The purpose here is to be quick, effective, entertaining and to make the audience feel secure. We remain at a considerable distance from the terrorist attacks; we hear about them when they are over, we only see the destruction that remains.

Even in the first scene of a bombing on a city bus, only the explosion is surprising.

We never really feel uncomfortable watching this attack; we remain safe. The scene is shot from the police viewpoint, far away from the bus. The camera doesn't want to come any closer. We have no images from the center of terror. The audience is not taken hostage with the other characters inside the bus. At different points in the movie, long-distance shots and slow-motion sequences are used to remind us that all of this is only cinema, that it is simulation and self-consciously artificial.

Now let's analyze this movie more closely. As Carl Boggs and Tom Pollard have pointed out in their essay "Hollywood and the Spectacle of Terrorism,"

"*The Siege* departs from earlier terrorist-action plots owing to its more complex, nuanced range of narratives and motifs."

Attacking America's model

What do the terrorists target in the movie? A city bus, a Broadway theatre, an elementary school and the federal building, which houses the New York headquarters of the FBI. The targets aim for the maximum number of casualties, we could at first think. More symbolically, as a Congressman points out in the film, "the terrorists are threatening our most noble values; we have to stop this!" It is the American way of life that is at stake. It is important to notice that the school, the place of education and transmission of American values, is the only terrorist operation that is stopped by the FBI. Agent Hub in person shoots the suicide bomber before he can activate his explosive device, all filmed in a very heroic way and in slow motion. The next generation of Americans remains safe, no matter who is attacking today.

When the terrorists blow the federal building up, New Yorkers are not the target, but the US government. The country as a single entity is the object of attack. The FBI team members are a symbol of American multicultural society, and we see an Arab agent, an Asian assistant, an Italian officer and a WASP agent working together under the authority of an Afro-American (Denzel Washington) to put an end to the attacks.

With the Broadway theatre explosion, we are told that "all the *who's who* of culture was there." This place is a metaphor for Hollywood, the showcase of the American way of life. By bombing it, the protest is against the symbolical power of the culture industry abroad. Similarly, Samir the terrorist has a curious line to deliver while speaking about his kamikaze brother. He says that "the only thing [my] brother liked was cinema," before explaining how an imam influenced him with the promise of 60 virgins in heaven if he became a suicide bomber.

The film is self-conscious about the possible effect it could have in blurring the lines between reality and fiction, or in putting the spectacle of destruction into images. As Annette Bening's character informs us, it is often the television cameras that matter most in hostage situations. And here it is the movie cameras, lending a deadly frisson of excitement to the blowing away of a city bus, a theatre, a school and a federal building.

Terrorism as the main threat to America

As Boggs and Pollard say, "with *The Siege*, we encounter terrorists who, though still evil, are dedicated to what they believe are noble aims." This is a major shift. Terrorism becomes the most important threat. Terrorists now offer a social counter-project to US society.

At the end of the movie, we could think that it is not only a fundamentalist reading of religion but Islam itself that is threatening America. Just before passing away, Agent Kraft and Agent Hub pray together saying the Lord's Prayer or "Our Father." After the chaos, the question of building a new American society is posed. The film answers, as the Pilgrim Fathers wanted, with the image of a society based on law-abiding citizens and Christianity.

This type of clear distinction would become less present on screen after 9/11. In the second part of my presentation, I will discuss the notion of Hollywood post-9/11 style.

Post-9/11 style?

In *Violence of the World*, Jean Baudrillard states that:

> an event is always unpredictable. Hollywood and the CIA imagined this scenario many times, but never as reality. It remained totally unexpected. Virtual scenarios may exhaust all the possibilities, but not the actual event. They are just continuity of causes and effects. The event itself, in its definition, comes from discontinuity and change. In this way, events worthy of being called 'events' are terroristic. It's a sort of symbolical acting out and this is why it's a source of strange fascination.[2]

An event of this scale obviously changed the film industry. Hollywood could not resist this "strange fascination." I will therefore begin this second part with some chronological remarks. In ten years, few films addressing 9/11 have been made. The average time to develop, produce, shoot and edit a movie in Hollywood is three years. This is why the film industry had to give a response to 9/11 by firstly using movies made before September 11, 2001. They were supposed to deliver a new narrative, to give some meaning to what had just happened.

In her essay "An Event 'Like a Movie'? Hollywood and 9/11," Christina Rickli suggests that as

> the devastating memory of the attacks [was drilled] deeper and deeper into the American collective unconscious, an unprecedented (self-)censoring of Hollywood movies occurred in the immediate aftermath of the attacks. Suddenly, the staging of a situation that

> might remind viewers of the attacks and that might be enjoyed due to its sublime aesthetics was deemed immoral.

For instance, Hollywood postponed the release of *Collateral Damage*, an action movie starring Arnold Schwarzenegger. Hollywood's first reaction was self-censorship. As French critic Emmanuel Burdeau said: "It will be one of the continuing surprises of our time: After September 11, 2001, the US has not produced any revenge cinema that puts the event into the frame of spectacle in order to stir the patriotism of the masses."[3]

The continuous retransmission of the traumatic images on TV, using redacted cinematic codes, surely reinforced the feeling of an event "like a movie." Using the semantics of fiction to describe an event that is now part of our reality is quite relevant. We are in the world of the *unspeakable* and the *unimaginable*, as W.J.T. Mitchell defines them in his famous essay about "Word and Image in a Time of Terror." "Trauma," Mitchell writes, "like God, is supposed to be the unrepresentable in word and image. But we incorrigibly insist on talking about it."[4] And a couple of years later, Hollywood was making movies about this trauma. The film industry did not tackle the attacks head-on; it rather followed a collective realization about terrorism. A couple of movies would address this "national nightmare" by using allegories and metaphors. Even blockbusters are now haunted by recollections of 9/11. Such is the case in Spielberg's *War of the Worlds* and in *Cloverfield*, directed by Matt Reeves. Both follow Mitchell's position: "Declare that something is invisible, inaccessible to visual imaging, and someone (usually an artist or scientist) will find a way to depict it."

Both films are catastrophe films, where invaders and monsters appear without any purpose other than that of decimating the human race. Just like the previous catastrophe films, nothing here is new. In *War of the Worlds*, we follow the escape of Ray (Tom Cruise) and his family, who are trying to survive the invasion of Earth by alien forces. In *Cloverfield*, we are supposedly watching an unedited amateur video of a giant monster attacking New York. The origin of this film is 9/11. The marketing campaign for the film was entirely based on the confusion between reality and fiction. Even before the film had a title it had a release date, as a promise that something was going to happen on that day. The trailer played with the "American collective unconscious" before we even knew that it was a monster movie.

9/11 visual style

The confusion, the possibility that an image from a catastrophe film could effectively be reality, is possible only in a post-9/11 world. The first attack by the invaders in *War of the Worlds* is a good example of how 9/11 defined a new visual style in blockbusters. Consider the moment in the movie when Ray (Tom Cruise) goes outside his house to investigate the curious storm that has just struck his city.

The aesthetic of terror and catastrophe has changed. *War of the Worlds* and *Cloverfield* are really dark in their narratives and their photography. They are shot most of the time with hand-held cameras, creating a very shaky and disturbing image. Cinema professionals began to mimic the documentary style, the *cinéma-vérité* that emerged from thousands of amateur videos of 9/11. The purpose here is the suspension of disbelief. These images are so realistic, why can't they be real? One could argue that this approach had already been implemented in movies like *The Blair Witch Project*. It is true, but how could this have been generalized in blockbusters without 9/11? The difference here with *The Siege* is clear; the way of filming action has changed. The experience of terror in cinema is now lived "from the ground," in the middle of the running crowd. Some in the audience may complain that they feel nauseous watching this type of film, even if this is precisely the point of a traumatizing spectacle.

In the midst of chaos, we can in both films see a wall of dust and people covered in dust. We see people instantaneously transformed into dust by the alien's weapons. Dust is used as a metaphor for the people who died when the Twin Towers collapsed. Dust did kill New York firemen and people who were living in the neighborhood. Public authorities announced that almost 19,000 people got sick because of inhaling the dust at Ground Zero. Later in *War of the Worlds*, a plane even crashes into the house where Ray and his children have found shelter.

Cloverfield and *War of the Worlds* don't dramatize empty myths, they rather question a past trauma as well as today's mobilization of the masses. Post-9/11 blockbusters depict an unknown and faceless threat. They also question the role of the image and evidence the impossibility of meaning.

Unknown and faceless threat

In previous terrorist films the face of the enemy, his citizenship and some of his motivations were known. In *The Siege*, for instance, the fundamentalist Muslim embodies the threat. Post-9/11 film portrays a new kind of threat, with no explanation. Where do monsters and invaders come from? The characters and the audience have no idea. The only thing we know is that *they were already here*, well hidden because nobody noticed. The invaders of *War of the Worlds* planted their deadly tripod a long time ago under US soil. The threat literally rises up from beneath. In *Cloverfield*, we acknowledge that the monster attacked first in Lower Manhattan, near the Statue of Liberty. This is a direct reference to the terrorist sleeper cells that struck on September 11, 2001. They are new form of domestic enemy.

What can we do against such aggression? Both films answer that there is nothing to be done. The scenes of military confrontation between the US army and the aggressor show the inability of soldiers to inflict any damage on the creature. The most powerful army in the world is impotent. Mitchell explains this situation as follows:

> Terrorists speak the language of the unspeakable. They perform and stage the unimaginable. Their acts as producers of words and images, symbolic forms of violence are much more important than their actual physical violence. . . . Terrorists do not occupy territory. They deterritorialize violence, making it possible for it to strike anywhere. . . . Of course all this means that conventional military means, most especially prolonged conquest and occupation of territory, are absolutely useless against terrorism.[5]

Post-9/11 Hollywood doesn't only reference this national nightmare, it also questions the place of the image and seems to conclude that meaning has become an impossibility.

Cloning terror, the place of the image, the impossibility of meaning

The experience of trauma is often defined as an experience of "missing," of not grasping or comprehending the experience at the time. In her essay "Unclaimed experience," Cathy Caruth defines trauma as a "breach in the mind's experience of time." Most of the time, we can barely see the monster or the invaders. The threat mostly remains off-screen. Even when we watch it face to face, the result is meaningless. There's no connection between the eye of the camera and the lethal creature. We just can't understand each other. They remain impossible to describe; they exist only in the domain of the unspeakable and the unimaginable.

It is clear that 9/11 not only reinforced paranoia in Hollywood cinema, it brought reflection about the *act of cloning terror* and the purpose of it. Mitchell's argument is that "the nature of both image-making and of war-making has undergone a radical transformation in our time, a transformation that can be summarized in the phrase, 'cloning terror.'" By this he means, "on the one hand, the reproduction or proliferation of terror, often in the very act of trying to destroy it; on the other hand the terror or horror of cloning itself."[6] I think *The Siege* did not really address the ideas of trauma and cloning terror. The attacks form timely happenings, diegetic moments gauged to keep the audience's attention; they do not really create trauma for the main characters. Their concern with respect to the threat is purely professional. Terrorism does not seem to affect them deeply and it does not seem to impact the rest of their lives. The film does not clone terror because it remains very optimistic about the future. The FBI, the CIA and American society are watching and are victorious in the end.

In Spielberg's and Reeves's movies, that is not true anymore. Both films picture a very pessimistic future. Something seems broken. *War of the Worlds* ends when invisible cells in the water poison the invaders. The human race cannot survive by itself; it needs Mother Nature's help.

Cloverfield ends when the last characters die. No exit is possible. The purpose in both films is not to understand what is happening, not only to experience trauma from the ground, but to keep watching, to record and to testify. "Cloning terror" is symbolized by the repetition of the image to infinity. In *War of the Worlds*, during the first attack, we notice people recording and taking pictures of the terrifying spectacle. We can see a man taking pictures of it. When the invaders begin to decimate the population, the audience sees it through the screen of a hand-held camera. The camera is the metaphoric tool that makes "cloning terror" possible. We also see the reflection of the tripod in the window of a shop.

The same idea underpins *Cloverfield*. Everything we see in *Cloverfield* was supposed to be recorded by the same camera, which goes from hand to hand between the characters.

The identity of the gaze changes, but the image that results does not change; the terror on screen is the same. In *Cloverfield*, the characters keep asking if someone sees something, wondering if the guy holding the camera is sure he has the monster on tape.

Cloverfield and *War of the Worlds* are cloning terror by putting recording material, screens, frames, windows and mirrors between the audience and the threat, living the traumatic experience again and again, with or without a filter. At the same time, both films are self-conscious traumas and do not help the viewer to understand anything at all.

To conclude, let us consider a still sequence from *Cloverfield*. It summarizes pretty well what I have tried to describe in this last part:

Cloverfield: clip of video in electronic store.

In this still, we see that the film tries to distance itself from what it shows. It is first an ironic comment on our technological society, where we cannot trust high technology (the cellphone battery is dead when you most need it). Some people are robbing the electronic store, but they stop to watch the news on TV. The camera is filming the screen where the news cameras are filming the monster in the streets from a helicopter.

The character, and the audience, feels safer this way. It is a strategy to distance us from the threat, seeing it from above, in place of going back to the street and facing the monster. Even in this desperate situation, people need to trust traditional media, probably the only ones which might help to understand the crisis. Confronting traumatic experience itself is too hard; we are looking for a filter. A study claims that Americans were watching an average of 8.1 hours of television on the day of the 9/11 attacks. As Christina Rickli states, "television, both on September 11 itself and in the movie, becomes an interface between the reality of the attacks and the shocked outside world that is left to watch the edited scraps of information offered on screen."

But what does TV think of all of this? Apparently nothing more than the rest of New York. One of the TVs is even screening animated cartoons. The entertainment society clearly seems to have no limit. What does the off-voice say on TV? Absolutely nothing that could give a bigger understanding than the image. Moreover, the speaker insists on the cinematic power of the vision of chaos: "We are getting some truly extraordinary images here!" The words on the screen – "New York under attack," "Panic in Manhattan live" – are empty words, a failed attempt to describe the unspeakable. *Cloverfield* doesn't really comment on our post-9/11 world. It challenges the idea of appropriation by the cinema of this national trauma. The all-image society does have certain limits. The scene is a sort of confession of the incapacity of our society to produce any meaning. Everybody can record the event live. But distancing itself, giving some understanding of the image, is very much harder.

Conclusion

To conclude, I would say that, before 9/11, Hollywood delivered a pretty accurate vision of what would happen if the US had to face a wave of terrorist attacks on its soil. The events of 9/11 influenced movie making in different ways, from the visual portrayal of terror to fiction writing. From my point of view, Hollywood has not responded to 9/11 in a way that marks a giant departure from previous norms. The shift is not a revolution. It finds its place in several old Hollywood traditions and motives.

Post-9/11 films dramatize an experience of trauma and cloning terror. Hollywood seems to struggle with the idea that filming the spectacle of terror, cloning it after 9/11, is not as simple, as inoffensive as it was before.

The representation of threat and terror is now marked by uncertainty. What happened on 9/11 brought new reflections into films, questioning the place of the image without concluding or being definitive. Post-9/11 films do dramatize anxiety about the future. Ten years on, the influence of 9/11 may find new ways to express itself in Hollywood, or it may become less present in movies, replaced, for instance, by the influence of the wars in Afghanistan or in Iraq.

Notes

1 Interview with Edward Zwick by Val Zavala on *Life and Times Tonight*, KCET, Los Angeles, on September 19, 2001, eight days after the terrorist attacks. Available online at http://www.thescreamonline.com/commentary/comment2-1/index.html (accessed June 8, 2012).
2 Author's translation.
3 Author's translation.
4 Mitchell 2005, 291–308.
5 Ibid., 298–9.
6 Ibid., 292.

References

de Baecque, A. (2001) "L'annonce de loi martiale faite à l'écan," *Libération.fr*, September 29, http://www.liberation.fr/evenement/0101388099-l-annonce-de-loi-martiale-faite-a-l-ecran (accessed June 8, 2012).

Baudrillard, J. and Morin, E. (2003) *La violence du monde*, Paris: Editions du Félin/Institut du monde arabe.

Boggs, C. and Pollard, T. (2006) "Hollywood and the Spectacle of Terrorism," *New Political Science* 9/06, http://www.ocnus.net/cgi-bin/exec/view.cgi?archive=103&num=26261 (accessed June 8, 2012).

Burdeau, E. (2007) "Terreur pour tous," *Les Cahiers du Cinéma*, 627, octobre 2007.

Caruth, C. (1991) "Unclaimed Experience: Trauma and the Possibility of History," *Yale French Studies, No. 79, Literature and the Ethical Question*, 181–92.

Mitchell, W.J.T. (2005) 'The Unspeakable and the Unimaginable: Word and Image in a Time of Terror," *ELH* 72, 2 , 2005, Baltimore: The Johns Hopkins University Press.

Page, M. (2008) *The City's End: two centuries of fantasies, fears and premonitions of New York's destruction*, New Haven: Yale University Press.

Rickli, C. (2006) "An Event 'Like a Movie'? Hollywood and 9/11," *COPAS*, http://www.copas.uni-regensburg.de/articles/issue_10/10_06_text_rickli.php, (accessed June 8, 2012).

Valantin, J.-M. (2010) *Hollywood, le Pentagone et le monde*, Paris: Editions Autrement.

CHAPTER 14

Visualizing 9/11

Christian Delage

The events of September 11, 2001 and specifically the attacks on the World Trade Center (WTC) which led to the death of almost three thousand victims, were copiously filmed, but what images were shown live on TV? Virtually none. Brief shots of people jumping from the towers were shown, but these were quickly removed from view. No traces of the bodies on the ground nor in the rubble. It is as if the images shot on that day offered nothing more than a confirmation of the destruction of the buildings and an idea of the number of the casualties. In general, a nation at war avoids showing the losses it suffers, so as not to demobilize combatants or demoralize the population. Nations always prefer to display the bodies of their enemies. But when atrocities are blamed on an enemy, do we not publish the photographs in the press, so as to attest in some way to their reality?[1] Three questions then arise: were the victims of the September 11 attacks filmed but not broadcast? Did the cameramen censor themselves? Or did they select only images that did not show bodies? To the filmmaker Jean-Luc Godard, the case is clear:

> no body, no traces of violence, nor fire, nor blood, but only the grandeur of the ruins ... Anything that could detract from the reality of the dead, anything deeper and more painful than the simple nomination of the "axis of evil," was systematically set aside. That citizens of the United States cannot stand seeing death face on

> is one thing, but the fact that they reshape the images of the event becomes very disturbing. You end up not having to show anything.[2]

The blood may well not have been seen, but the fire was shown! This, however, was precisely the show that the terrorists wanted to inflict on America, by attacking the symbols of its financial (New York) and geo-political (Washington DC) domination, and we must recognize that their project was successful far beyond their expectations when the two towers collapsed, covering lower Manhattan with a huge cloud of dust and debris. This was indeed an image that the author of these attacks apparently liked to watch in his refuge in Afghanistan, as seen in Figures 14.1 (*a*) and (*b*).

Figure 14.1(a) and 14.1(b) Bin Laden watching videotapes related to 9/11 in Afghanistan. All rights reserved.

The whole American nation – ordinary citizens as well as political elites – had to undergo the experience of the event by watching the implacable live broadcast of the day. Godard thinks that there were ideological reasons lying behind the U.S. media not showing the bodies of the victims of the attacks. For Yves Michaud, it is rather moral conditions and a certain sensitivity that imposed a spontaneous, indeed natural, censorship of the horror and obscenity, and particularly of the violence. The reasons for the censorship, he adds, are threefold:

> I do not see how anyone could object to them. There were first the simple demands of human dignity, and in particular the dignity of victims. It is hard enough to be tortured, lynched, disfigured, or disemboweled, without then being exhibited like a carcass on a butcher's slab. Then you have the demands of political accountability: showing clusters of unfortunate victims jumping into the void from the WTC towers on September 11, 2001 would require also taking responsibility for the race riots which occurred the same

> night against certain Arab American neighborhoods .... These requirements of sensitivity and modesty are the result of criteria and sensibilities generated and administered by law, including laws guaranteeing victims the right to protect their image.[3]

One can only agree with these criteria of sensitivity and modesty put forward by Michaud. It seems, however, that the first requirement should be that of truth and fidelity of the images to the event: it is therefore more a matter of generating a distance, empathy, respect for the individuals filmed, regardless of their physical condition. The reference to the law is more complicated: on the one hand, Article 3 of the Third Geneva Convention of 1949, defining the treatment that should be reserved for "persons taking no active part in hostilities," states that their "dignity" must be protected, and they should be protected from "humiliating and degrading treatment." Since the photographing and filming of war became possible, public authorities have sometimes needed to add to written accounts a visual report of atrocities against combatants and civilians. The specification of such procedures always advocates, among other things, the identification of bodies, examination of injuries and the establishment of specific causes of death. All this information should be collected in such a way that it could, if necessary, serve as forensic evidence. It may also be subject to public dissemination, to contribute to the authentification of an unacceptable and scarcely credible reality.

The attacks of September 11 have therefore led some commentators to provide an analysis of the responsibility of the U.S. federal government for the censorship of images that recorded the events of that day. The United States faced a double problem: those who hijacked the planes for the attack on the WTC towers were among the victims of the day, while the organizer of the attacks was invisible, at least at the beginning.[4] It seems that the U.S. authorities were far from being able to control what the media could or would show in the course of the day. As the official report of the investigation commission shows,[5] confusion reigned instead in the different departments concerned, as well as in the the administration, as to the sequence of the attacks and as to what should be shown. In the higher echelons of the Federal Government, communication between the President and Vice President appears to have been difficult and sporadic. It therefore makes most sense to ask to what extent the events of the day were apprehended and comprehended in New York.

When the suicide attack on the WTC began on the morning of September 11, 2001, the first images released did not come from the network channels, as they were not able to cover the first attack live. On the internet, only one photograph was available at the time. It showed the two towers, one of which bore the traces of an explosion. This photo was accompanied by a short mention of a possible accident involving a light aircraft. Actually, it was a still image that came from a CNN video camera. A well-known news network, created during the first Gulf War, CNN had installed two permanent surveillance cameras pointing at Manhattan, one from the north, the other from west Brooklyn. It is interesting to note that nobody stands behind these cameras: they are anonymous and, therefore, offer no point of view on the so-called "breaking news."

The President, at a distance

The still image, although apparently taken from a considerable distance, was remarkable for its clarity: on the day the sky was completely cloudless, but the early morning sunlight was not yet overwhelmingly bright and still permitted an image with great depth of field. In the foreground, the Twin Towers stand out clearly. Their environs – the famous skyline of Manhattan – looks familiar to anyone who has already seen this iconic view disseminated countless times in the form of postcards or as eye-catching images in publicity brochures around the world. But the legibility of the image almost contradicted the brutal events that had just taken place. Nothing about it was really extraordinary except the traces of yellow, red and black that cut across the north tower of the WTC.

When the President of the United States, George W. Bush, was informed of the "accident" that had occurred at the north tower of the WTC at 8:46 a.m., he was far from New York City, as well as from the White House. He had just arrived at the Emma E. Hooker elementary school in Sarasota, Florida, where he was to talk on the necessity of reading as part of the education of young students. His opinion was that the accident was due to pilot error, a viewpoint that was not denied by his National Security Advisor, Condoleezza Rice, whom he reached by phone. There is evidence now that much of the information he would receive during the day, and especially with regard to the sequence of events, was directly linked to the images constantly replayed on the networks throughout the day of September 11.

Just after he arrived in the classroom, his chief of staff, Andrew Card, whispered in his ear, in the presence of local television and journalists covering his visit: "A second aircraft has crashed into the second tower. America is under attack." After waiting a few minutes, the President went into an improvised meeting room where he could communicate with the White House, while watching on a television screen images of both towers burning.

Figure 14.2(a) and 14.2(b) As Director of Communications Dan Bartlett points to news footage of the WTC towers burning, President Bush gathers information about the attack (left). Bush, White House Chief of Staff Andy Card and Admiral Richard Mies conduct a video teleconference at Offutt Air Force Base in Nebraska (right). Photos by Eric Draper, courtesy of the George W. Bush Presidential Library.

From the school, Bush addressed the nation on television and invited viewers to meditate with him in honor of the victims. He then boarded his plane, *Air Force One*, but the security services discouraged him from returning to the capital. By 9:45 a.m. the long journey has begun that will allow the President to return to the White House by the late afternoon and then to deliver a speech to the nation at 8.30 p.m. Throughout this period, in the air or on the ground, it was the television sets that allowed Bush to see what was happening in Washington DC, where the Pentagon was attacked, and it was also by means of video-conference that he communicated with his administration.

Images as witnesses

The President and the U.S. population alike discovered what happened over the course of the day – the sequence of events, the continuity – via the multiplicity of media images that were rapidly produced and repeatedly broadcast. Most New Yorkers admittedly had difficulty in believing what was happening before their very eyes. Their first amazement derived from the fact that the more they saw the same images, whether amateur or professional, and the more they were almost mesmerized while watching them, the less they were able to persuade themselves that this was really possible. Nevertheless, the repeated airing of some images, at least for the first few times, permitted the extension of the duration of the event and gave the time that was needed to comprehend the way in which the facts were connected to each other.

One of these images, taken from the same angle as the one beamed over the internet, allowed the viewer to anticipate the arrival of the second Boeing plane. At first, it could be seen as it moved furtively behind the two towers, but then it came through onto the side where the camera was placed, in other words directly in front of the viewer, even if now in the unrecognizable form of debris and flaming jet fuel. This image triggered visual memories of the kind of trick shots that often appear in low-budget telefilms,[6] which use smoke to obscure violent scenes whose reconstruction would have been too expensive or which would have been hard to watch if seen from too close up. Even though television viewers are accustomed to looking at a scene from different angles in the movies, when a single shot does not provide enough information to grasp everything that is happening, they were still, however, able to sense the gap between the enormity of the event and the relatively elliptical way in which it was being represented. They were also able to understand that the reductive character of the first photograph was connected to the fact that it was a video image, an excerpt from a televisual recording of the event.

What followed was experienced as a kind of contradiction: the reality of what had been filmed did not rise to the level of fiction. The very popular genre of disaster films is rooted in a hyperrealism that immediately engrosses viewers.[7] What was lacking in the real images was something that would establish a connection between the visible destruction of the blazing towers and the way a human being could come to terms with such a terrorist act.

Three sets of images

Several sets of images were going to come to fill this need: those taken by amateurs close to the event; those, quasi-official, showing the President returning to Washington DC; and those, finally, made by two French documentary film directors accompanying a team of firefighters inside and around the towers.

The images from the first series not only took advantage of being at the heart of the event: one of them, filmed from a low angle, simultaneously captured the crash of the second Boeing and the startled reaction of a man filmed in close-up, whose gaze was not at first directed toward the WTC, but who jumped at the moment of the explosion. The impression of realism is all the stronger when there is a human figure in the frame. It was thereby rendered much more vivid, even though one was seeing images from which victims had been excluded.

One knows that placing a third party between the spectator and what is filmed is the basis of our belief in the truth of images. Now there was someone not only behind the camera but also in front of it. We were provided with a space for viewing by the intermediation of indispensable witnesses. Their very presence authenticated the truth of the audiovisual recording and allowed us to share, even from a distance, the sensations of the impact felt at the site.

After the fact, many New Yorkers, but also those who came from other American states or from countries such as Italy or England, became direct witnesses by going close to "Ground Zero" one week after the attack, carrying little cameras and photographic equipment. "They Came to See, and Believe" was the way Dean E. Murphy titled his article in the *New York Times*.

To see in order to believe: these masses of visitors took the same path as the one followed sixty years earlier by US congressmen visiting the Nazi camps. At the time, U.S. cameramen and photographers, present at the opening of the camps, had given an important place to their own comrades, prisoners of war, in order to promote belief at a distance and through images of the fate of the deportees. Then they had to confront the radical otherness of the atrocities committed by the Nazis, which could create an effect of terror damaging the credibility of the images captured as well. The cameramen, the first in the position of eyewitnesses, did not hide their shock: they made it visible by including themselves in the frame.[8] Barbie Zelizer, in a continuation of her book on the first images of the Nazi camps,[9] went so far as to link public reactions to the opening of the camps and those related to September 11. The inability to see the bodies in 2001 would be offset by the vivid memory of those shown in 1945: "There was, in effect," writes Zelizer, "no need 'to see' the bodies in the later event, for the structural similarities in presentation called to memory the corpses of earlier times."[10]

In 2001, however, the event was not far from the New Yorkers, or their representatives, but a part of their life, and of their immediate preoccupations; they dispatched photos and texts, here and there in Manhattan, to alert people to the disappearance of their relatives. In order to avoid too tragic a memory of the event, President Bush came to the foot of the WTC, three days later, and put his arm in a rather forced way around the fire chief with a view to taking advantage of the heroism of the firefighters by posing with them in front of the cameras. But, first, he needed to get back to the East Coast, and fit a familiar narrative schema in the United States.

It involved showing the return of President Bush to the White House. Here, then, were the images of his plane, *Air Force One*, and of Bush himself, returning to the federal capital seven hours after the beginning of the attacks. The presidential aircraft was at first filmed in a sky free of all other planes except for the F-16s protecting him from a possible surprise attack. Given the normal daily density of air traffic over American territory, this situation was extraordinarily symbolic, recalling the moment when Lyndon B. Johnson took the oath of office on *Air Force One* and assumed the presidency after the assassination of John F. Kennedy. The first response to the terrorists came when the President took to the skies and transformed his plane into the center of the political crisis in an America in complete disarray. Bush allowed himself to be filmed in the interior of the cabin, standing in front of a battery of television screens, appearing to address some words to an interviewer outside the frame, as if to signify that he was master of the situation.[11] Apparently banal, although obviously very contrived, this image is nonetheless replete with meaning, one that overflows its bounds: the President would undergo his first great test and, like the middle America he incarnates to the point of caricature, he was obviously not prepared for such an event.

The second part of the sequence confirms this reading. It shows him as he descends from his helicopter and re-enters the White House. As one knows, it is customary to film the departures and arrivals of the President as ceremonies that are both partly solemn and partly informal. Not infrequently, for example, journalists covering the White House throw out a

Figure 14.3 George W. Bush in *Air Force One*, September 11, 2001. Photo by Eric Draper, courtesy of the George W. Bush Presidential Library.

question to the President, or may ask him to comment about one event or another, which he then fields in an improvised way. It is a practice that would be somehow unthinkable in France. It is precisely because such a moment has been filmed hundreds of times that it was easy to read the unease, the anxiety, in Bush's movements. Because these few steps were ostensibly filmed to symbolize the return of the chief executive to Washington, we regard them as if they were performed by an actor. The real Bush, however, was all too visible within his role. He wanted to give the impression of determination, but his body suggested that the contrary was true.

The third series of images, taken by Jules and Gedeon Naudet, have a very different status. The two French directors had, since July 2001, been making a documentary called *Une caserne de pompiers de Manhattan* (A Manhattan Fire House). When, on the morning of September 11, 2001, Chief Joseph W. Pfeiffer receives a call indicating that there is a smell of gas at the corner of Church and Lispenard Streets, he goes there along with the second cameraman, Jules Naudet.

In the noisy atmosphere that characterizes the city, Pfeiffer looks up after hearing the sound of a plane flying over Manhattan and then returns to his work. Jules, in a better position, notes the unsually low trajectory of the aircraft, and films the plane striking the north tower.

"Instinctively, I am with the camera," says Naudet. "I see the plane hit the tower, but I do not understand, it has no sound. Then the sound of the explosion reaches us. A vision, a mirage, the tower is on fire. The Chief

Figure 14.4 Screen shot of Jules and Gedeon Naudet's *9/11*, first hit on north tower, September 11, 2001. © Goldfishpictures.

returns to the car, I rush to take my usual place at the back and I film all the time. Meanwhile, Chief Pfeiffer understands immediately and conveys the message on the radio: 'This is a direct attack. The aircraft had the tower as a target.'"[12]

From the images collected when following the firefighters, the brothers Naudet direct a film, entitled *9/11*, which would air on CBS in March 2002. They were the only ones to enter the north tower after the attack: "On the side, two people burned to the ground, apparently still alive, they move and scream. I don't turn the camera to film them. Almost unconscious self-censorship. Nobody wants to see that."

Yet, without showing death, it is present during the long period of time that the firefighters were trying to organize the rescue of survivors. It takes a particularly distressing form when, at regular intervals, a loud noise is heard, corresponding to the fall to the ground of people who have thrown themselves from the windows of the tower. This is probably all that an ordinary viewer can tolerate.

From the 19,700 fragments exhumed from the rubble of the WTC and transported to a former open dump in Staten Island, only 1,092 victims have been identified.[13] Near the WTC, photographs showing the faces of the dead were posted everywhere, along with handwritten messages. As has been shown by Béatrice Fraenkel, these texts eventually became a sort of obituary.[14] The *New York Times* has published a list of the dead victims by portraying them with ID photos. As you read this special issue, if you look at the images, all the same size, and remember the sound of falling bodies, everyone can imagine what, without having been shown, has been made visible. The "self-censorship" of professional witnesses – reporters, photographers, cameramen – whether it was internalized, concealed or otherwise declared, was neither an obstacle to grasping the event nor to starting the work of mourning for the relatives of the victims, along with the work of knowledge. "This combination of violent moments and focus on an expanded story without establishing any narrative structure riveted people to their TV screens and gave them the impression that they were living the trauma in real time, something newspapers can't offer. It was time, on September 11, and during the following days, to build a tale of heroism."[15]

During the Vietnam War, reporters working for the networks were able to come very close to the fighters[16] and to film war in a way that eventually shocked Americans: the death of young soldiers, thrown into a conflict that dragged on and was going nowhere. Shown every night on television, these images had an effect completely contrary to what William Westmoreland, the commander of US forces, had wished. His opinion was that he had been betrayed by the "rear." Remembering this failure, media strategists in the

Pentagon imposed more stringent conditions for later wars, filtering access to the field of battle by requiring that journalists be embedded with military units.

During the Gulf War of 1991, continuous TV coverage by CNN did not significantly change the situation: failing to control the news, the military could still decide what was to be filmed or not, at least on their side. Knowingly, the September 11 terrorists decided that they should take into account the strengths of the channels providing 24-hour television news coverage: U.S. officials would be informed of the event along with ordinary citizens, and under the gaze of viewers worldwide. In this relatively unique situation, and the chance presence of a French film crew, some New York firefighters were filmed during the whole day as a small community of professionals was plunged into the heart of the event. But, against their will, and even though they allowed some of those working in the towers to escape unharmed, their helplessness in the face of the fire and the collapse of the towers provided an image of an America losing its luster, fostering the spirit of revenge and of an aggressive war declared by the Bush administration.

These political and military decisions were considered a second disaster by many Americans, especially New Yorkers, and this is partly the reason why the memorial erected on the site of the WTC, and inaugurated ten years later, offers nothing but emptiness. The architect, Michael Arad, was chosen, from more than 5,000 entries from around the world, to build the memorial. His proposal was for a "reflecting absence," with a pair of pools where the Twin Towers once stood, flanked by waterfalls and surrounded by low walls lined with the names of the people who died on September 11, 2001.

Between the two pools a museum will be erected, due to open in 2013, whose entrance is already built, and which will cover the last segment of the WTC site as an icon of its destruction. But you can hardly see these ruins, as the glass wall that protects them blurs any clear view, allowing the other buildings, and, more generally, Manhattan's skyline, to reflect in them. This space is not a sacred one, it is in the heart of the city and gives everyone the opportunity for a sort of internal reflection, a meditation. "How do you design it so that people can form a space of their own, and feel quiet and contemplative?" Arad asked in *The New Yorker*. "I hope for the experience of people standing together, turning their backs to the city and facing this, and hearing the leaves rustle."[17]

What then has happened to the images of the attacks? Of course, a memorial does not usually mean showing pictures, even if this is the most likely thing for a museum today to do. The previous and inaugural example of a memorial museum erected soon after a tragic event took place is Hiroshima. In 1955, ten years after the bombing, the Japanese government

Figure 14.5 Michael Arad's sunken pool lined with waterfalls, 9/11 Memorial, New York, September 2011. © Christian Delage.

sought by every means possible to represent the consequences of the nuclear explosions realistically. They even went so far as to stage, in fictional films, scenarios that they did not have enough physical evidence to display in the memorial museum. In her screenplay for the 1959 film, *Hiroshima mon amour*, Marguerite Duras describes how a woman tries to convince her Japanese lover that, by going to the site of impact and to the museum, she has actually *seen* Hiroshima, as well as witnessed and to some extent understood the devastation that resulted from the nuclear bombing. Each time she says that she can visualize it, her interlocutor replies: "You have seen nothing of Hiroshima."

In New York City, the first act of recollection was to erect a Memorial Museum. The museum, originally scheduled to open at the same time as the memorial, in 2011, has faced some problems, particularly related to the physical, as well as visual, presence of the victims.[18] The controversy concerned the remnants of the bodies and the gruesomeness of some of the images available. The representatives of the victims argued that "putting the remains in an underground museum is a disgrace; they would prefer that the remains be placed in a spot outside the museum, in a manner similar to the Tomb of the Unknowns at Arlington National Cemetery", as Patricia Cohen reported in *The New York Times*.[19] Concerning the images, photographs, unlike video, can be shown, but no visible blood or possible identification of faces. Yet, this was precisely what was required from the US cameramen and photographers sent in 1944 in Europe to account for the Nazi Atrocities.[20] In any case, the photographers, amateur and professional, have played an unwitting part in the event itself, namely in relaying attacks that were staged precisely so as to achieve the maximum possible publicity. In the best case, for example that of the Naudet Brothers,[21] the images taken and shown on the day offered a narrative that allowed the spectators to identify with what they saw, while protecting them by generating a certain distance from the violence of the events. Ultimately, the question that the committee of experts convened by Alice Greenwald, director of the memorial, could have addressed as a priority was not so much whether or not to show the images of Sept. 11, but how those images constitute a part of the event and not a subsequent representation.

Notes

1 André Gunthert, "L'image de la guerre dans la presse illustrée allemande, 1938–1945," *Voir, ne pas voir la guerre*, Paris: Somogy/BDIC, 2001, 109–13.

2 Entretien accordé à *Libération*, 7 avril 2002, translated by Peter Goodrich.

3 Yves Michaud, "Critique de la crédulité," *Études photographiques*, 2002, 12, pp. 111–25. Translated by Peter Goodrich.

4 On December 13, 2001, a videotape of Osama bin Laden talking with others, translated from Arabic into English, was issued by the U.S. Department of Defense. Bin Laden, claiming responsibility for the attacks, explained: "The brothers, who conducted the operation, all they knew was that they have a martyrdom operation and we asked each of them to go to America but they didn't know anything about the operation, not even one letter. But they were trained and we did not reveal the operation to them until they are there and just before they boarded the planes" (transcript of Osama bin Laden videotape, CNN.com, December 13, 2001).

5 *The 9/11 Commission Report: Final Report of the National Commission on Terrorist Attacks Upon the United States*, New York: W.W. Norton & Company, July 22, 2004.

6 On the imaginary visual of the images of 9/11, see Clément Chéroux, *Diplopie: L'image photographique à l'ère des médias globalisés. Essai sur le 11 septembre 2001,* Cherbourg: Le Point du jour, 2009.

7 Anthony Lane, "This is not a movie", *The New Yorker*, September 24, 2001, pp. 79–80.

8 Christian Delage, "Image as Evidence and Mediation: The Experience of the Nuremberg Trials", in Michael Freeman (ed.), *Law and Popular Culture*, Oxford: Oxford University Press, 2005, pp. 491–503.

9 Barbie Zelizer, *Remembering to Forget. Holocaust Memory through the Camera's Eye*, Chicago and London: The University of Chicago Press, 1998.

10 Barbie Zelizer, "Photography, Journalism and Trauma," in Stuart Allan and Barbie Zelizer, *Journalism after September 11*, London and New York: Routledge, 2002, p. 65.

11 This image was used again to publicize the interview George W. Bush gave on the National Geographic Channel on August 28, 2011, ahead of the commemoration of the tenth anniversary of the attacks.

12 *Le Monde*, March 7, 2002.

13 Bruno Cabanes and Jean-Marc Pitte, *11 Septembre : La grande guerre des Américains*, Paris: Armand Colin, 2003, pp. 93–4.

14 Béatrice Fraenkel, *Les Écrits du 11 septembre, New York 2001*, Paris: Textuel, 2002.

15 Carol Gluck, "11 Septembre. Guerre et télévision au XXIe siècle", *Annales HSS*, 2002, 1, 141.

16 On the issue of photographing and filming dead soldiers, see Susan Sontag, *Regarding the Pain of Others*, New York: Picador, 2004, and Errol Morris, *Believing Is Seeing: Observations on the Mysteries of Photography*, New York: Penguin Press, 2011.

17 *The New Yorker*, October 12, 2009.

18 On the entanglement of politics and memory following 9/11, see the novel, Any Waldman, *The Submission*, New York: Farrar, Strauss, Giroux, 2011. Amy Waldman is a former reporter for the *New York Times*.

19 At Museum on 9/11, Talking Through an Identity Crisis, *New York Times*, June 2, 2012.

20 See *From Hollywood to Nuremberg. John Ford, Samuel Fuller, George Stevens*, Paris: Icarus Films, 2012, a documentary directed by Christian Delage.

21 A conversation with Jules Naudet took place during a conference on "Visualizing 9/11" at the Cardozo Law School in New York City on September 9, 2011. See <http://culturevisuelle.org/figuration/2011/09/05/visualizing-911> (accessed June 19, 2012).

Portfolio: 9/11 visual memories

Peter Goodrich and Linda Mills,
Edward Hillel, Richard Sherwin

Peter Goodrich, Linda Mills and their son Ronnie live in downtown Manhattan in the neighborhood known as Tribeca. Their loft, located on Murray Street, is just three blocks from where the World Trade Center once stood. Ronnie, 5, started kindergarten at Public School (P.S.) 234 on September 6, 2001. The school is located three blocks from where the north tower fell. Peter, Linda and Ronnie were displaced for six weeks following the attack on the World Trade Center. Ronnie's school was relocated twice. P.S. 234 became the Red Cross Command Center and the school did not return for eight months.

Richard Sherwin is a Professor and Director of the Visual Persuasion Project at the New York Law School, located at 185 West Broadway in Manhattan. On the morning of 9/11, he came to work, ten blocks from the World Trade Center, with a recently purchased camcorder.

Edward Hillel, a photographer and multidisciplinary artist, was living and working in downtown Manhattan on September 11, 2001.

In the following pages, I have collected their visual and written memories of 9/11.

Christian Delage

Figure P.1 Sketch of the WTC on 9/11. © Edward Hillel, 2011.

On the morning of September 11, 2001 when the first airplane smashed into Tower #2, my television was turned on. We live a few hundred yards directly north from the World Trade Center, the 'Twin Towers' always stood over my neighborhood like the two legs of a celestial giant. Since I tend to question the truth of what the media tells us, I didn't pay much attention when the CBS Morning News announced that a plane flew into one of the towers. But no commercials followed, no weather or sports news. By the time I went downstairs and ran outside, the street was full of people looking up into the blue sky. Men and women in suits on their way to Wall Street jobs.

– *. . . oh my God.*
– *A plane went right into it . . . !?*
– *Was it a small Cessna?*
– *They are saying it was a 767 jet . . .*
– *Oh my God . . .*
– *It's not possible. How can a jet go into the World Trade Center? . . .*
– *Must be an accident . . . Remember that Egyptian pilot who crashed a plane last year? . . .*
– *Mentally unstable . . .*
– *Oh my God . . .*
– *Hello Joanie, listen, tell Al I won't make it for the board meeting . . .*
– *It's Bin Laden again. Who else could do this?. . .*
– *It must be an accident. I refuse to believe terrorists would do this until I have hard evidence . . .*

Edward Hillel

Figure P.2 "The first sight that greeted my eyes as I emerged from the Chambers Street subway." Screen shot of image taken on 9/11. © Richard Sherwin, 2001.

Figures P.3 and P.4 "The towers are ablaze. Amazement at the sheer absence where the first tower stood." Screen shots of images taken on 9/11. © Richard Sherwin, 2001.

Figures P.5, P.6 and P.7 "A billow of smoke and debris shot down Church Street. A car emerges from the smoke and debris of the fallen tower, trailing white silt." Screen shots of images taken on 9/11. © Richard Sherwin, 2001.

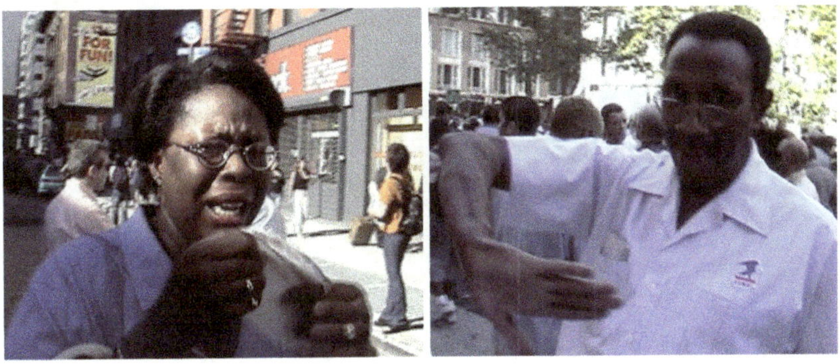

Figures P.8 and P.9 "A distraught employee grieves for her fellow workers, trapped on a high floor in one of the towers (left). A postal service employee demonstrates how the first plane hit (right)." Screen shots of images taken on 9/11. © Richard Sherwin, 2001.

Figure P.10 "A man's haunted expression." Screen shot of image taken on 9/11. © Richard Sherwin, 2001.

Figure P.11 Sketch of the World Trade Center on 9/11. © Edward Hillel, 2011.

Suddenly a bicycle jerks to a stop beside me and a tall muscular man wearing shorts and a helmet screams out:

"*Jesus Mother God Mother of Jesus Jesus Man! Is that really burning like it looks?*"

As if to answer his own disbelief he screams again, "*Goddam Motherfucker Jesus Shit Man I gotta deliver this package urgent in two minutes. Jesus hold this will ya man?*" he says and pushes the bicycle at me. He pulls out a brass monocular from his back pocket, aims it at the World Trade Center and starts to scream and cry hysterically, but the words come out like a whisper:

"God Almighty Jesus what should I do now? I gotta go in there and deliver this envelope!" He pulls out a mobile phone to call his dispatcher and hands me the lens. I raise it up to my right eye. Through an amazingly long telephoto, I am staring at only blackness spewing out thick smoke from a gaping hole on the top corner of the building. Adjusting my eyes I remark the circumference's torn edges of metal and glass glistening from the sun's reflections. I see objects falling out from the hole, falling from the sky.

Edward Hillel

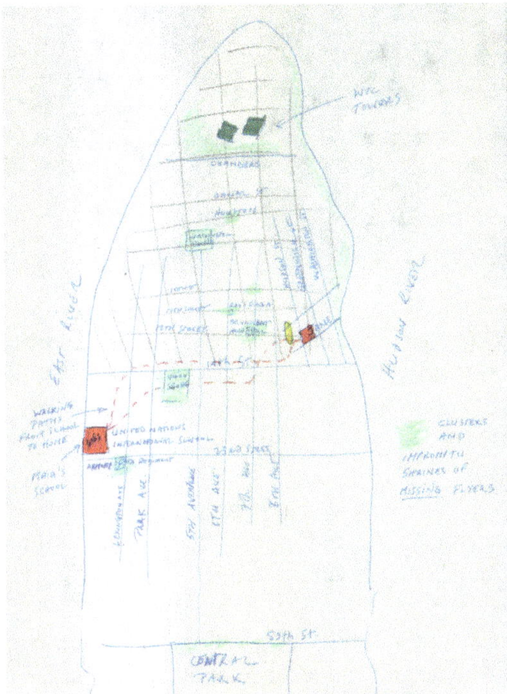

Figure P.12 Sketch of downtown Manhattan on 9/11. © Edward Hillel, 2011.

Two days later, walking with my seven-year old daughter home from school, we noticed that the city had transformed into a makeshift shrine: flyers screaming "MISSING" were taped everywhere, surrounded by candles, flowers, billboards, the cityscape. They usually included a recent portrait and some text, about what the person was wearing, where he or she was last seen or heard from, description of a tattoo or jewelry they wore, and a telephone number to call. New York, the largest city in the world, had become a backdrop for an impromptu memorial. It was the purest form of hybrid art, performance, public exhibition and as close to the rawness of life as you can get. And it was beautiful.

My daughter said:

"*Daddy, each of these papers is a story about someone's life.*"

This is the magic of innocence. While I saw only death and destruction, she could see life and hope. Picasso, after painting *Guernica*, said: "Creation and destruction are simultaneous actions."

Edward Hillel

Figures P.13 and P.14 Murray Street after our return in late October 2001 (left). 37 Murray Street, terrace of the building. Piece of one the planes which crashed into the World Trade Center (right). © Peter Goodrich and Linda Mills, 2001.

September 23, 2001.
9:30 a.m.
Our neighbors, Melvin and Helen, invite us to Long Island. Their house, they say, will be empty. We are torn between staying in the city and never coming back. We reluctantly agree to go.
10:30 a.m.
The phone rings. Melvin and Helen call back. "*Linda, one of the plane's engines landed on a terrace on the top floor of the building. The piece tore the roof open. The rain penetrated the fifth floor apartment and probably yours,*" Melvin shouts into the phone. "*We won't know if there is damage until the building is cleared for re-entry. The FBI is investigating.*" "*Thanks,*" I say, a bit dazed by what I am hearing.

September 24, 2001.
8:00 a.m.
I open the door for the people who have been hired to remove the dust. I see that the rain damage is significant but contained. I survey the damage from the roof. A large piece of the fuselage sits atop my building. Just landed there on a 2' x 6' terrace. I am grateful that it is plane and not body.

Linda Mills, "What He Knew Before It All Changed: A Narrative From Ground Zero", 2002

Figure P.15 *9.11/5-10.* © Edward Hillel, 2001.

How can one convey an event after it has happened but before it has been explained, before its memory has faded, and before its history has been taken over? A work that hovers in the realm of the in-between: in between reality and disbelief, in between living and dying, in between reportage and memorial.

The "Missing" flyers began to appear on the streets of New York City on the same day as the attack on the World Trade Center, September 11, 2001. I made over 100 photographs from September 13 to September 30, 2001. By mid-October, due to rain, wind, neglect and vandalism, most of them had disappeared.

This work is about people like us, who are us, and who happened to be at the wrong place at the wrong time. It is a collective portrait of humanity in our time: urban, a random mix of races, colors, religions, classes and families, living their fragile existence while sharing their days and their dreams. MISSING is a celebration of life, a memorial to that day, and a form of resistance. This is the legacy of 9/11 that I want to remember.

Edward Hillel

Figure P.16 *9.11/3-25.* © Edward Hillel, 2001.

Figures P.17 and P.18 Ronnie Mills-Goodrich, drawings of the WTC before and after 9/11. © Peter Goodrich & Linda Mills, 2001.

When I ask Ronnie what he thinks he is full of hope: "*I want to go back to P.S. 234, Mommy. I want to walk to the school so I can learn more.*" When I ask him about what happened, he is full of optimism: "*I feel bad about the people in the building, the people who died, but I think a hundred people got out.*" "*I want them to develop one World Trade Center that is real high so only a little tiny part falls off, instead of half.*" "*I feel it is special to live here Mommy because there's a gate so if a part of the building falls down it will land on the gate and none of the people will die.*" And sometimes he is full of surprises: "*I thought all the planes were dead,*" he tells Peter when he notices a plane in the sky six weeks after the event. "*I thought all the planes crashed into the World Trade Center.*" I realize that my son is not so oblivious as I may think.

Linda Mills, "What He Knew Before It All Changed: A Narrative From Ground Zero", 2002

Figure P.19 Ronnie's class, P.S. 234. © Peter Goodrich & Linda Mills, 2001.

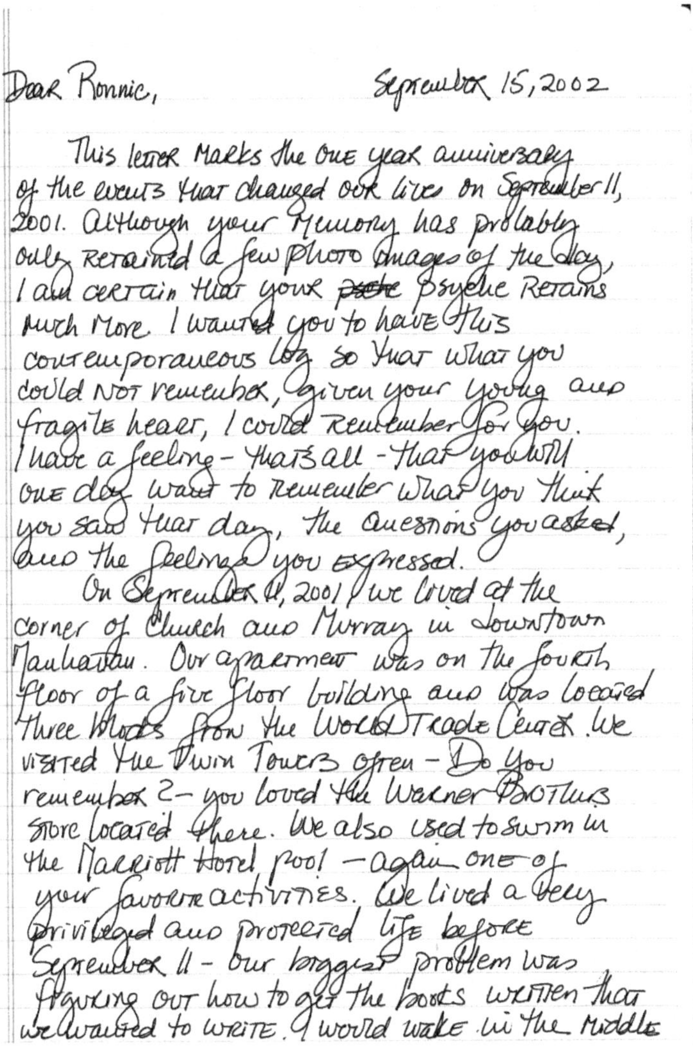

Dear Ronnie, September 15, 2002

This letter marks the one year anniversary of the events that changed our lives on September 11, 2001. Although your memory has probably only retained a few photo images of the day, I am certain that your ~~psyche~~ psyche retains much more. I wanted you to have this contemporaneous log so that what you could not remember, given your young and fragile heart, I could remember for you. I have a feeling – that's all – that you will one day want to remember what you think you saw that day, the questions you asked, and the feelings you expressed.

On September 11, 2001 we lived at the corner of Church and Murray in downtown Manhattan. Our apartment was on the fourth floor of a five floor building and was located three blocks from the World Trade Center. We visited the Twin Towers often – Do you remember? – you loved the Warner Brothers store located there. We also used to swim in the Marriott Hotel pool – again one of your favorite activities. We lived a very privileged and protected life before September 11 – our biggest problem was figuring out how to get the books written that we wanted to write. I would wake in the middle

Figure P.20 Linda Mills, "Letter to Ronnie" (extract), September 15, 2002. © Linda Mills, 2002.

Index

www.ingramcontent.com/pod-product-compliance
Lightning Source LLC
LaVergne TN
LVHW021038011026
849160LV00008BA/521
9780415688956